LINCOLN SHIRE

NOTTINGHAMSH

LEICESTERSH

RUTLAND

NORTHAMPTON SHIRE

HUNTINGDON

CAMBRIDGESH

NORFOLK

SUFFOLK

BEDFORD SHIRE

BUCKINGHAM SHIRE

HERTFORDSH

ESSEX

MIDDLESEX LONDON

OXFORDSHIRE

BERKSHIRE

SURREY

KENT

SUSSEX

HAMPSHIRE

Isle of Wight

The Wash

River Thames

Straits of Dover

CHANNEL

Gainsboro, Caistor, Saltfleet, Bawtry, Tickhill, Blythe, Worksop, Market Raisin, Alford, Wragsby, Lincoln, Burgh, Spilsby, Bolingbroke, Tuxford, Newark on Trent, Waynflet, Southwell, Tattershall, Boston, Nottingham, Sleaford, Kirkton, Gosberton, Grantham, Folking-ham, Holbeach, Lynn Regis, Spalding, Bourne, Corby, Stamford, Thorney, Wisbeach, Downham, Swaffham, Peterboro, Whittlesea, Aphall, Methwold, Walton, Rockingham, Oundle, Hunt-ingdon, Sutton, Ely, Brandon, Thetford, Attleborough, Kettering, St Ives, Mildenhall, Newmarket, Bury St Edm., Ixworth, Northampton, Kimbolton, Cambridge, Caxton, Linton, Haverill, Clare, Needham, Bildeston, Wellborough, Northampton, S. Neots, Royston, Saffron Walden, Sudbury, Hadleigh, Ipswich, Towcester, Stoney Stratford, Bedford, Baldock, Habstead, Manningtree, Harwich, Daventry, Silsoe, Hitchin, Steven-age, Thaxted, Col. Chester, The Naze, Buckingham, Dunstable, Luton, Braintree, Witham, Maldon, Bicester, Woodstock, Tring, St Albans, Ware, Ongar, Chelmsford, Oxford, Aylesbury, Thame, Cheshan, Watford, Hoddesdon, Epping, Rayleigh, Wallingford, High Wycomb, Barnet, Enfield, Rumford, Horndon, Barking, Wantage, Henley, Maidenhead, Hounslow, Kingston, Dartford, Gravesend, Sheerness, Reading, Windsor, Chertsey, Staines, Bromley, Eltham, Rochester, Margate, Newbury, Kingsclere, Odiham, Guildford, Croydon, Godstone, Seven Oaks, Maidstone, Canterbury, DOWNS, Deal, Andover, Basingstoke, Ryegate, Tunbridge, Ashford, Wye, Sandwich, Dover, Stockbridge, Alton, Godalming, Dorking, East Grinsted, Salehurst, Tenterden, Winchester, Petersfield, Haslemere, Horsham, Cuckfield, New Romney, Lidd, Fareham, Midhurst, Petworth, Rye, Hastings, Havant, Arundel, Steyning, Lewes, Battel, Dunge Ness, Gosport, Chichester, Worthing, Brighton, Beachy Head, Cowes, Spithead, Selsey Bill, Newport, St Catherines Point, Calais, Boulogne

UNDER TWO MANAGERS

UNDER TWO MANAGERS

The Everyday Life of the Thornton-
Barnett Theatre Company
1785-1853

Paul Ranger

Society for Theatre Research
2001

First Published 2001
by the Society for Theatre Research
c/o The Theatre Museum, 1E Tavistock Street,
Covent Garden, London WC2E 7PA

ISBN 0 85430 069 4

by the same author
for the Society for Theatre Research:
"Terror and Pity Reign in every Breast":
Gothic Drama in the London patent theatres (1991)

(Edited and extended:) *Theatre in the Cotswolds:*
the Boles Watson family and the Cirencester theatre
by Anthony Denning (1993)

Designed and typeset by
Blot Publishing (www.blot.co.uk)

Printed by E. & E. Plumridge Ltd
41 High Street, Linton, Cambs CB1 6HS

To

W. A. F.

who has patiently lived with stories of Henry Thornton
for the past thirty years

CONTENTS

LIST OF ILLUSTRATIONS

FOREWORD

Where did the English find the mania for the theatre that swept the country in the eighteenth and nineteenth centuries? The greater part of the population could not read. But plays were written not to be read but acted. And plays were acted in country houses by aristocratic amateurs, and in country barns by troupes of itinerant players who gained almost nothing from this exercise. The theatre was somewhere in London and a few cities, but Theatre was something that existed all over the country. The chief examples of this were the circuits of often unsuitable buildings that were adapted for acting in every county in the land, and the troupes of performers who would travel from one to the others, often on foot, to play in them.

Paul Ranger has already whetted out appetites in his study of early nineteenth-century gothic melodrama and his careful treatment of Theatre in the Cotswolds, both published by the Society for Theatre Research. Now in this study of one particular theatrical circuit he has produced a definitive account of a movement that was struggling to express itself all over the country. Every researcher into our theatre history will be grateful. Every more general reader will find much to discover and enjoy.

GEORGE SPEAIGHT
For the Society for Theatre Research

INTRODUCTION

In this work I have concentrated on the establishment of a circuit of theatres by a middle-aged man of unlikely origins for such a task. Henry Thornton began to create his circuit in 1785 when he was twenty-five years old. By the time of his retirement in 1817 he managed more than twenty theatre buildings. A nucleus of the more stable of these passed to his son-in-law, Edward Barnett, who kept them going until his own retirement in 1853. Threats of invasion, European wars, social upheaval, the agricultural revolution and changes in politics and monarchies rumbled on in the background of the lives of these two men. To some extent their theatres reflected the surrounding turmoil but the chief glory of the two managers was their ability to keep their stages lit come what may for nigh on seventy years.

This book, however, is not a biography of two men, although their own lives are inseparable from their band of actors. It aims to be a study of the life of a company working from the reign of King George III to that of Queen Victoria. The everyday practical challenges confronting any theatre manager - how to get a company together, financial disbursements and embarrassments, the plays which will appeal to an audience, how to stage the text, the journeyings around the circuit, visiting stars - are tackled thematically, chapter by chapter. The development of the theatre in any given location on the circuit is best studied with the help of the index although chapters two to four give a chronological account of the establishment of individual playhouses. Notes on sources and apparatus appear in Appendices 1 and 2.

I must record my gratitude to the staff of the various libraries and other institutions itemised in Appendix 1 for their professional help which often went well beyond the demands of my questions. I am also most grateful to those who have spoken personally to me giving me verbal information; of these I owe a special debt of gratitude to Dr Arnold Hare who first introduced me to Henry Thornton. Many years ago when I began to research the Thornton family I received financial help from King Alfred's College, Winchester and recently the Society for Theatre Research has given me a handsome disbursement from the Anthony Denning Research Award; to both I owe my thanks. I am grateful to the Society for readily publishing this work and to Derek Forbes for so ably editing the typescript with skill and dealing with my various lacunae with perspicacity and tact. For me, this has been an enjoyable experience.

Paul Ranger, Oxford

The Church of Saint Peter and Saint Paul, Clare, Suffolk.
(Author's collection)

CHAPTER 1
THE FORMATIVE YEARS

The Family Background

Clare is a pleasant small town on the banks of the River Stour, some six miles outside Sudbury, Suffolk. In previous days its wealth had been gained from making say, a type of serge.[1] Prosperity is still evident in the imposing gothic church of St Peter and St Paul. Henry Thornton, the future theatre manager, was born in the town and baptised in the parish church on 6 March 1750.[2] His parents were Daniel and Elizabeth Ford; Henry was their fifth son. When they arrived in Clare is not known, nor is the father's occupation recorded, although many were locally employed in the manufacture of cloth. He appears to have been a steady and respectable townsman for eleven years later he became a member of the parish council.[3] The reason for Henry's later change of name from Ford to Thornton is also unknown, although at much the same period another would-be actor, Thomas Court of Edinburgh, changed his surname to Collins on travelling southwards to Southampton.[4] Henry Ford attended Clare School where he was taught by Thomas Crick.[5] The question naturally arises: did the future theatre manager get his first taste of the playhouse in his home area? Sudbury possessed a barn theatre and there is just a chance Thornton would have walked over to the town to spend an evening captivated by the players.[6]

Whilst still a teenager the young man travelled to London and became a resident student at the Inner Temple where he struck up a friendship with William Hough, later the prompter of the Belfast Theatre and stage educator of the juvenile phenomenon William Henry West Betty.[7] However, Thornton did not make a formal enrolment; he possibly decided that a life on the stage held more excitements for him than one in the law.

1

Strolling Player

For a while Thornton disappears until in 1773 John Bernard, a stage-crazed youth, caught sight of him in Chew Magna, Somerset, as the leader of a 'band of dramatic desperadoes'.[8] Thornton appeared at his most buckish in scarlet coat, laced hat, embroidered waistcoat, buckskin breeches and topboots. Possibly he was dressed in the best of the theatre wardrobe but the remaining costumes were in tolerable condition and to accompany them was a series of scenes. Thornton had set up his temporary theatre in a malt house and, short of actors, he searched for these at a 'spouting club', an informal gathering in which aspirants to the stage recited set speeches from plays. Bernard's youthfulness and agility appealed to Thornton and he was snapped up to appear in 'juvenile tragedy... and genteel comedy'. The takings during the four-week season were variable; at one performance the box office receipts came to £9.00 and at the share-out Bernard received eight shillings and three tallow candles.

Keynsham, the next stopping place, afforded few profits and a rapid move was made to Glastonbury. Thornton's response to two of the local facilities is an indication of his opportunism. Stroud, an eccentric resident, had written a play located in the Somerset countryside, entitled *The Fiend in the Air or The Glastonbury Apparition*. This, Thornton determined, must be presented. The fiend with a glowing head and tail of exploding crackers was made and the manager decided that it could be used in a startling advertising project. A large kite and a frightened cat were fixed to the monster which was taken during the night to the top of the Tor and flown, awakening the startled inhabitants and imposing on the play the similitude of a documentary.[9]

In this theatrical progress Chard and then Taunton were each visited. The latter was a clean and cheerful town and the wealthier families were known to patronise the play.[10] A second playwright, Mrs Skinne, with two dramas to her credit, was encountered here. Living a life of fantasy - she pretended to the West Country folk that she was the wife of the Persian ambassador - she agreed to take part in Thornton's staging of *The Wonder*, appearing as Violante. Her appearances were short-lived for at dawn the next day she left Taunton to begin a national crusade against the penury in which the actors existed.[11] Audiences were sparse and the actors starved. Bernard claimed that Thornton worked a share system, dividing the box office income amongst the company only after awarding himself a heavily loaded share, with the result that he was able to lodge comfortably in Somerset inns.[12]

2

The usual practice for a wandering manager was to establish through yearly repetition a walk and, although possibly enlarging it or buying the walk of a retiring manager, keeping to a set pattern of times and locations. With scant regard for the convention, Thornton suddenly dashed over to Essex to play at Brentwood. In later years he was to return to the county to manage the playhouse at Chelmsford and to assist the Petre family at Thorndon Hall with their private theatricals. Whilst here, Thornton received a letter from Thomas Holcroft - then nearing thirty and to become a highly successful playwright - asking for an engagement which would mean leaving Roger Kemble's well-established company in the

Thomas Holcroft, Playwright.
(Author's collection)

Midlands.[13] Strangely Thornton found the letter 'deficient in orthography and etymology', and sent a surly reply that 'he would treat with no person to become a member of his company who could neither read nor write'.[14] Was this a joke? A number of performers in Kemble's company at this time, Holcroft himself, the Hatton family, the West family and Downing, were to become involved in Thornton's future management.[15]

The Whitley and Herbert Company

One wonders whether the management of this touring enterprise failed, as three years later Thornton's name is to be found amongst the lists of players in Whitley's and Herbert's company. From mid-eighteenth century James Augustus Whitley had established a Midland circuit with theatres at Wolverhampton, Shrewsbury, Stamford, Warwick, Derby, Nottingham and Leicester, amongst other towns. This was a large circuit and the intricacies of its management may have had an influence on Thornton, although Tate Wilkinson noted that the 'dominions' were 'here today and gone tomorrow'.[16] After the death of his wife in 1769 Whitley joined forces with Nathaniel Herbert who managed the Lincoln and East Anglian circuit. Newark and King's Lynn became the principal bases of the combined circuits.[17]

When cast, Thornton was often paired with Thomas Shafto Robertson, a clownish fellow whose line allowed him to double the roles of the Grave Digger and Polonius in *Hamlet* at King's Lynn.[18] The two men engaged in a speculation of their own in Tewkesbury, an enterprise which gives an insight into the politics of provincial theatre. The manager of the Rugby company, Mark Moore, attempted to perform in Tewkesbury but found his way blocked by the magistrates who claimed the town had suffered 'great inconveniences' through the players.[19] Earlier an officer in the Royal Navy, Moore was able to invoke an Act of Parliament that former officers should 'set up those trades or occupations as they are most apt for and those who oppose them shall pay double cost of suits'.[20] The ploy worked and Warren, a local builder, erected a temporary theatre in a meadow known as 'The Pantry'. Still bent on opposition the magistrates invited Thornton and Robertson to come from a neighbouring town and play in Tewkesbury under their patronage. The pair arrived, built a temporary theatre in the Rails Meadow, and began a smear campaign suggesting that Moore would be unable to meet the costs of setting up his playhouse which came to £63. Roger Kemble, who was playing at his theatre in Warwick, advanced Moore the necessary cash for completion and visited Tewkesbury himself to play. The ensuing three month season was so successful that Moore claimed his rivals 'fled the field'.[21] Thornton appears to have been philosophical about the incident and when he was his own manager again, invited members of the Kemble family to perform on his stages. Robertson, for his part, eventually became manager of the Lincoln circuit.[22]

Yet again obscurity hides the daily events of Thornton's life, although it should be noted briefly at this point that it was prior to 1780 that he became married to the provincial actress Elizabeth Pritchard who was related by marriage to his friend Robertson.[23] Thornton and his wife next appear in Plymouth.

4

Plymouth and Brighton

A bill for the Frankfort Gate Theatre, Plymouth, containing the names of Thornton and his wife as members of the company, suggests the difficulties encountered by provincial playhouses, even in the remote stretches of the West Country.[24] The entertainment, given on 19 July 1780, was presented under the euphemism 'A Concert of Music' followed by the additional information that Richard Sheridan's operetta *The Duenna* would be presented 'Gratis' between items. This kind of circumlocution, a defence against the punitive measures of Sir Robert Walpole's 1737 Act forbidding non-patent theatres to operate, was rarely used by 1780, although years later Thornton was forced to employ the term 'Readings' for performances at the Oxford Theatre. A friend from Whitley's company, James Wheeler, was also playing in Plymouth; a singer as well as an actor his forte was the role of Macheath. Soon Wheeler was to obtain the deputy managership of the Portsmouth Theatre, said to be the 'handsomest out of London'.[25] He did not forget the colleague he was leaving behind.

A brief spell at the Brighton Theatre, then managed by Joseph Fox, followed. Here Thornton met Edward Cape Everard, singer, dancer and actor, together with his wife. The two families struck up a friendship that was to continue, sometimes turbulently, over a number of years.[26] One of the few recorded performances of this interlude was a reversed production of John Gay's *The Beggar's Opera* in which Everard played Jenny and Mrs Thornton Filch.[27]

To choose a company for the Portsmouth Theatre, Wheeler paid a visit to Brighton and selected half a dozen performers, including the Everards. His long-standing friend was invited to become prompter of the Portsmouth Theatre, an important position which Thornton accepted. In all, a party of eighteen set off in a 'kind of caravan' after an abortive attempt at sailing along the coast.[28]

A Prompter at Portsmouth

Sheridan is reported to have said that the prompter was the corner stone of a well-regulated theatre; that had become Thornton's responsibility.[29] His duties were multifarious: he sent out the commands of the manager, smoothed relationships backstage, filled in a role if an actor was suddenly indisposed through sickness or accident, supervised the script-in-hand rehearsals, detailed the exits and entrances, the statuesque atti-

THEATRE, FRANKFORT-GATE.

By Their Majesties Servants.

On *WEDNESDAY*, *July* 19, 1780,
Will be PERFORM'D

A CONCERT of MUSIC.

BOXES 3 s.— UPPER BOXES 2 s. 6 d.— PIT 2 s.— GALLERY 1 s.

TICKETS to be had at Mesrs. Wallis and Haydon's, Booksellers; Mr. Weatherley's, Printer; King's-Arms, and London Inns; Mr. Ord's Tavern, Plymouth:—The Fountain, and King's-Arms, at Dock; and at the Theatre, where Places for the Boxes may be taken.

The DOORS *to be opened at* SIX, *and begin presisely at* SEVEN *o'CLOCK.*

Between the several Parts of the CONCERT, will be presented GRATIS,

A New COMIC OPERA, *call'd*

The DUENNA:

Or, The DOUBLE ELOPEMENT.

Don Anthonio by Mr. CUBITT,
Don Ferdinand by Mr. BARRYMORE,
Don Carlos by Miss JARRATT,
Isaac Mendosa by Mr. T. BLANCHARD,
Father Paul by Mr. BROWNE,
Father Augustine by Mr. BLANCHARD,
Lay Brother by Mr. THORNTON,
Lopez by Mr. SMITH,
And Don Jerome *(for the first Time)* by Mr. FOOTE.

Donna Louisa by Mrs. WELLS,
Donna Clara by Mrs. JEFFERSON,
Nun by Mrs. DAVIS,
And the Duenna by Mrs. THORNTON.

End of Act I. a DANCE, *by Miss* BRADSHAW.
End of the Opera a HORNPIPE *by Mr.* T. BLANCHARD.

To which will be added a FARCE, call'd

Three Weeks after Marriage:

Or, What we must all come To.

Sir Charles Racket by Mr. JEFFERSON,
Mr. Woodley by Mr. THORNTON,
William by Mr. SMITH,
And Old Drugget by Mr. FOOTE.

Lady Racket by Mrs. JEFFERSON,
Dimity by Mrs. THORNTON,
Nancy by Mrs. WELLS,
And Mrs. Drugget by Mrs. BRADSHAW.

N. B. No Person can possibly be admitted behind the Scenes; at which, it is humbly presumed, no Gentleman can be offended.

PLYMOUTH: Printed by R. TREWMAN, and B. HAYDON, in Pike-Street.

Playbill, Frankfort Gate Theatre, Plymouth.
(Devon Library Services)

tudes the actors were to adopt and the emphases to be made in the speeches. Furthermore the ancillary staff such as the seamstresses, wig-makers, carpenters and painters were directly under his control. During performances, if he were not acting, he would sit in a leather armchair from which he could watch the stage with the playtext in hand. Amongst other marginalia in this, were the letters 'R' and 'W', indications of the junctures at which the prompter would ring a handbell for the orchestra to start the music or blow on his whistle to galvanise the scene shifters into action.[30]

The manager of the Portsmouth Theatre was George Mattocks, for a while the manager at Plymouth, whose northern theatres often drew him away from the seaport leaving the daily running of the playhouse to Wheeler.[31] The business of getting the repertoire on the stage must have taken up the greater part of Thornton's time but events of local and national importance broke into the pattern of days. Let us take an example of each. The cheapness of the life of a member of the theatre team is indicated in the incident of the stage carpenter who bumped into a mid-shipman backstage. The carpenter remonstrated with the officer who exclaimed, 'I'll use you ten times more,' which he did by driving a dirk through the workman's left arm and chest. Four days later the wounded man died. The sailor was taken to Winchester where it transpired at his trial that he was related to two admirals; the information acted as a rein on justice and he was acquitted with a shilling fine.[32]

A rival theatre, the Sadler's Wells, was built in 1782 on the edge of Portsmouth. The name indicated that the entertainments consisting of 'singing, dancing, tumbling, slackwire, rope dancing, interlude and pan-tomime' were the staple fare as at the Islington house of the same name. One of Wheeler's actors, James Perry, had an altercation with the manag-er and left the theatre to direct Sadler's Wells and then attempted to coerce various members of the company to join him: Everard responded but Thornton remained with the drama. No sooner had the theatre opened in August, than it was forced, as was the principal playhouse, to close for a period of mourning: the *Royal George* had sunk in Portsmouth Harbour with the loss of Admiral Kempenfelt and four hundred seamen.[33]

Thornton's remaining months in the town were obscure, probably con-sisting of nothing more than the everyday round of administration and appearance. This offers a chance to take stock. By the time Thornton had reached his mid-thirties he had worked as leader of a company of strollers, actor, singer and in the highly responsible position of prompter. The remaining role of his life, Thornton the manager, was about to be assumed.

1. G A Thornton, *A Short History of Clare* (Brentwood, 1963), pp 17 and 19.
2. Suffolk Record Office, Bury St Edmunds: Baptismal Register of the Parish of Clare, Suffolk, FL 501/3. The date of Thornton's birth is uncertain. Some theatre historians place this in 1748 as John Bernard stated that Thornton was aged twenty-five when he met the man in 1773. Bernard was not strong on dates and it seems unlikely that Thornton's parents would wait two years before the baptism of their son. The matter seems to be clinched by the Burial Register at St Mary's Cathedral, Chelmsford, which gives Thornton's age at death in 1818 as 68. See: book 16, p.67.
3. Suffolk Record Office: Church Wardens' Books, no 1, entry for 23 March 1761.
4. City Archive Office, Southampton: SC/4/3/1153.
5. Suffolk Record Office: Wardens' Books, 1, entry for 26 August 1744.
6. Elizabeth Grice, *Rogues and Vagabonds* (Lavenham, 1977), pp 102-3.
7. *Reading Mercury*, 14 March 1805. Giles Playfair, *The Prodigy* (1967), pp 20-1.
8. John Bernard, *Retrospections of the Stage* (Boston, 1830), p.41.
9. *ibid*, p.49
10. S W Ryley, *The Itinerant* (1805), 1. 317.
11. Mrs Skinne appears not to have published any of her plays.
12. Bernard, *Retrospections*, p.73.
13. F Grice, 'Roger Kemble's Company at Worcester', *Theatre Notebook*, 9 (1954-5), 73-5. From 1771 - 8 Holcroft worked with a number of provincial companies. At much the same time as he wrote to Thornton he also contacted, following an introduction given by William Hatton, C J Booth who managed a circuit which included some of the towns of Northumbria. See Philip H Highfill, jnr, Kalman A Burnim, Edward A Langhans, *A Biographical Dictionary of Actors, Actresses, Musicians, Dancers, Managers and Other Stage Personnel in London, 1660-1800* (Carbondale and Edwardsville, 1973-93), 7. 359-60.
14. Bernard, *Retrospections*, p.98.
15. *Berrow's Worcester Journal*, 10 December 1772.
16. Tate Wilkinson, *Memoirs of His Own Life* (York, 1790), 3. 162.
17. *The Thespian Dictionary* (1805), np. J L Hodgkinson and Rex Podgson, *The Early Manchester Theatre* (1960), pp 51 ff.
18. British Library: Burney Collection of Playbills, 1, King's Lynn, 3 March 1774.
19. Mark Moore, *Memoirs and Adventures of Mark Moore* (1795), pp 121-2. Gloucestershire County Records Office, Gloucester: Prohibitions of theatrical performances, 1775 and 1777, Q/TS (addn).
20. *Statute Books*, 22 George II.
21. James Bennett, *A History of Tewkesbury* (Tewkesbury, 1830), p.205n. Moore, *Memoirs*, pp 121-2.
22. Lincoln Central Library: Letters of Thomas Robertson to James Winston, 380131-6.
23. *The Thespian Dictionary*, np. S[ybil] R[osenfeld], 'The Theatrical Notebooks of T H Wilson Manley', *Theatre Notebook*, 7 (1952-3), 2. Highfill, *et al, Biographical Dictionary*, 12. 167-8.
24. West Devon Records Office, Plymouth: Playbill collection, 19 July 1780.
25. Harvard University, Boston, Mass, Theatre Collection: Manuscript notebook of James Winston, TS 1335.211.
26. Edward Cape Everard, *Memoirs of an Unfortunate Son of Thespis* (1818), p.102.
27. Henry Porter, *History of the Theatres of Brighton* (Brighton, 1886), p.11.
28. Everard, *Memoirs*, p.103.
29. Cited by W J Lawrence, *Old Theatre Days and Ways* (1935), p.41.
30. The list of the prompter's duties is based on: Richard Cross, *The Early Diary of Richard Cross, Prompter to the Theatres*, ed H W Pedicord (Manchester, 1955), p.507. Pierce Egan, *The Life of an Actor* (1892), p.254n. *The Prompter*, 12 November 1734.
31. James Winston, *The Theatric Tourist* (1805), p.33. Highfill, *et al, Biographical Dictionary*, 16. 30-1.
32. Everard, *Memoirs*, p.105.
33. Theatre Museum, London: Peter Davey manuscript notebooks, 3, Portsmouth. W G Gates, *Records of the Corporation* (Portsmouth, 1928), p cx. Everard, *Memoirs*, p.207. Peter Davey was a manager of the Portsmouth Theatre. He collected material for a history of the theatres of southern England, a project which he never completed.

CHAPTER 2
THE CIRCUIT: BEGINNINGS

Planning the Circuit

The circuit of theatres which Thornton established appears to have been carefully planned with a clear foresight. When his playhouses are plotted on a map of England it is evident that the majority run along three of the principal coach routes of the eighteenth and nineteenth century, the roads from London to Bath, London to Chichester and London to Portsmouth.[1] One questions how these first theatres were financed. Thornton's marriage to Elizabeth Pritchard brought him into the thick of a theatrical family and it is possible that those members who joined his company made monetary contributions.

With the passing of the 1788 Act, life for a manager became much easier. No longer was he and his company treated, as in the 1737 Act, as a rout of vagabonds wandering the country, illegally staging plays and liable to heavy financial penalties. In place of these strictures the manager was allowed to play for up to sixty nights in any one location, with the exception of London and the two university cities of Oxford and Cambridge. This gave stability to the manager's enterprises. The theatres at Andover and Newbury seem to have begun functioning during the 1784-5 season; these and the theatres at Henley and Farnham were set up in leased barns or warehouses and in contrast, subsequent to the Act, those following at Reading and Guildford were purpose-built. However, it has to be pointed out that even after 1788 Thornton would guardedly open a new location in temporary premises - for example, a barn in a muddy farmyard in Windsor - and if he found the territory advantageous, he would then set up his permanent playhouse.

Newbury

To the north of Newbury, Berkshire, the road running westwards from London to Bath intersected with the northbound road from Southampton to Oxford. This convergence made the town a convenient overnight stop for coaches as the number of inns here testifies; amongst them was the Pelican, since demolished, at which the actor James Quin had stayed and was surprised by the 'enormous bill' he ran up.[2] The town enjoyed the nearby residence of a number of landed gentry, some of whom, such as Lady Elizabeth Craven, later Margravine of Anspach, at Benham Park and Mrs Elizabeth Montague of Sandleford Priory, were enthusiastic supporters of the drama. The geographical position, overnight visitors and the interest of wealthier residents pointed favourably to setting up a theatre in the town. Less advantageous was the general employment of the local community in shops, tavern keeping and farming; such Berkshire workers, as will be seen when looking at Reading, tended not to patronise the play.

Thornton, undeterred, leased premises above a warehouse situated in a narrow thoroughfare, Northcroft Lane, surrounded by similar warehouses as well as taverns.[3] Lying near to the parish church of St Nicolas and the River Kennet, the place was dangerously dark at night in the absence of lamps and when patrons arrived at the building they discovered ignorant and uncivil money takers, uncarpeted boxes and a shortage of playbills, then often used as programmes.[4]

Andover

James Winston in *The Theatric Tourist*, a guide to the provincial theatres of Britain, asserted that Andover, Hampshire was an unpropitious town in which to open a theatre; nevertheless, the place had a theatrical history.[5] A widely spread circuit had been built up by the manager of the Poole Theatre, [Robert?] Bowles, which included several of the locations to be used in the future by Thornton: Andover, where Thornton was to perform regularly for a period, Colnbrook, a location for one or two visits, Wallingford, Dorchester and Windsor, the latter town eventually to house a highly prestigious theatre built, owned and managed by Thornton. At Andover Bowles arrived every two or three years. After his retirement Hounslow's company visited the town. Both performed in a barn or malthouse. Then a theatre was opened in the Market Place, possibly in the old guildhall, the upper part of the Market House, a popular venue, served by Hambling and his players.[6]

10

The yard of the Angel Inn, Andover, in which the theatre building stood. (R. H. Tilling)

Thornton began his visits by settling with Buckland, the landlord of Winchester College's Angel Inn, to rent a large thatched barn in the yard for £10 a year. The landlord was a carpenter by trade and agreed to enlarge the building and put it into repair with the result that the construction and decorations were tolerable. They served well enough for those roughs who congregated in the gallery and made it, in the words of one resident, Turner Poulter Clarke, 'the noisiest in the kingdom'.[7] Buckland was obviously a theatre enthusiast. By 1788 he was scene painter, assisted by Gilbert White, son of the vicar of nearby Fyfield.[8]

Henley

A malthouse and a barn in the yard of the White Hart Inn were the first theatrical locations used in Henley, Oxfordshire by a succession of managers which included Bayliss, Samuel Johnson, and William Smith; the latter also managed the Weybridge, Wokingham, Reading and Sonning theatres.[9] The yard of this Elizabethan inn had been used in earlier days for the entertainment of bear-baiting.[10]

Thornton leased a building in the yard of the Broadgates Inn on the High Street, a good location but indifferent premises; the stage was built

11

into a stable and the pit was a warehouse. However, in an attempt to compensate, the place was 'ornamented with every theatrical decoration'; full houses and distinguished audiences were attracted.[11] There was a worth in the company which contrasted with the short-term visiting actors the town had previously seen[12].

Farnham

A correspondent in the *Reading Mercury* claimed in 1787 that Thornton was manager of a theatre at Farnham and Peter Davey noted that the location here was a barn. If this is correct, presumably the venture did not pay. There is an absence of advertisements and no permanent theatre seems to have been built by Thornton in the town.[13] If it was the same location in which Jackson had earlier worked, a room in the Black Bull, then it was inconveniently rudimentary:

> [Jackson] suspended a collection of green tatters along [the middle of the largest room in the inn] for a curtain, erected a pair of paper screens right-hand and left for wings; arranged four candles in front of said wings, to divide the stage from the orchestra (the fiddlers' chairs being the legitimate division of the orchestra from the Pit) and with all the spare benches of the inn to form Boxes, and a hoop suspended from the ceiling (perforated with a dozen nails to receive as many tallow candles) to suggest the idea of a chandelier; he had constrtucted and embellished what he denominated a Theatre![14]

A collection of four temporary theatres in gimcrack accommodation, made over several years, was an unadventurous start in creating a circuit and it was not until the first of his permanent playhouses was built that Thornton began to demonstrate the flair which made him one of the most successful managers of the Georgian stage.

Reading

Reading, Berkshire, was a town of contrasts. In Thornton's day much of its mediaeval plan remained with a network of narrow, winding streets, including quarters devoted to various foodstuffs, such as Butcher Row with carcases overhanging the way.[15] To one side of the old town were wide Georgian thoroughfares, one of which was Friar Street, a visible token of the 'elegant sociability in the manners of the inhabitants which is irresistably attractive to strangers,' on which Thornton chose in 1788 to build his theatre, situated at number 121.[16] James Winston claimed that Thornton was gripped by a 'constant rage for building' and the Friar Street playhouse flags the start of this activity.[17] Nothing now remains of the building.

There was already a tradition of drama within the town. The headmaster of the Grammar School, Dr Richard Valpey, gave regular presentations of Greek and Roman plays in the original languages with the opportunity for the audience to buy in advance an annotated text.[18] In comparison with this scholarly drama that of the visiting companies lacked finesse, so much so that Samuel Johnson's players drew the comment that the men were 'all rogues' and the women 'whores'.[19] Their behaviour upset the town council who decided to prohibit incoming theatricals. Mark Moore stormed the gates as he had at Tewkesbury and, finding no welcome, appealed to the Attorney General, basing his case on the 1748 Act. He was successful and appeared under his stage name of Signor Moroni.[20] A large building in Pangbourne Lane was fitted up as a playhouse by Smith in the summer of 1781. At first the interior consisted only of pit and gallery; several weeks later boxes were added. Prior to the Reading visit the company performed at Sonning.[21] Yet another attempt at establishing a theatre was made in 1786 when Mrs White, proprietor of the New Inn, formerly the Marquis of Granby, and manager of the Maidenhead Theatre, opened a short season at the inn. After a production of *The School for Scandal* the quality of the 'decorations' and dresses was highly commended and under pressure of popular demand the magistrates extended the short season they had allowed.[22]

Conveniently the Bath Road ran through the town which gave Thornton easy access to Newbury. There were, however, disadvantages. The council opposed a regular theatre which must have been a difficult hurdle to cross; Everard remarked that on this ground Thornton engaged in 'many and great struggles'.[23] Other managers had dealt successfully with the council but, lacking perseverance, their enterprises had failed. Not so Henry Thornton. By May 1788 the theatre was ready. The doors opened at 6.00 pm with a start at 7.00 pm. Generous provision was made for people in the boxes where it was reported two hundred could be accommodated. At first one purchased seats from the 'principal inns', from James and Trendell at their hairdressing salon or from the manager at his lodgings in Gun Street, St Mary's Church Yard. By the following year, however, a box office keeper, Mr Crockford, had been established in the house next to the theatre.[24]

The Reading Theatre from The Theatric Tourist *by James Winston (1805)*
(The British Library)

The first season was lively. As well as a varied range of plays, which included some Shakespeare in adaptation and numerous operettas, a procession of stars made their way to Reading. John Bannister and his daughter led, followed by Stephen Kemble and his wife both of whom Thornton had known in his Portsmouth days.[25] Thomas Ryder, the former manager of the Smock Alley Theatre, Dublin, appeared in *The Miser*, in which the Thorntons also played, for no fee other than than his benefit; Anna Maria Crouch, the singer and actress, also entertained.[26] The highlight of this galaxy was Dorothy Jordan who played the part of Peggy in David Garrick's *The Country Girl* before she left to present the same character in Cheltenham on the occasion of George III taking the waters at the spa.[27]

This first season was highly successful artistically but even with full houses, the small theatre could not yield enough profits to make the speculation pay. Everard felt that if Thornton had presented only the permanent company, which gave decent performances, the audience would have been satisfied and the manager some hundreds of pounds in pocket.[28] The Reading Races were held at the end of August and Thornton maintained his season to cover these, a ploy which became habitual with him (as with many other managers) for they drew larger audiences to the theatres.

Guildford

Whilst Thornton was playing in Reading he decided to build a permanent theatre at Guildford, Surrey. An application, reminding the town council of the 1788 Act, was immediately successful.[29] Why had Thornton selected Guildford as the next station on his circuit? Its position on the Portsmouth Road was obviously the principal reason, especially as he was considering the feasibility of working his way down that route to the coast. At Reading he had discovered that a racecourse in the vicinity could be a useful means of enticing people to the playhouse in the evenings; this Guildford, too, possessed.[30] The ease with which the manager was able to lease a site for the new theatre at the reasonable rent of £10 per annum suggests that he may have known the owner of the land, Fletcher Norton, Lord Grantley of Wonersh Park, Recorder of Guildford and a former speaker of the House of Commons. Norton had bought half of the Red Lion Inn, Market Street, and it was in the yard that Thornton erected the playhouse.[31]

Charles Witherby's map of Guildford clearly shows the site. The High Street and North Street are two parallel roads following the steep downward slope of the land to the River Wey. Market Street is a narrow intersection between the two. In Thornton's day the pattern was exactly the same. Much of the western side of this narrow passage was taken up with the Red Lion Inn and its outbuildings. The theatre abutted onto the end of these and was in turn conjunct with a cockpit at its northernmost flank.[32] That the site was cramped is even more evident from the dimensions of the building which measured only 63 feet by 38; nevertheless, it was said to have an extensive stage and to be capable of seating four hundred.[33] A rough drawing from memory by a local resident, Mr L Ellis, shows a plain rectangular red brick building of two storeys with a steeply pitched slate roof. A single entrance with the term 'Theatre' above served for all classes and the stage door, as shown, is unimpressive.[34] Crowds, propelled by curiosity, attended the theatre at its opening in April 1789.[35] That audience was faithfully served by Thornton for the rest of his working life.

Lord Grantley and his successor rapidly improved the immediate surroundings, thus raising the status of the theatre. The Assize Court was built in Market Street by Grantley and the Earl of Onslow the year after the opening of the theatre and by 1800 the use of the cockpit had changed from fighting to the sale of dairy produce.[36]

Charles Witherby's map of Guildford (1839) showing the position of the Market Street and the theatre. (Guildford Museum)

Horsham and Dorking

Thornton did not always act with such certitude as he had done at Reading and Guildford. In a number of towns he leased a rough building and tested the response of the local people to the theatre. This happened in 1789 at Horsham, Sussex and Dorking, Surrey. The two places, only thirteen miles apart, lay on the route of the London to Chichester road. However, visits to the towns were brief and the project abandoned after a short time.

In Horsham John Baker, a local lawyer, recorded that the Town Hall had been utilised as a theatre by a company performing *Midas* and *Harlequin Skeleton* in July 1772.[37] Towards the end of the century and into the following it was put to further theatrical use. However, most of the applications to perform in Horsham simply referred to 'The Theatre' leaving the location open. These included Charles Osborne, who claimed he would open a 'Histrionic Academy', Edward Cape Everard, Sampson Penley and John Jonas, then joint managers of the Lewes and Eastbourne theatres, John Diddear of Brighton who wanted to hold a winter season, an idea welcomed by the military of the garrison, and Thomas Haymes.[38]

A theatre of sorts also existed in Denne Road, used by a variety of players; at other times it was employed, typically, as a store or, strangely, as a room for dissecting corpses from the town gaol.[39] Possibly this was the venue in which Thornton played in 1789 when he announced that he had opened a theatre. He made a return visit in September 1791 but by the end of the following month a sad note appeared in the newspaper:

> The Theatrical Corps, lately on service at Horsham, was last
> week suddenly disbanded by their Commander in Chief after a
> short, and we believe, not very successful campaign.[40]

The premises must have been in a parlous state as the town magistrates declared that they were unsafe in 1804; earlier Fox had brought the Brighton company to perform and rejected the theatre for the Town Hall, a pleasant market house type of building, although it seems to have lacked boxes.[41] In 1806 the manager of the Worthing Theatre, Thomas Trotter, established himself at the King's Head Hotel, at the intersection of East and North Streets, in spacious accommodation said to hold 700 people.[42] Thornton must have left the way clear for him.

The theatre at Dorking was as insalubrious as that in Horsham's Denne Road. A once-stylish hostelry, the King's Arms Inn, situated on the corner of West Street, had ceased business and over the years the building had become ruinous. In this state it was let as units to shopkeepers and poor families who could afford no more than a single room. A long gallery was occasionally leased to theatre companies.[43] Here, conceivably, Thornton's company performed. Whilst half of the ensemble was playing at Horsham in 1789, the other half played simultaneously in Dorking.[44] An alternative would have been the barn in which Penley later played in 1797.[45]

Chelmsford

The pattern of working along the Bath Road and the routes from London to the south coast was interrupted when Thornton announced in the *Chronicle* during the summer of 1790 that he was to play in Chelmsford, Essex.[46] There may have been several reasons for his change of plan. In looking at the later aberrant positioning of several theatres it becomes obvious that nostalgia could be as good a reason as any for selecting a location. Thornton's childhood had been spent in Suffolk but the Norwich Company and David Fisher's players traversed that county and Norfolk; there were fit-ups playing spasmodically in Clare, Thornton's birthplace, and Fisher and William Scraggs conducted business in the earlier-mentioned barn in Sudbury.[47] Chelmsford was possibly the nearest suitable town to Thornton's childhood haunts; furthermore he had made trips to Essex whilst managing the band of strollers in his twenties[48]. Emotion was tempered by opportunism, however. Defences against the possible incursion of Napoleon and the French troops were being set up along the south and south-east coasts. Around Chelmsford martello towers were constructed. Within the next six years four thousand military personnel moved into accommodation rapidly rising in Wood Street and Barrack Square. A captive audience waited for amusements in the evenings.[49] Socially, too, the town was of some consequence: the assizes were held here and assemblies proliferated. Another draw to the town was the race course, situated on Galleywood Common, which enjoyed the privileged gift of an annual plate donated by Queen Charlotte.[50]

Minor theatrical activity had spread in and around the town. In 1773 strollers performed at the Shears Inn in Colchester (now Springfield) Lane on the edge of the town. The same year some of the townspeople, possibly by way of response, turned a room at the White Horse Inn, centrally located opposite the Shire Hall, into a playhouse where they gave a piece with a local flavour, *The Merry Midnight Mistake* by David Ogborne who also was responsible for painting the scenes.[51] Three years later the six year old equestrian child prodigy, Samuel Thomas Russell, a later rival of Thornton in Oxford, was presented by his parents, giving, as well as his horsemanship display, 'imitations' and an address.[52] When Thornton was ensconced, travelling players known as the Phoenix Company performed nearby at Bocking, Dunmow and Castle Hedingham and Johnson and Son brought their players to Maldon just before the end of the century. More permanent enterprises demonstrated that theatre could succeed in East Anglia: Hounslow managed a theatre at Bishop's Stortford and Bartrum of the Norwich Company managed theatres at Colchester and Ipswich.[53] During his first visit to the town Thornton made an excursion to the Assembly Rooms at Ongar to perform. Possibly he was considering using Chelmsford as the hub of a series of nearby forays, a plan he later abandoned.[54]

Thornton's first season was a success, - so much so that by August 1790 the manager had announced that he would build a permanent theatre at Chelmsford.[55]

Gosport

> A theatre is opened at Gosport by Mr Thornton, formerly
> prompter to Mr Wheeler's company at Portsmouth, and we
> understand is likely to meet with encouragement.[56]

Perhaps there is a clue in the wording of the above announcement which appeared in the *Hampshire Chronicle* at the beginning of 1791 to the choice of Gosport, Hampshire, for Thornton's next theatre. Working on the 'nostalgia theory' propounded earlier, the manager may well have yearned to return to the south coast in the vicinity of Portsmouth. Indeed, two years previous Wheeler had invited Thornton and Everard to Gosport to act in the temporary playhouse he had set up in the yard of the India Arms Hotel. Wheeler used the fit-up on nights that the Portsmouth Theatre was closed. However, the houses could be poor and the company had sometimes receipted no more than £5.[57] There were a number of other difficulties Thornton would have to face. Thomas Collins leased a small theatre off the King's Arms Passage in Gosport as well as managing his flourishing theatres in nearby Portsmouth and Chichester.[58]

The place had advantages as well. A social consciousness began to pervade the town expressed in the provision of assemblies in the coffee room of the White Lion Hotel and the dancing lessons given by French teachers; the theatre could be a useful adjunct to this activity. Gosport was the victualling yard of the Royal Navy, crowded with sailors, traditionally patrons of the drama, during the Napoleonic Wars. A penny ferry (three pence on rough days) linked with Portsmouth, a work-a-day town with few carriages - hence a restricted society - but again a naval and military base.[59] On a larger scale a regular ferry service to Havre de Grace was evolving, so bringing overnight visitors to Gosport.[60]

Unfortunately Thornton's place of playing is not known. It would not have been Wheeler's fit-up as the interior had been dismantled. Nor does the local paper carry any news of the season. It appears to have been a budget venture, relying on members of the family as performers rather than the employment of expensive London theatre people.

Windsor

By April 1791 Thornton was advertising that he had obtained in Berkshire the Windsor Theatre.[61] The old pattern of infilling the Bath route with theatres continued. However, in this instance the building was no great catch but simply a barn standing in a muddy farmyard at the lower and wetter end of Peascod Street[62]. The interior seems to have been an improvement for the *Public Advertiser* speaks of the 'very neat manner' in which the playhouse was fitted up.[63] Two stage boxes were provided with decorative canopies and side and front boxes had been painted two years earlier.[64] Geographically the position made it an excellent choice: the theatre was near the houses at Reading and Henley and London was only 20 miles away on a direct coach route.[65] Whether Thornton envisaged performing before the court at Windsor is impossible to tell; certainly the approach to the theatre would have been unsuitable.

There were various formalities to be undergone. George III's approval of the new manager had to be obtained before the theatre could be opened. Possibly the Lord Chamberlain who licensed the theatres in such places of royal residence as Brighton and Richmond was the liaison. One of the conditions of approval was that the company would only perform during the holidays of nearby Eton College; these lasted for a month at Christmas, beginning on the second Monday of December; the spring holiday took place during Holy Week, traditionally a week in which theatres closed, and Easter Week; and the summer Bartlemtide holiday was for four weeks from the first Monday in August.[66] A town guide clarifies how this limited the seasons. The company could be seen

> from the middle of December to the latter end of January and
> from the last Monday in July to the end of September. With

permission from the Magistrates of Windsor and that of the
Provost and Master of Eton School, it has been usual for them to
perform during Ascot Races...[67]

Obviously Thornton would be unable to take full advantage of the pro-
visions of the Sixty Day Act.

In spite of these restrictions Windsor had enjoyed theatrical entertainments in the past. As early as *c.*1705, when Queen Anne was at Windsor, a
Mrs Carrol (the future Mrs Centlivre) 'put on her Breeches again and acted
[at court] the part of Alexander the Great, in the tragedy of that Name'.[68] In
1748 Richard Yates opened a booth theatre, presumably either in the yard
of an inn or in a field on the edge of the town.[69] Later the town became a
stopping place on the circuit of Bowles of Poole. For eleven years from 1778
Francis Godolphin Waldron, also manager of the Richmond Theatre, Surrey,
had been manager in Windsor. He was a literary person, writing a number
of plays for the various theatres in which he performed, as well as a vast
number of tracts and books on the drama; he also ran a bookselling business.[70] Above all he was a man of the theatre, learning his craft under David
Garrick at Drury Lane and serving as George Colman the Younger's
prompter at the Haymarket Theatre.[71] Members of his Richmond company
played regularly in Windsor.[72] He was succeeded by Berkley Baker who on
his retirement from management a couple of years later opened a public
house, The Merry Wives of Windsor, and also undertook acting tours in
London and America.[73]

Thornton made little of the presentations at the Windsor Theatre. They
received scant notice in the *Reading Mercury*. At first the regular company was rarely augmented by London personalities. Indeed some of the original Waldron company remained, the most strong-willed of which were
probably the Bensons. On one occasion Robert Benson absented himself
from the part of Orlando (*As You Like It*) piqued at the engagement of two
London actresses who played some of the roles his wife usually undertook.[74]

Arundel

Thornton visited Arundel, Sussex, in 1791, playing in a temporary theatre. Finding circumstances to his liking, the following year he advertised
that a new theatre was in the course of erection. Possibly this, too, was
no more than a barn which could be let between infrequent visits.[75] Its
site is unknown although William Douglas writes that Thornton later used
a building in the yard of the Angel Inn as a venue.[76]

This was an unusual town in which to build a theatre: not only was it very small, the limited number of bedrooms in the houses suggested that there was no regular influx of resident visitors for events such as race meetings or assemblies. The Duke of Norfolk presided from his hillside castle over the compact society. It was some 40 miles from Thornton's firmly established south coast theatre at Gosport but a coach ran to Fareham, providing a convenient link and one could travel northwards to London via Horsham.[77] Thornton may have set his sights on nearby Chichester which possessed a new, attractive theatre, also opened in 1792 but if he had designs on this, he was thwarted for the building was managed by Thomas Collins and forty years were to elapse before the Thornton-Barnett company played a season there.[78]

1. See: *Britannia Depicted*, based on John Ogilby's Maps, rev Ino Owen (1730). pp 8-10, 22 ff and 71.

2. Cecil Roberts, *And So to Bath* (1940), p.287.

3. Berkshire Record Office, Reading: Borough of Newbury, Council Minute Book, 1742-1785, pp 613-4, AC 1/1/2.

4. *Reading Mercury*, 5 December 1785.

5. *Salisbury Journal*, 13 December 1784. *Biography of the British Stage* (1824), p.199. Winston,*Tourist* , p.8.

6. *Salisbury Journal*, 8 December 1777 and 13 November 1779. Birmingham Central Library: Winston collection, Andover, letter of Thomas Rawlins to James Winston. Winston, *Tourist*, p.8.

7. Arthur Bennett and Edward Parsons, *A History of the Free School of Andover* (Andover, 1920), p.81.

8. Bodleian Library, Oxford: Diaries of the Revd Henry White, 4 February - 12 March 1788, *passim*, Diaries 42111-12. Gilbert White was the nephew of the famous Selborne naturalist of the same name.

9. Birmingham Central Library: Winston collection, letter of M Andrews to James Winston.

10. John Southern Brim, *A History of Henley on Thames* (1861), p.20.

11. Birmingham Central Library: Winston collection, Henley, letter of M Andrews.

12. *Reading Mercury*, 19 February 1787.

13. *Reading Mercury*, 19 February 1787. Theatre Museum: Davey manuscript notebooks, 28, Farnham.

14. Bernard, *Retrospections*, p.11.

15. W M Childs, *The Town of Reading during the Early Part of the Nineteenth Century* (Reading, 1910), p.11.

16. William Mavor, *A General View of the Agriculture of Berkshire* (1809), p.463. *The Post Office Reading Directory* (Reading 1842), p.37.

17. Winston, *Tourist* , p.8.

18. eg *Reading Mercury*, 6 October 1806.

19. Birmingham Central Library: Winston collection, Reading, letter of Smart and Carslade to James Winston.

20. Moore, *Memoirs*, pp 121 and 156.

21. *Reading Mercury*, 23 April, 14 and 21 May, 18 June and 30 July 1781.

22. *Reading Mercury*, 16 October 1787. Thomas Sheridan, '500 Years of Reading Theatre', *Reading and Berkshire Review*, 11 (1952), 14.

23. Everard, *Memoirs*, p.135.

The Circuit: Beginnings

24. Harvard Theatre Collection: Winston's manuscript notebook, TS 1335.211. Winston, *Tourist*, p.18. Everard, *Memoirs*, p.135. *Reading Mercury*, 12 and 19 May 1788 and 30 November 1789. Information supplied by Daphne Phillips.

25. *Reading Mercury*, 2 and 9 June 1788.

26. *Reading Mercury*, 7, 21 and 28 July 1788

27. *Reading Mercury*, 16 June 1788. Claire Tomalin, *Mrs Jordan's Profession* (2nd edition, 1995), pp 79-88.

28. Everard, *Memoirs*, p.135.

29. Guildford Muniment Room: Petition of Henry Thornton and Licence to erect a theatre, BR/QS/2/7(1) and (2). *Reading Mercury*, 25 August 1788.

30. J and S Russell, *A History of Guildford* (Guildford, 1801), p.177.

31. Guildford Muniment Room: lease (1792), RB 274; 'Catalogue of the Papers of the Grantley Estate', biographical note on Fletcher Norton.

32. Charles Witherby, Map of Guildford (1839).

33. J and S Russell, *History of Guildford*, ed F Laurence (Guildford, 1845), p.187. E R Chamberlin, *Guildford. A Biography* (1970), pp 169-70.

34. Local Studies Library, Guildford: drawing of the theatre by L Ellis. Comments on it are contained in a letter dated 28 June 1948 from the Chief Librarian of Guildford to Richard Southern.

35. *Reading Mercury*, 20 April 1789.

36. W C Smith, *Rambles round Guildford* (Guildford, 1828), p.49; *A Handbook to Guildford and its Environs* (Guildford, 1862), p.97; Shirley Corke, *Guildford. A Pictorial History* (Chichester, 1990), fig 71.

37. John Baker, *The Diary of John Baker*, ed P C Yorke (1931), p.239.

38. Horsham Museum: letters and applications to the Horsham bailiffs and magistrates to perform in the town, HM333.

39. Maria Theresa Odell, *More about the Old Theatre Worthing* (Worthing, 1945), p.28. Francis Steer, 'Sources of Information on 18th and Early 19th Century Theatres in Sussex', *Theatre Notebook*, 12 (1957-8), 62.

40. *West Sussex Advertiser*, 28 November 1791.

41. Harvard Theatre Collection: Winston's notebooks, TS1335.211. Folger Shakespeare Library, Washington D C: Winston's notebooks, T.a.65.

42. Odell, *Worthing*, p.13. Susannah Lee was landlady at the time of Trotter's visit, see *The Horsham Companion*, ed Susan C Djabir. The hotel is still flourishing but no remains of the theatre exist.

43. John Timbs, *A Picturesque Promenade around Dorking* (1823), p.63. Although Timbs refers to the hotel as the King's Head, it is possible he has muddled the name with another Dorking inn. Alan A Jackson, ed, *Dorking. A Surrey Market Town through Twenty Centuries*, (Dorking, 1991), p.63.

44. Everard, *Memoirs*, p.136.

45. Folger Shakespeare Library, Washington D C: Winston's notebooks, T.a. 65.

46. *Chelmsford Chronicle*, 2 July 1790.

47. Grice, *Rogues and Vagabonds* pp 102-3.

48. Bernard, *Retrospections*, p.97.

49. Britton, J and Brayley, E W, *The Beauties of England and Wales* (1801),5. 26

50. *Universal British Directory* (1793), pp 513 and 515.

51. Charles Dibdin, *Observations on a Tour throughout almost the Whole of England and a considerable Part of Scotland* [1801-2], 2. 52. Essex Record Office, Chelmsford: W A Mepham, 'History of the Drama in Essex from the Fifteenth Century to the Present Time', typescript doctoral thesis, University of London, 1988, pp 341-344. David Ogborne's play had been published in 1765.

52. *Universal British Directory* , pp 513 and 515. Mepham, 'Drama in Essex', p.345.

53. *Chelmsford Chronicle*, 13 July, 2 November 1798; 4 January, 5 April, 10 May, 7 June 1799. Britton and Brayley, *Beauties*, 5.260. Phyllis Hartnoll, *The Concise Oxford Companion to the Theatre* (1972), p.386.

54. *Chelmsford Chronicle*, 17 September 1790.

55. *Chelmsford Chronicle*, 6 August 1790.

56. *Hampshire Chronicle*, 24 January 1791.
57. Harvard Theatre Collection: Winston's manuscript notebook, TS 1335.211. Everard, *Memoirs*, p.136.
58. H T Rogers, 'Gosport's Lost Theatres', *Gosport Records,* 3 (1972), 13.
59. *HampshireTelegraph*, 28 August 1809. *Portsmouth Telegraph*, 19 May 1800. Tate Wilkinson, *The Wandering Patentee* (York, 1795), 3. 172.
60. *Hampshire Chronicle*, 29 June, 7 September 1791. *Universal British Directory*, 3. 182.
61. *Reading Mercury*, 18 April 1791.
62. Winston, *Tourist*, p.54.
63. *Public Advertiser*, 17 August 1779. Harvard Theatre Collection, Winston's manuscript notebook, TS 1335,211
64. *Reading Mercury*,14 December 1789.
65. A Robertson, *The Great Road from London to Bath* (1792), np.
66. Eton College Library: a manuscript paper by Thomas James, 1766.
67. *The Windsor Guide* (Windsor, 1811), p.24.
68. Thomas Whincop, *Scanderberg or Love and Liberty to which are added a List of all the Dramatic Authors ...to the Year 1747* (1747), p.188.
69. Winston, *Tourist*, p.54
70. *The Thespian Dictionary* , np. F G Waldron, *The Literary Museum* (1792), *passim*. *Gentleman's Magazine*, 88 (1818), 283-4. Winston, *Tourist*, pp 54-5.
71. Leslie Stephen and Sidney Lee, eds, *Dictionary of National Biography,* 20 (1909), 484-5.
72. eg *Public Advertiser*, 17 August 1779.
73. Highfill *at al*, *Biographical Dictionary* 1. 219.
74. Winston, *Tourist*, p 54. Harvard Theatre Collection: Winston's manuscript notebook, TS 1335.211.
75. Everard, *Memoirs*, p.146. *Sussex Weekly Advertiser*, 23 April 1792. Odell, *Worthing*, p.25.
76. New York Public Library: Manuscript notebook of William Douglas.
77. John Tompkins, *The Tompkins Diary*, ed G W Eustace (Cambridge, 1930), entry for 21 December 1809.
78. Arnold Hare, *The Georgian Theatre in Wessex* (1958), pp 169-170.

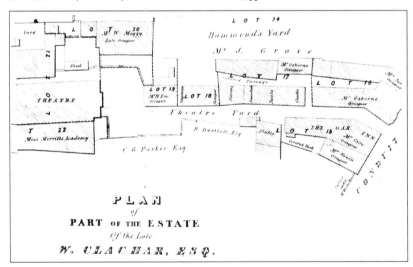

Plan of part of Chelmsford from the sale catalogue of William Clacher's estate. (Essex Record Office, Chelmsford)

CHAPTER 3
THE CIRCUIT: EXPANSION

Chelmsford

At Chelmsford Thornton had been as good as his word. A small purpose-built theatre situated off Conduit Street was ready to open in July
1792.[1] Patrons turned down Theatre Yard beside the Oak Inn and at the
end found a small rectangular brick building, 30 feet wide and 66 feet
long. Attractive gardens leading down to the River Can lay behind the
structure and were used, with lanterns hanging in the trees, for dancing
on fine evenings.[2] The theatre was erected by William Clachar, the proprietor and printer of the weekly local newspaper, the *Chelmsford
Chronicle*, on his own land, with his works partly hiding the playhouse
from the main street. Clachar was also a bookseller and stocked more
disparate commodities such as rat poison and purging elixir as well as acting as a fire agent.[3] Out of the theatre season, Clacher used the playhouse
as an auction room.[4]

Although small, 'neat' was a word often applied, the interior of the theatre was attractive. The decorations - as also was the scenery - had been
painted by William Johnson, an artist of Chelmsford. A correspondent to
the Chronicle thought the building to be

> one of the most elegant and splendid little theatres he has seen
> in the country and that the decorations, etc. etc. will be equal in
> taste, richness and fancy to be found of those of the first the-
> atres.[5]

For the opening night Thornton wrote and delivered a rhymed address
- he enjoyed this labour - between the two plays, *The Road to Ruin* and
The Lying Valet. The prices and the starting time were as at his other theatres. The season coincided not only with the Races but also with the
Assize Week and a Flower Feast at the Shire Hall.[6] During the races the

theatre was open every evening except Sunday at a time when many provincial theatres opened only four times a week and Saturday was often regarded as a closure night.[7]   Additionally Thornton experimented with the innovation of matinée performances, prior to the race meetings, on Tuesday, Wednesday and Thursday.   The manager tended to grind his performers into the ground, a habit on which Winston commented:

> Mr T is of the opinion that six bad nights per week are better
> than three middling ones and consequently works his actors.[8]

Southend

In the early summer of 1793 Thornton was not only preparing to open a new theatre at Windsor, but also one at Southend, Essex. In all, this was an unproductive venture and he appears to have lasted only four years in the town. A temporary structure was used, probably stables, in the grounds of Lawn House which stood near the foreshore. This humble building unfortunately did not live up to the hopes of Thomas Archer in his long prospectus poem written as new buildings in the town were rising:

> And soon Thalia's pleasures shall be shar'd,
> A decent Theatre is now prepar'd.[9]

Thornton advertised the opening night, 26 August 1793, in the *Chelmsford Chronicle* (*Everyone Has His Fault* was given together with *Rosina*) but refrained for a while from further newspaper notices.[10]

By 1797 Ralph Wewitzer, a member of Thornton's troupe, was granted a licence to bring a company to Southend. Thornton usually relinquished temporary leadership to members of his family only and one wonders whether Wewitzer had struck out on his own. During the next few years Thomas Trotter brought the Worthing company to play at various venues in the town. In 1800 a room in the Grand Hotel was used and by 1804 he had opened a new purpose-built playhouse located near to the Castle Inn. The circumstances were highly unusual: Thornton, who enjoyed a fight to preserve territorial rights, seems to have been driven from the town by two other managers. What attracted him to Southend in the first place? From 1790 thoughts of speculation were in the air: the building of the Royal Terrace and its accompanying Royal Hotel and the nearby Subscription Library had begun and the plan of the High Street was laid out. However, the sale of properties hung fire and the speculators ran into financial difficulties. Possibly Thornton's departure was an exercise in cutting one's losses as the anticipated extent of a graciously planned Southend failed to materialise.[11]

Windsor

If members of the court were to attend the theatre in Windsor, then Thornton would need to build a suitable venue in the centre of the town. This he did at 27 (56 according to the numbering at the time of writing) High Street, at the foot of the Castle ramparts. By July 1793 Thomas Sandby, the draughtsman and architect who lived in the Great Park, inspected the premises and found them safe.[12] The king also paid preliminary visits to look around the theatre before the official opening, expressing himself pleased with the result.[13]

In the previous months several curious claims to the ownership of the theatre had been made by Benson, the member of the company mentioned earlier. The first of these appeared in a report of the 1792 season in the *Thespian Magazine*, based possibly on information supplied by the actor:

> This little theatre [ie that in Peascod Street] which has the privilege of opening during the Eton vacation has had a tolerable season and produced the manager, Mr Benson of Drury Lane Theatre, we should think a plentiful harvest;...[14]

The next claim appeared the following year and this time referred to the High Street theatre:

> We are happy to find that a new theatre is now erecting in the middle of Windsor (a plan which has been presented and approved of by his Majesty) and will be entirely finished by July - Benson, of Old Drury Lane, is appointed Manager, and we are informed Mr Thornton and Company are engaged to perform with him.[15]

A slight clue is offered in *The Theatric Tourist*, written twelve years after the events, in which Winston notes that Waldron 'having lent to Benson some scenery for a country scheme, the hero in return got Windsor from him'.[16] Was the Peascod Street theatre security for the scenery? If so, Benson must have imagined he had done rather well. Thornton's rebuttal of the situation did not appear until August but it was decisive:

Various reports have taken place who are proprietors and managers of this undertaking. The public prints have mentioned a
joint concern of different parties; but we assert with an authori-
ty and confidence that defy contradiction, this elegant theatre is
the sole property of Mr Thornton the manager, who as well as
sole proprietor, is the sole manager.[17]

The Windsor Theatre from The Theatric Tourist *by James Winston (1805).*
(The British Library)

The internal structure of the building consisted of two tiers of boxes,
slips, pit and gallery with the prices ranging from 4/- to 1/-, an increase
on Thornton's other theatres in the price of the superior seats. The
building held £70, a goodly increase on the £25 that the previous building had accommodated.[18] When the royal family attended, then extra
revenue was made by dividing the pit with ropes into 'boxes' with
appropriate charges and applying these also to the gallery slips.
Charles Knight, who became the editor of the *Windsor and Eton Express*,
recorded his childhood memories of the building. The stage box and
the line of lower tier boxes on the prompt side of the house accommodated the royal family and court on their visits. Rarely could the
monarch have been so close to a gathering of his subjects:

The Circuit: Expansion

> ...the pit, where some dozen persons might be closely packed on
> each bench, separate the royal circle from the genteel parties in
> the opposite tier of boxes. With the plebeians in the pit the
> Royal Family might have shaken hands.[19]

In earlier days the king had been a keen performer and still maintained a lively interest in both plays and players.[20] A comedy was much to his taste but George complained to Fanny Burney 'of the great want of modern comedies and of the extreme immorality of most of the old ones'.[21] Thornton, bearing this in mind, selected John Quick to take the role of Scrub in the king's choice of *The Beaux Stratagem* for the court's first visit to the Windsor Theatre on 2 September.[22] This was the first of a series of visits and the routine was repeated at each: accompanying the royal family was a 'considerable bevy of ancient maids of honour and half pay generals', all making their way on foot from the apartments in Windsor Castle to the theatre door; there, at precisely seven o'clock, they were met by the manager at the entrance to his house, adjoining and connecting with the theatre; carrying a candelabra in each hand and walking backwards, he escorted the visitors into the auditorium where the audience rose as the six violins struck up the National Anthem; the king nodded to his people and, together with the queen, took his seat in the stage box; the satin bills of the day, which had lain on the seats, were displayed, a sign for the performance to begin.[23] At the end of the third act of the main piece the royal family retired to take coffee whilst in the gallery a local brew, Queen's Ale, circulated. Performances finished at about 11.00 pm when 'God Save the King' was repeated, the monarch bowed to the house amidst applause and the royal party followed the manager either to the waiting carriages or joined the link boys for the walk up the slope to the castle apartments. On nights when a royal visit was expected, the remainder of the audience arrived at staggered times: admission to the gallery was from 5.45 pm, to the pit 6.15 pm and the box doors opened at 6.30 pm ready for a 7.00 pm start.[24]

One of the highlights of the first season at the theatre was Quick's benefit. The choice of plays was again in the hands of the king - 'an honour almost unprecedented', remarked the *Thespian Magazine* - who selected another Farquhar comedy, *The Recruiting Officer*, and John O'Keeffe's *Wild Oats*.[25] A further favourite of the king appeared in the course of the season: Richard Suett travelled down from Drury Lane to play Alscrip in *The Heiress* during which the king's voice rang out at each of his quips, 'Bravo! Suett!!', a response engendering a roar of loyal sympathy in pit and gallery, although the boxes 'were too genteel for such emotional feelings'.[26]

Towards the end of the season the *Thespian Magazine* commented that the company

> upon the whole have met with wonderful encouragement, as
> indeed both him [Thornton] and them richly deserved. His
> attention and judgement are equal to any manager whatever.[27]

In that phrase 'upon the whole' is a hint of a difficulty that was to increase: when the royal family attended, the theatre was overflowing but on other nights attendance fell below an economic level and eventually was to become a serious financial hazard.[28] In spite of that, Thornton was justly proud of his new-found position as entertainer to the king and queen. Although his name appears on none of the royal household lists, Thornton was to refer to his company, wherever they played, as 'Their Majesties Servants from the Theatre Royal, Windsor'.

Croydon

The Croydon theatre which Thornton first leased in 1794 was a timber barn, 'a good deal decayed and very incommodious' standing on Crown Hill.[29] Patrons with box places were admitted by a central doorway cut into the stucco front of the building and above this a long window was set which gave the gallery - to which an outside wooden staircase led - limited ventilation.[30]

This was not the manager's first experience of playing in the Surrey town, for two years earlier he had set up in temporary accommodation at the Croydon Fair, an event which opened annually on 2 October.[31] Here he was in company with other well-known managers. One of these was the popular conjuror and puppeteer, [Daniel?] Gyngell with his fleet of caravans; an elderly resident remembered that he leased a wooden building as his theatre and drew up his vehicles alongside. John Richardson, who was to extend his circuit of fairs from the towns around London as far afield as Oxford, Newmarket and Winchester, was another visitor.[32] Each of his shows was reputed to last twenty minutes, reminiscent of the later penny gaffs.[33] This is the only known record of the established Thornton performing at a fair. On taking a lease of the permanent theatre, he relinquished the booth.[34]

Presumably the public response to the players was encouraging enough for Thornton to take a risk, contravene the 1788 Act and rent on a regular basis a playhouse at a location only ten miles (ie ten miles nearer than the stipulated limit) from Westminster and the City. Possibly the size of the location with its five thousand inhabitants was an inducement.[35] Other Croydon managers had opened their theatres in previous years with impunity. There was the Widow Yates whose company performed in a 'Large Theatrical Barn facing the Boarding School'.[36] Carr had begun at Croydon performing in a tavern before coming to the Crown Inn Yard where he kept a small company; his circuit consisted of a number of towns, including Deptford, on the edge of London.[37] He was succeeded by Berkley Baker, former manager of the Windsor theatre.[38]

A building to the north of Crown Hill, Croydon, almost opposite the opening of Surrey Street, had come into the hands of John Fly. His son, John Moys Fly, transformed this into a playhouse and immediately afterwards claimed it was worth £2,000. Behind the stage was a series of outhouses consisting of a stable with three horse boxes, a barn and a cart shed. Over the first of these the dressing rooms were situated.[39] Thornton first leased this in 1800 for an annual visit.[40] There was nothing exceptional in the building and the remarks made about it were the sort used in descriptions of Thornton's other new theatres: it was considered a 'perfect bijou, small but compact' playhouse.[41] William Douglas noted that the playhouse was 'nearly on the plans of the then London Theatres', an imprecise remark capable of several meanings.[42] Over the proscenium arch the legend, 'All the World's a Stage' was scrolled, later changed to 'Multum in Parvo'. Seating consisted of two tiers of boxes, pit and gallery bringing the box office takings to £30.[43] A narrow passage took pit and gallery patrons alongside the building and through the yard, replete with its pig sty, belonging to A. Burnett, a corn merchant.[44] This 'rough and dirty lane' could become so muddy that an ostler would be needed to carry one to the entrance.[45] Thornton usually arrived at Croydon in time to give a performance on 2 October, the opening day of the fair, which then continued for two more; he went on to play for six to eight weeks. The remaining part of the year the building was leased to other professional companies or to groups of amateurs.[46]

The theatre and company pleased the people of Croydon. A correspondent to the *Monthly Mirror* wrote: 'The scenery [is] of unparalleled variety and excellence for a country theatre, and the whole of the company respectable in every way...'.[47] This approbation notwithstanding, by 1810 Thornton was ready to relinquish the lease and the theatre was sold to Robert William Elliston, the Drury Lane actor.[48]

31

Henley

The theatre at Henley was among Thornton's first cluster of playhouses. Surprisingly, for it was conveniently located within easy reach of Windsor and Reading and houses there appear to have been well-attended, he decided in 1795 to sell the building at the Broadgates to two reputable managers, Penley and Jonas.[49] As the building served for a further ten years, one presumes that it was in a reasonable state of repair.

East Cowes

During 1795 Thornton's company played at East Cowes, on the Isle of Wight, and Fareham and both were to be visited in future years; yet almost nothing is known of either theatre.

The establishment of a playhouse at East Cowes was only to be expected when sea-bathing became fashionable. The other accoutrements of the seaside had been provided, 'genteel and reasonable lodgings' and a fleet of bathing machines.[50] East Cowes, the area in which the theatre was situated, was approached from West Cowes by a ferry.[51] It served as the sorting and reloading base for the Carolina rice ships as well as for boats bringing tobacco, employing large numbers of workers as did the expanding dockyards.[52]

Fareham

On the return journey the company played at an unknown location in Fareham, but without Everard who had become dissatisfied with his terms of employment. There can be little doubt that a theatre building of sorts existed in the town: earlier in the century Charlotte Charke had performed with a small troupe.[53]

Gosport

The unidentified, temporary theatre in which Thornton's company had camped during their visits to Gosport was replaced with a permanent structure in 1796. Situated in Middle Street, now the High Street, and conveniently near to the King's Arms Hotel, a double fronted house gave the manager a residence and his patrons a coffee shop and tavern; the flanks of the building were separated by an archway through which theatre-goers made their way to the small auditorium beyond. This held a box office income of £50; reputedly there was room for 500 (some claim as many as 800) spectators.[54] A newspaper report, possibly written by the manager himself, speaks in glowing terms of the town's new acquisition:

> We learn that this very elegant Theatre, erected by Mr
> Thornton, proprietor and manager of the Theatre Royal,
> Windsor, etc. opens on Monday next; and we are informed by
> an intelligent correspondent it is fitted up in a style of elegance
> and splendour superior to any other provincial theatre, and
> that the man whose spirit, judgement and taste is universally
> known and acknowledged has confined himself to no expense
> whatever in the completion of this undertaking....[55]

The Winchester firm of William Cave and Son was hired to create new scenes; there is a distinct possibility that the auditorium decorations were also in their hands.[56]

Both Wheeler and Collins had retired from the town, although Collins was flourishing in nearby Portsmouth. Within Gosport Thornton had a clear coast; appreciating this, for some winters he and his family resorted to the town, braving the sea winds, in order to play a lengthy season.

*The Gosport Theatre, standing on the right hand side of the present
High Street, c1890.*   (Author's collection)

Weybridge

It may have been a pleasant surprise for Thornton to be asked by Frederica, Duchess of York, who, since her marriage in 1791 resided at Oatlands House, Weybridge, to manage the theatre in the town. Scruffy, it was a 'barnlike' building in Back (now Baker) Street. As this was an unfit place for the reception of the Duke and Duchess, a small portico with a central opening was added externally and inside a stage box for the royal pair was constructed.[57] The building had been in theatrical use since 1751.[58] Although in the past a success with nearby playhouses, the manager William Smith and his wife had grown too old to cope with the company. Thornton accepted the commission and generously allowed his elderly predecessors to live in the theatre residence. The Duchess would have seen Thornton's company perform at earlier appearances in Weybridge in 1794 and 1795 as well as coming in contact with the players when she and her husband were staying at Windsor Castle.[59]

Frederica Charlotte, Duchess of York.
(Elmbridge Museum, Weybridge)

In a town of only 700 inhabitants there would be no opportunity for lengthy seasons, so Thornton took the opportunity to let the building to the Methodists during the company's absences, a surprising arrangement as the sect was overtly anti-thespian.[60] Guildford, where Thornton held regular seasons, was only a dozen miles away, allowing for occasional nights in Weybridge and at such spasmodic times as he played at Dorking and Farnham he again found himself near to the little town. Members of Smith's company were presumably subsumed into Thornton's. By August 1797 refurbishment was completed and at the command of the Duchess *A Cure for the Heart Ache* opened the new season.[61]

After Thornton's appointment in 1797 little appeared to happen. William Smith died in 1799 and was interred in the burial ground of Weybridge parish church.[62] The year following the building was acquired by Lady Tuite who owned other small properties in the town. Winston reported that Osborne was manager in 1803 but by 1810 the building would appear to have been relinquished as a playhouse.[63]

Remarkably few playbills of the Thornton management at Weybridge remain. A bill exists for one of his early short seasons at the 'New Theatre' where the company performed under the sponsorship of the Hon Mrs Petre. Many of the family as well as the Hattons are named in this as appearing in the musical entertainment *My Grandmother*.[64] A later bill of 1804 is for a benefit performance of *The Review* given for a mason, Simpson, and his wife. On the bill Simpson grumbled about the 'standard expenses of this theatre'.[65]

Little took place in Weybridge at the beginning of the nineteenth century to interest or detain Thornton and at the end of the first decade he left the town without ceremony.

Oxford

Since 1584 the Vice-Chancellor of the University of Oxford, later strengthened by a ratification of the Privy Council, had forbidden professional companies of players to perform within the city and even the relatively liberal 1788 Act prohibited theatrical entertainments within fourteen miles of Oxford.[66] Pleas for the repeal of these injunctions had been made; the reasoning of the correspondent in the *Gentleman's Magazine* is typical:

> If it should be urged that the introduction of a company of
> players might be the cause of breeding many disturbances
> amongst the 'gens togata' I answer, Why is not this the case in
> the music room? Or why is it not as likely that a play of
> Shakespeare would be heard with as much attention as the
> finest piece of music whatever.[67]

Illegally theatres had opened on a regular basis in the neighbouring towns and next to nothing was done to inhibit performances. Abingdon, five miles away, boasted of a long theatrical tradition with companies visiting since the mid-century. The Lamb Inn at the side of the Sheep Market (now the Square) and the Market House were the locations in which the companies of the elderly Linnett, Penshard and Wood performed.[68] Henry Lee remarked that Oxford students were wont to travel to the town to see plays, viewing them with undue merriment.[69] At the time of his visits to Abingdon Linnet visited Woodstock, too, playing at the Town Hall until he was banned from using it and resorted to the Six Bells (later 16 Oxford Street).[70] Was it his actors whom Josiah Wedgwood in 1765 dismissed as a mess of 'poverty, rags and blunders'?[71] Northleach, Burford, Eynsham and Wallingford were other neighbours enjoying presentations.[72] Within the city itself the Great Room of the Mitre and a room capable of holding a large audience at the Wheatsheaf, off the High Street, were used for entertainments such as the fantoccini and one man shows. A Mr Collins, for example, gave an entertainment 'An Evening Brush for Rubbing Off the Rust of Care'.[73]

Possibly these examples of past theatre offered Thornton cause for hope. For how long he battled with the University authorities is not known, but by 1799 he was ready to open a theatre. Possibly his connections with the royal family had helped and it is possible that George III himself intervened on his behalf.[74] On some points Thornton had to defer to the authorities. Firstly, the playhouse would open only during long vacation when the majority of students were absent from the city. Here was a parallel with the arrangements at Windsor in which the theatre opened during the absence of the boys of Eton College. Secondly, the actors would read their parts rather than simulate naturalism. An advertisement in *Jackson's Oxford Journal* advised that 'We learn on Monday evening next the READINGS will open at the Rackets Court....'[75] This restriction caused some quiet amusement:

> The performances are called 'Readings' but this is a subterfuge; plays and farces are exhibited in an entire state, the actors only now and then affecting to look at their parts which they carry in their hands.[76]

As his base the manager took a lease on the indoor tennis court of Merton College, still standing opposite the main gate in Merton Street, an ironic choice of venue considering the attitude of the University. Compared with Thornton's other theatres the court was spacious, 93 feet long, almost 32 feet broad and at its highest point 26 feet to the eaves. Rebuilt only the previous year, it was in pristine condition. Two earlier courts had occupied the site, one of which had been used by the King's Players and the Duke of Ormonde's Players each on a visit to Oxford in

1680.[77] The walls, floor and ceiling of the hall were painted with a dark substance, a compound of bullocks' blood, lamp-black and ox galls which made the auditorium considerable darker, although illuminated, than those of other theatres.[78] A protected covered way, the dedans, probably doubled as boxes during the season.

1. *Chelmsford Chronicle*, 6 July 1792.

2. Essex Record Office, Chelmsford: Sale Catalogue of the Estate of William Clacher (1837), B4070. 'A Tour in 1776', *Essex Chronicle*, 15 April 1938. Gilbert Torry, *The Book of Chelmsford* (Buckingham, 1985), p.54.

3. *Chelmsford Chronicle*, 20 July 1792.

4. Local information.

5. *Chelmsford Chronicle*, 6 July 1792.

6. *Chelmsford Chronicle*, 27 July and 17 August 1792.

7. The Bath company serves as an example; in 1793 it gave three performances at its home base each week and a further night in Bristol. See Arnold Hare, ed, *Theatre Royal, Bath. A Calendar of Performances at the Orchard Street Theatre, 1750-1805* (Bath, 1977). The entry for the week beginning Monday, 25 November 1793, is typical and illustrates the point.

8. Winston, *Tourist*, p.54.

9. Thomas Archer, *A Poetical Description of New South-End* (1793), p.16.

10. 23 August 1793.

11. Stephen Pewsey, *The Book of Southend-on-Sea* (1993), p.28.

12. *Reading Mercury*, 23 July 1793. Luke Herrmann, *Paul and Thomas Sandby* (1986), pp 51-4.

13. *Reading Mercury*, 12 August 1793.

14. *Thespian Magazine*, 1 (1792), 155.

15. *Thespian Magazine*, 1 (1793), 256

16. Winston, *Tourist*, p.55.

17. *Reading Mercury*, 5 August 1793.

18. Harvard Theatre Collection: Winston's manuscript notebooks, TS 1335.211.

19. Charles Knight, *Passages of a Working Life, during Half a Century* (1873), pp 46-7.

20. J C Long, *George III* (1960), pp 26, 32, 34.

21. Charlotte Louise Henrietta Papendiek, *Court and Private Life in the Times of Queen Charlotte* (1887), 1. 206.

22. *Reading Mercury*, 2 September 1793.

23. Charles Knight, *A Volume of Varieties* (1804), p.71. Winston, *Tourist*, p.54.

24. Theatre Royal, Windsor: playbill, 23 September 1793.

25. *Thespian Magazine*, 2 (1793), 260

26. Knight, *Working Life*, p.46.

27. 2 (1793), 261.

28. *Thespian Magazine*, 3 (1794), 33.

29. *Monthly Mirror*, 10 (1800), 260. Ronald Bannerman, *Forgotten Croydon* (Croydon, 1933), p.27.

30. *Surrey Magazine*, September 1904, p.323. Croydon Archives Service: Ronald Bannerman, ed, 'A Scrapbook of Old Croydon', p.3. Theatre Museum: Peter Davey manuscript notebooks, 6, Croydon.

31. *Thespian Magazine*, 1 (1793), 177.

32. Sybil Rosenfeld, *The Theatre of the London Fairs in the 18th Century* (Cambridge, 1960), p.68. Highfill et al, *Biographical Dictionary*, 6. 472-4 and 12. 364-7. Thomas Frost, *The Old Showmen and the London Fairs* (1834), p.23. Croydon Archives Service: William Page, 'My Recollections of Croydon Sixty Years Ago', typescript.

33. Bannerman, *Forgotten Croydon* , p.27.

34. Theatre Museum: Peter Davey Notebooks, 6.

35. *Statute Books*: 28 George III, 30, 1788. RCW Cox, 'The Old Centre of Croydon: Victorian Decay and Redevelopment' in *English Urban History*, ed Alan Everitt (1973), p.186.

36. Croydon Archives Service: playbill, 2 October 1755.

37. Highfill *et al*, *Biographical Dictionary*, 3. 82-3.

38. Harvard Theatre Collection: Winston's manuscript notebooks, TS 1335.211.

39. Croydon Archives Service: Collection of deeds belonging to the firm of Marshall, Liddle and Downey, conveyance to Daniel Watney, 10 February 1810 and mortgage of the Croydon Theatre, 7 August 1819.
Fly's estimate of the building's worth was greater than usual at the turn of the century. Possibly high costs were incurred in paying extra attention to the foundations, as the construction was on a slope running sideways. Additionally Fly lacked experience in theatre conversion or building and may have been overcharged. Or his reckoning may have been inflated.

40. Croydon Archives Service: J Corbet Anderson, File of Notes and Cuttings. Birmingham Central Library: Winston collection, Croydon, Letter of Moys Fly to James Winston, 24 March 1804.

41. Croydon Archives Service: Page, 'Croydon Sixty Years Ago'.

42. Johannesburg Central Library: William Douglas manuscript notebook.

43. *Monthly Mirror*, 10 (1800), 260.

44. Croydon Archives Service: Crown Hill (Croydon Theatre), pencil drawing, 143.4, Crown Hill.

45. George Raymond, *The Life and Enterprises of Robert William Elliston* (1857), p.322.
Occasionally written recollections of the two Georgian theatres muddle the features of one for the other.

46. Birmingham Central Library: Winston collection, Croydon, letter of Fly to Winston.

47. *Monthly Mirror*, new series, 7 (1810), 70.

48. Croydon Archives Service: Marshall, Liddle and Downey deeds, 7 April 1810 and 7 August 1819. Raymond, *Elliston*, 1. 413-4.

49. Birmingham Central Library: Winston collection, letter of M Andrews to James Winston. Jonas managed a troupe of players which travelled to fairs in London and Hertfordshire. He sometimes performed with Sampson Penley. At the beginning of the nineteenth century the pair opened theatres at Eastbourne and Folkestone and later managed the Peckham Rye Theatre in South London. See Highfill *et al*, *Biographical Dictionary*, 8. 219-220.

50. A Cunningham, ed, *The Southampton Guide* (Southampton, 1787) cited in *The Hampshire Antiquary and Naturalist*, 2 (1892), 7.

51. *A Companion in a Tour round Southampton* (Southampton, 1801), p.252.

52. W H Davenport Adams, *The History, Topography and Antiquities of the Isle of Wight* (Ryde, 1856), p.166. *The Victoria History of the Counties of England. Hampshire and the Isle of Wight* (1912), vol 5, ed William Page, p.197.

53. Charlotte Charke, *A Narrative of the Life of Mrs Charlotte Charke* (1755), p.211.

54. Folger Shakespeare Library: Winston's manuscript notebooks, T. a. 65. Rogers, 'Gosport's Lost Theatres', *Gosport Records 3*, p.13.

55. *Hampshire Chronicle*, 5 November 1796.

56. Barbara Carpenter Turner, 'A Notable Family of Artists', *Proceedings of the Hampshire Field Club*, 22 (1961), 30-33. *Hampshire Chronicle*, 19 November 1796.

57. G B Greenwood and A B Martine, *Walton-on-Thames and Weybridge. A Dictionary of Local History* (Weybridge, nd), pp 59-60. The exterior of the theatre is illustrated in D M and J L Barker, *A Window on Weybridge* (Addlestone, nd), p.25.

58. M E Blackman and J S Pulford, *A Short History of Weybridge* (Walton and Weybridge, 1991), p.26.

59. Everard, *Memoirs*, pp 152-5. *Reading Mercury*, 23 April 1791.

60. Chertsey Reference Library: Wetton Scrapbook, manuscript table of inhabitants, anonymous. Weybridge Museum: Theatre Folder, typescript, anonymous.

61. *Chelmsford Chronicle*, 4 August 1797.

62. Weybridge Parish Church: Register of Burials, entry for 29 June 1799.

63. Weybridge Musuem: typescript on the history of the buildings of Weybridge. Folger Shakespeare Library, Washington D C: Winston's manuscript notebooks, T.a.65.

64. Essex Record Office, Chelmsford: Playbill, 22 September 1794, D/DP F263.

65. Folger Shakespeare Library: playbill, Bill Box G3 W54tr 1804.

66. Strickland Gibson, ed, *Statuta Antiqua Universitatis Oxoniensis* (Oxford, 1931), p.432. *Acts of the Privy Council*, 24. 427-9. *Statute Books*, 28 George III, 30. Frederick Boas, 'The University of Oxford and the Professional Players', *The Times Literary Supplement*, 14 March 1929.

67. *Gentleman's Magazine*, 4 (1785), 591-2.

68. *Jackson's Oxford Journal*, 1 and 8 February 1755, 15 December 1762, 5 February 1774.

69. Henry Lee, *Memoirs of a Manager* (Taunton, 1830), 2. 53.

70. *Jackson's Oxford Journal*, 16 and 22 March, 18 May 1771. *Victoria History of the Counties of England, Oxfordshire*, ed C R Elrington (1906), 12. 332.

71. Josiah Wedgwood, *Letters of Josiah Wedgwood*, ed Katherine Euphrensis Farrer (1903), 1. 67.

72. Everard, *Memoirs*, p.174.

73. *Jackson's Oxford Journal*, 17 February 1784, 19 May and 17 November 1787. Bodleian Library: Minns Topographical Scrapbooks, High Street north and south, fol 1, Mss Top Oxon d 498.

74. R Compton Rhodes, 'The King's Players at Oxford, 1661-1712', *The Times Literary Supplement*, 21 February 1929.

75. *Jackson's Oxford Journal*, 17 August 1799.

76. *Monthly Mirror*, 4 (1802), 206-7.

77. E G Scanlan, 'Tennis Courts in England and Scotland', *Theatre Notebook*, 10 (1955), 10-15. Sybil Rosenfeld, 'Some Notes on the Players in Oxford', *Review of English Studies*, 19 (1943), 366-375. Anthony a Wood, *Life and Times* , ed A Clark (1891-1900), 1.111.

78. Morys George L Bruce (Lord Aberdare), *The Story of Tennis* (1959), p.59.

Under Two Managers

40

CHAPTER 4
THE CIRCUIT:
REBUILDING THEATRES

For Thornton the years after 1800 were a time of rebuilding the existing theatres at Reading, Andover, Newbury and Arundel. In each case the new building replaced one that had been used for several seasons to gauge the reliability of the ongoing patronage. The compactness of the new theatres sometimes received comment and in making them so Thornton seems wisely to have aimed at the cheerfulness of full houses, even though on celebration nights this could involve refusing admission. Numbers were regulated sometimes by charging box seat prices for a place in the pit.

Reading

Possibly not so much a rebuilding as a refurbishment, the Reading Theatre reopened in August 1801. The work had been undertaken by the local building firm of Stokes and Knight; Harvey, the theatre carpenter and painter, had taken the opportunity to make new scenery and machines.[1] A clear impression of the neat building may be gained from J C Stadler's engraving accompanying *The Theatric Tourist.* The theatre entrance juts from a plain rectangular building situated immediately behind a pump, a gathering place from which to read the bills and discuss the previous evening's offerings. The door and its frame are classical and make a dignified impact with the royal arms set in the pediment, although a playhouse without a royal patent had no right to display these.[2] The newspaper advertisements were similarly emblazoned.[3] Patrons who made their way into the building found the lobby spacious but when this branched into the corridors that led to the three parts of the house, box, pit and gallery, the ways became claustrophobic.[4]

Hungerford

In September 1802 Thornton's company was performing in Hungerford, Berkshire's westernmost town situated on the Bath Road ten miles from Newbury.[5] Admittedly small, it would have drawn the surrounding villagers to itself and the Napoleonic Wars had resulted in an influx of Swedish sailors.[6] The venue was the Town Hall - a typical market house built in 1786 with colonnades at ground level and above a large room for council business and that of the townspeople as well as entertainment - standing in the Market Place opposite Cow Lane, now Park Street.[7] Thornton seems not to have repeated his visit here.

Hungerford Town Hall
(Hugh Pihlens)

Newbury

The building in Newbury's insalubrious Northcroft Lane was not ideal as a theatre. Strangely, when Thornton applied for a licence to erect one in the central area of the town this was refused by the magistrates.[8] The reason is not known and the council minute books throw no light on the matter. Whilst the players and audiences at Northcroft Lane seem to have observed due order, something of the evil cluster of tenements, public houses and warehouses may have rubbed off on to Thornton's reputation.[9] His retaliatory ploy was to look northwards, beyond the area over which the magistrates held jurisdiction to Speenhamland's Oxford Road off which Gilder, a local speculator, was in the process of building a residential square, subsequently named after himself.[10] Although the houses in Oxford Road forming one side of the square were spacious, the flanking sides consisted of thirteen two-storey brick and tile artisans' cottages. The far end of the square was terminated by a wall behind which was some waste ground. After consultation with Thornton (this is an assumption but it is inconceivable that a builder would construct a theatre purely as a speculation and then attempt to attract a manager and a licence) Gilder built an attractive playhouse of brick and slate measuring 75 feet by 35 feet.[11] Tenements were incorporated into the sides of the playhouse, each with its door. The building gained greatly in dignity with the addition of a splendid portico consisting of four ionic pillars and a pediment bearing a carving of the royal arms, to which Thornton claimed an entitlement on behalf of his company. James Winston thought that the portico columns had been purchased from St John's College, Oxford, but there is no corroborative evidence.[12] An illustration in *The Theatric Tourist* shows a detail of the imprints of carriage wheels, which made a tight circuit of the small square, entering through an archway in Oxford Road and leaving by a similar. Residents in the larger houses were disturbed; one of the arches was filled in with the result that patrons had to

The Newbury Theatre, Speenhamland, from The Theatric Tourist *by James Winston (1805).* (The British Library)

43

walk across the square to their transport.[13] The interior of the building was attractive. The auditorium consisted of gallery, pit and boxes with the latter lined in crimson velvet. The centre box at the rear was larger than the others and reserved for the Margravine of Anspach who lived nearby at Benham Valence and under whose patronage the theatre was built.[14] Above the parts of the house a moulded plaster ceiling coloured cream and brown attracted favourable attention.[15] In spite of the smallness of the structure, an indication of the possible box office takings is given in the remark in the local newspaper that on an evening at the beginning of March 1803 'the receipt of the house was the largest ever known in Newbury being no less than £50. 0. 6d'.[16]

The change of location had advantages. Nearby the road from London to Bath carried coaches and a variety of inns stood in the vicinity welcoming travellers at the end of a long day's journey from London: the Pelican was a stone's throw away, the Maidenhead (now the Bacon Arms) and the Castle on Speen Hill all provided sojourners as theatre patrons.[17] Thornton's notable patrons, the Margravine of Anspach and her youngest son the Hon Keppel Craven, were able to get to the playhouse along the Bath Road without traversing the town.

On 16 November 1802 the 'New Theatre, Newbury and Speenhamland' opened quietly for a highly successful season which lasted until April 1803. Excursions were made to Reading from Newbury for some of the weeks.[18] After April the company made its way to Andover. A new theatre was ready to open there.

Andover

Thornton seems to have rested content with his theatre at the Angel Inn, Andover, but in 1800 the lease expired and the building was sold to the local Society of Friends to be used as a Meeting House. For a couple of years the manager was homeless until around Christmas 1802, searching in the town for premises superior to his former, he entered into an agreement with Thomas Rawlins, printer, bookbinder and stationer.[19] Rawlins outlined the arrangement:

> I... showed him my premises, and proposed building all the shell
> of a theatre at my expense if he would agree to give me a rent
> accordingly and take a long lease, which he very readily agreed
> to.... The inside work was done at the expense of the manager
> and fitted up in a very neat manner.[20]

44

The Circuit: Rebuilding Theatres

The premises mentioned were off the Andover to Newbury road from which a rough and dirty track near to the Angel Inn led to the new establishment. Rawlins managed to make this presentable, since when it became known as Rawlins Lane.[21]

The Andover Theatre, Rawlins Lane, from The Theatric Tourist *by James Winston (1805).* (The British Library)

Walking up the lane the theatre-goer was faced by a neat building of brick and slate with a central entrance framed by fluted pilasters; above this were windows and the facade was topped by a triangular pediment containing the royal arms resting on the legend, 'From the THEATRE ROYAL, Windsor'.[22] In his description of a plate of this theatre Winston noted:

> To induce a belief of its being a patent theatre, the words 'From the' are written so faintly, as to be scarcely legible, while 'Theatre Royal', appears in striking characters, followed by an almost invisible 'Windsor'.[23]

The letters were picked out in gold on a blue background. Internally the theatre was only half the size of Newbury and said to hold just over £30. Into this small space was deftly fitted gallery, pit, and boxes, both lower and upper. Thornton described the interior thus:

45

...[it] is formed and fitted up with every attention to Dramatic
order and elegant neatness, the boxes lined, cushioned, carpet-
ed, etc. and rendered perfectly convenient and commodious.[24]

At the end of each season Rawlins patiently dismantled the stage and
proscenium arch and then used the place as a honey store. The appropriate name of the box-keeper, Mr Treacle, amused Winston. Perhaps this
was Thomas Treacle, a local resident and broker who undertook the work
on behalf of the company; his wife, Rebecca Treacle, was a milliner and
possibly of use in the costume department.[25]

The theatre opened at Easter 1803, every night during the holiday
week and thereafter on Monday, Wednesday, Friday and Saturday.[26]
There was no pattern in future visits although Thornton attempted to
make a visit to Andover at least once every two years.

Alresford

Mary Russell Mitford recorded that at the beginning of the 1790s she
was taken to see a troupe of strolling players in a barn at Alresford; her
remark is vague on the location and the company, but she did remember
the fantasy and atmosphere of the occasion:

...I have a dim recollection of a glimmering row of candles dividing the end which was called the stage from the part which did
duty as pit and boxes, of the black face and the spangled tur-
ban, of my wondering admiration, and the breathless interest of
the rustic audience.[27]

Ten years later, according to Peter Davey, Thornton opened a theatre
in the town.[28] It lay six miles north-east of Winchester on the way to
Alton, consisting principally of two streets of Georgian houses and shops
which were a rebuilding after a succession of fires in the seventeenth and
eighteenth centuries, and contained less than 170 families.[29] So few people would provide an audience for only a couple of nights, although numbers were augmented by those on the many coaches passing through the
town who broke their journey there.[30] Again, the location of the theatre
is difficult to establish. The Swan had a large Assembly Room and on the
first floor of the Bell was a Market Room used for entertainments but it
has to be admitted that a barn in the yard of any of the Alresford inns -
possibly the very one used by the strollers - might equally have served for
a temporary playhouse.[31]

The Sale of the Windsor Theatre

In this period of consolidation it is surprising to find that Thornton's prestigious theatre at Windsor was up for sale. In July 1806 it was bought by James Mudie, who, together with his wife and six year old child, had been members of Thornton's company.[32]

The difficulty noted earlier, that nights on which the royal family were absent from the theatre drew the smallest of audiences, was by this time exacerbated. Porphyria held the king in its grip and his eyesight became gravely defective; additionally there was a rift between himself and Queen Charlotte.[33] Henry Thornton had enjoyed styling himself 'manager, proprietor and Sole Patentee of the Theatre Royal, Windsor', but this was becoming an expensive luxury, forcing him to face the fact that a sale was inevitable.[34]

The limitation of the seasons at Windsor to the holidays of Eton College left the Mudies free to continue to act in Thornton's company. Whilst alterations to the relatively recent theatre building in Windsor were taking place in the summer of 1806, the new managers played in Chelmsford and Newbury.[35]

A Change of Venue at Oxford

The rackets court which Thornton leased in Oxford was hidden from the main thoroughfares of the city and easily forgotten by patrons so when an opportunity to transfer to the court of Christ Church occurred in 1802 Thornton welcomed it.[36] Although the building lay behind one of the well-known hostelries of Oxford, the Bull Inn, which fronted onto St Aldates, this was the beginning of a busy road leading from Carfax to Abingdon, thus helping to make the theatre more conspicuous. Patrons for the boxes made their way through 'Mrs Sabine's house in Blue Boar Lane', which ran alongside the theatre, and those making for 'the pit and standing places' went through Mrs Venables' yard.[37] Venables is given as the landlord of the Bull Inn in a directory of 1823 and the route may be through part of the tavern.[38] By 1807 the entry arrangements were clarified on a playbill: the pit and boxes were approached through the Bull and the gallery entrance was in Blue Boar Lane.[39] The Revd Dr Whittington Landon, the Vice-Chancellor, refused permission for plays to be performed by professional companies from 1803, but on the completion of his term of office in 1806 the former arrangement was reinstated.[40]

The Bull Inn frontage to Oxford Theatre, St Aldates.
(The Bodleian Library, University of Oxford)

In subsequent years, until 1815, Thornton used one or other of the rackets courts, without giving any reason in the newspaper for the relocations. Before his final visit, though, he received a jolt in the person of Samuel Russell, an actor of the Haymarket Theatre and the Theatre Royal, Drury Lane. It was a coincidence that Russell, as a child equestrian, had appeared in 1776 at a theatre in Chelmsford, one of Thornton's later seats of management.[41] With his guileless face, the adult Russell made a name for himself in the role of Fribble in David Garrick's comedy *Miss in her Teens*, a character he performed many times in Oxford. Russell arrived to play in the Christ Church court in 1810.[42] His adaptation of the building was thorough and attractive with two artists, Latilla and Smith, employed to make alterations and decorate the premises.[43] As did Thornton, Russell alternated appearances at Christ Church and Merton. For several years Thornton's season followed immediately after Russell's. In 1815 Thornton appeared at the Christ Church courts and Russell at those of Merton where he built an amphitheatre in front of the stage ('fitted up in a most commodious manner, and is much superior to any Circus that ever yet opened in Oxford') so that hippodramas could be presented in style and safety.[44] For their part Thornton's actors offered an ultimatum, refusing to team with horses on an unadapted stage.[45] In addition to horse troops, Russell had invited a bevy of stars over his annual seasons (Makeen's Stud of Horse, Kean, Mrs Johnstone, Dowton, Betty, George and Sarah

Bartley, Mrs Cobham, Miss Feron amongst others) which tended to dim the lustre of Thornton's offerings.[46] Russell was canny enough to out-number the sentimental dramas which Thornton staged and these were an attraction in Oxford. There may have been an initial retaliation on Thornton's part: during Russell's first season he had to remonstrate publicly with youths in the gallery creating disturbances during the shows.[47] One wonders whether they were paid by Thornton to do this. After his 1815 season Russell worked with Elliston and then took up the management of the Brighton Theatre.[48]

Arundel

That same year Henry Thornton came to an arrangement with Joseph Hinde of Arundel, the freeholder of a malthouse in Old Market (now Maltravers) Street, to convert the building into a theatre which he, Thornton, would lease each year for a season.[49] The building was squashed in between two houses one of which belonged to the mother of John Tompkins, a factor and future mayor.[50] According to Tompkins the conversion cost £1300 on leasehold ground for sixty years. A drawing by Winston shows the minute building of white bricks with an undecorated entrance door, above which is a large window; it is topped by a slate roof.[51] The Duke of Norfolk was consulted about the design made con-formable to his taste to the extent that a rear wall was gothicised, thus preserving a unified outlook from the castle.[52] At the back of the build-ing was a domestic apartment for the manager.[53]

Thornton played for only two seasons in the new theatre. After 1808 it housed the Worthing company under the management of Thomas Trotter.[54] Why Thornton would have disposed of the building so quickly is difficult to determine. There is scant likelihood that the journeys from Gosport were difficult. Maybe the sparse numbers of people living in Arundel, around 2,000 by the beginning of the nineteenth century, made the venture impractical; possibly the theatre was too small for profitabil-ity. This must be balanced with the remark of the Arundel local histori-an, G W Eustace, who stated that many of the nobility and gentry attend-ed the theatrical winter seasons and that 'Brighton as a residence was con-sidered dull in comparison'.[55] The temporary theatre had opened in 1792; by 1808 Thornton would have been conversant with the disadvan-tages of the place. Did he live in the unfulfilled expectation that Arundel's fortunes were on the upturn?

Ryde

Having established a theatre at Cowes on the Isle of Wight as early as 1795 it is to be expected that Thornton would set up another at Ryde, a larger and busier watering place on the island. A makeshift playhouse existed in the town with which Thornton seems to have been unconnected; Peter Davey claims that the lessee was James Shatford, the manager of the Lymington theatre.[56] Amateur companies sometimes performed here; an example is that of the Academy of the Abbé de Grenoble which for the benefit of the poor presented *Richard III*.[57]

From 1810 a market house on the western side of St Thomas's Square was in the course of erection by a joint stock company. The financing for this failed and it was decided to convert the structure to a theatre, employing Atkey, a local builder whose workmanship was praised.[58] On this Henry Thornton took up a lease. The following year there was an assignment of shares to a number of local businessmen, including George Player, the lord of the manor and ground landlord. In later years the place appeared mean: 'The theatre [in 1856] is a very paltry, insignificant erection...' but one of the strong points of the building was its situation at the centre of the town; on a neighbouring corner stood the Crown Hotel with The Colonnade and Durham College on the northern corner.[59] Thornton opened the building on 23 June 1813.[60]

The circuit completed

The Ryde theatre was the last addition Thornton made to his circuit. As his working life ended four years later it is difficult to surmise whether in 1813 Thornton regarded his collection of playhouses as complete. Certainly the complexity of the operation taxed his strength and one gains the impression that for him the number of theatres and their geographical spread was enough. This was by no means the largest of the Georgian circuits but for Thornton it formed a series of bases which satisfied the performance needs of his company of actors. Barnett, his son-in-law, rested content with a considerably smaller operation. If, however, one plots the spread of the Thornton theatres on a map, it is evident that the threefold strand along the Bath, Chichester and Portsmouth roads had been achieved.

The Circuit: Rebuilding Theatres

1. *Reading Mercury*, 24 August 1801.
2. Birmingham Central Library: the Winston collection, Reading.
3. *Reading Mercury*, 24 August 1801.
4. Winston, *Tourist*, p.18.
5. Harvard Theatre Collection: Winston's manuscript notebooks, TS1335.211.
6. W H Summers, *The Story of Hungerford in Berkshire* [1926], p.148.
7. Hugh Pihlens, *The Story of Hungerford* (Newbury, 1983), p.44. Britton and Brayley, *The Beauties of England and Wales*, 1.124.
8. Winston, *Tourist*, p.30.
9. Berkshire Records Office, Reading: Borough of Newbury, Council Minute Book 1786-1829, p.30.
10. Harvard Theatre Collection: Winston's manuscript notebooks, TS 1335.211.
11. *Newbury Buildings Past and Present* (Newbury, 1973), p.96. Sale notice of the Theatre, 18 September 1883, seen in 1976 at the Newbury Archive Room, Newbury Mansion House. *Newbury Weekly News*, 20 September 1883.
12. Winston, *Tourist*, p.31. Local information from the bursar of St John's College, Oxford, 6 January 1975.
13. *Newbury Buildings*, pp 96 and 114.
14. Harvard Theatre Collection: Winston manuscript notebooks, TS 1335.211. Winston, *Tourist*, p.30.
15. Richard Southern, *The Georgian Playhouse* (1948), p.52.
16. *Reading Mercury*, 7 March 1803.
17. Walter Money, *A Popular History of Newbury in the County of Berks from Early to Modern Times* (1905), p.102.
18. *Reading Mercury*, 15 and 29 November 1802, 31 January, 7, 14 and 21 February 1803.
19. *Universal British Directory*, 2.51.
20. Birmingham Central Library: Winston collection, Andover, letter of Thomas Rawlins to James Winston, 12 January 1804.
21. Harvard Theatre Collection: Winston's manuscript notebooks, TS1335,211.
22 Coloured aquatint published by T Woodfall (1804) to accompany *The Theatric Tourist*.
23. Winston, *Tourist*, p.10.
24. *Salisbury Journal*, 11 April 1803.
25. *Universal British Directory*, 2. 51.
26. *ibid.*
27. Mary Russell Mitford, *The Dramatic Works* (1854), p.viii
28. Theatre Museum: Peter Davey Notebooks, 22.
29. Hampshire Record Office, Winchester: James Rodney, 'A History of Alresford', typescript.
30. William Page, ed, *The Victoria History of the Counties of England* (1908), 3. 352.
31. *Hampshire Chronicle*, 21 January 1799.
32. Public Record Office, Chancery Lane, London: The Lord Chamberlain's Papers, LCS/163, p.234.
33. Stanley Ayling, *George the Third* (1972), pp 433 and 442.
34. Essex Record Office, Chelmsford: Petition of Henry Thornton, Q/SB6 368/4.
35. *Chelmsford Chronicle*, 20 June and 4 July 1806. *Reading Mercury*, 18 August 1806.
36. *Jackson's Oxford Journal*, 14 August 1802.
37. *Jackson's Oxford Journal*, 10 August 1811. A plan of the jig-saw of houses, yards and the theatre is given in H E Salter, *Cartulary of Osney Abbey* (1929-36), 2. 596.
38. *Pigot's Directory* (1823), p.448.
39. Cheltenham Museum and Art Gallery: Playbill Collection, 28 August 1807.
40. Raymond, *Elliston*, p.85. Christopher and Edward Hibbert, *The Encyclopaedia of Oxford* (1988), p.526.
41. *Chelmsford Chronicle*, 26 January 1776.
42. *Jackson's Oxford Journal*, 4 and 18 August 1810. *Thespian Dictionary*, no pagination. William Clark Russell, *Representative Actors* (1872), p.286. Samuel Russell was often known as 'His Innocence'.
43. *Jackson's Oxford Journal*, 11 August 1810.

44. *Jackson's Oxford Journal*, 17 June 1815.
45. *Jackson's Oxford Journal*, 16 and 23 September 1815.
46. *Jackson's Oxford Journal*, 1 August, 22 September 1810, 17, 24 June, 1 July 1815
47. *Jackson's Oxford Journal*, 18 August 1810.
48. *Gentleman's Magazine*, new series, 23 (1845), 446.
49. Steer, 'Theatres in Sussex', *Theatre Notebook*, 12 (1957-8), pp 58-64 and 107-8. Arundel Castle: Archives of the Duke of Norfolk, title deeds of the site of the theatre.
50. Tompkins, *Diary*, entries for 5 October 1807 and February 1808.
51. Harvard Theatre Collection: Winston manuscript notebooks, TS1335.211.
52. *Hampshire Telegraph*, 12 December 1807.
53. *The World's Fair*, 1 November 1958. Information snippet by 'Southdown' citing an unattributed report dated 24 October 1808.
54. Odell, *More about the Old Theatre, Worthing*, p.25.
55. G W Eustace, *Arundel Borough and Castle* (1922), p.232.
56. Theatre Museum: Peter Davey Notebooks, 6. *Hampshire Chronicle*, 5 September 1810.
57. *Hampshire Chronicle*, 3 December 1810.
58. Local information: Mr R E Brinton.
59. Adams, *The Isle of Wight* , p.89. Ordnance Survey Map, 1863.
60. *Hampshire Telegraph*, 28 June 1813.

CHAPTER 5
THE COMPANY AND ITS ROLES

The nucleus of the Georgian theatre company consisted usually of the extended family of the manager. To this was added a number of husband and wife teams, together with some of their children, as well as single people as required. These constituted the regular company. Additionally there were visiting performers; some would arrive for as long as a season, whilst those at the top of their profession and thereby expensive, such as Dorothy Jordan, Sarah Siddons, Richard Suett and John Quick, would be employed for a few nights only. Most of the performers within the company were hired by the manager for the portrayal of stock types; these varied from romantic young lovers who, as well as acting, would also be required to dance and sing, to the heavy villain or the matronly tragic heroine.

Henry Thornton

As manager Thornton only infrequently performed with his company. From middle age he contracted gout which severely hampered his ability to walk and left him in continual pain. Having said that, there were occasions he deputised in a role when an actor was ill or had suddenly abandoned his position. Presumably, too, the cares of management, especially from the time when he sectionalised his players into two or three subsets which performed simultaneously in a number of locations, some of them distant from each other and all demanding his oversight, prevented him regularly taking part in the repertoire. To become aware of the kind of role for which he had a natural flair, one has to look at the man in his younger days.

During his time with Herbert and Whitley's company he seems to have favoured colourful, bravura roles on stage, indicated here by the parts he took during the 1774 season at St George's Hall, King's Lynn; several times he was cast as Tony Lumpkin - with interpolated songs - in *She Stoops to Conquer*, Bob Acres in *The Rivals*, the title role in *Harlequin Fortunatus* and the same part in *Theatrical Candidates*, Edmund the Bastard in *King Lear*, Petruchio in *Catherine and Petruchio*, the drunken Stephano in *The Tempest*, the sentimental Belcour in *The West Indian*, Young Wilding in *The Lyar*, Captain Macheath in *The Beggar's Opera* and Hodge in *Love in a Village*. His rendering of Thomas Arne's setting of parts of 'An Ode to Shakespeare' by David Garrick, together with his success in performing in operettas, suggests his ability in singing which would have extended his range of characterisations.[1] He was valuable in taking roles which demanded powers of sustaining; examples are Philotas in *The Grecian Daughter*, played at Lincoln the previous year, Ranger in *The Suspicious Husband* and, in 1776, the title role in *Comus*, a reshaping of John Milton's poem by George Colman.[2] In most of these roles may be seen the stock, dashing hero, able to draw a sword when needed, to conjure romance and to warm the hearts of his audience. During his promptership at Portsmouth Thornton took on a wider range of parts, revealing, as a man in his early 30s, his growing maturity on the stage: there was Bedaman in *Venice Preserved*, in *The West Indian* Belcour had been discarded for Captain Dudley, just as Osric had made way for the Player King in *Hamlet*, Tybalt in *Romeo and Juliet* and Blandford in *Oroonoko*.[3] Ralph Wewitzer took on several of Thornton's former roles including Harlequin, leaving the latter to play Pantalone, the elderly rich Venetian merchant.[4]

When he was forty-five, Thornton appeared in a series of walk-ons at the Haymarket Theatre in London during March 1795. Invited to play at Everard's benefit on 22 April, Thornton took the role of Lord Ogleby, a part Everard yearned to play himself, in *The Clandestine Marriage* by George Colman the Elder and David Garrick. Even Winston commended the performance in which the actor 'represented the antiquated debauchee with uncommon éclat'. The afterpiece was *Mrs Doggett in Her Attitudes or The Effects of a West Indian Ramble*, an anonymous trifle, in fact by Sarah Gardner who appeared in both plays; Thornton spoke her lengthy prologue and also provided without charge the costumes for the evening, a saving to Everard of £3. These appearances seem to be the only ones Thornton made on the London stage.[5]

As a prompter Thornton would often have stepped into the role of an absent actor, remembering as best he could the lines. Possibly adept at this, the facility unfortunately was his undoing in preparing his own roles. Combined with a forgetfulness and ingenuousness in everyday matters - on

Caricature, reputed to be of Henry Thornton.
(The Royal Collection ©2000, Her Majesty Queen Elizabeth II)

one occasion he went on tour wearing the six shirts his wife had set aside for him, discarding the topmost as it became soiled - the result of his characterisations was frequently unsatisfactory. '...He can bustle through a part with considerable ease, though unacquainted with the author's words,' penned a writer in the *Thespian Dictionary* citing the remark of George III when Thornton played Old Dornton in *The Road to Ruin*: 'It was very well, but an entire new edition, being quite different from the Old Dornton which Munden represented in London'.[6] Even on stage, the manager demonstrated a lack of concentration. At Gosport, whilst playing Biron (*Isabella*) Thornton made a stage death, forgetting first to hand over that letter on which the unravelling of the plot depended. Prompted by a performer, the dead Biron leapt to his feet and apologised:

> One thing I had forgot through a multiplicity of business. Give
> this letter to my father: it will explain all.

Death again assailed him.[7]

In Thornton's hands the plot could be mangled but in deputising for an absent colleague, the original dialogue became lost in a series of wild improvisations. Miss Ivers, the daughter of one of the violinists, narrated that when she played the role of Miss Blandford in Thomas Morton's *Speed the Plough* she acted opposite an unprepared Thornton cast as her stage father, Sir Philip Blandford. Whilst dressing for the part the manager rapidly digested the essentials of the plot:

> ... read over the part to me while I'm dressing - there, there,
> that will do; oh! aye, a murder - a castle - well, well, I know
> enough to go on for it.

Thornton floundered through business and dialogue until he arrived at his recitation of the crimes committed against Bob Handy. Morton's text ran: '...with one hand I tore the faithless woman from his damned embrace, and with the other stabbed my wretched brother to the heart', which Thornton transmitted: 'I tore the faithless woman from his damned embrace; with one hand I stabbed my wretched brother to the heart, and - what do you think I did with the other?'[8] One feels that there could be a modicum of truth in Winston's assertion that Thornton inserted words from a favourite play into whatever role he was performing, a trait which 'brought him off with laurels'.[9]

There was, though, one activity in which Thornton became an adept, writing rhymed addresses which he recited in the course of an evening; those at the opening of the rebuilt theatre at Windsor and his 'Thoughts on the Slave Trade' given at Reading are examples.[10] At the end of his career in 1817 Thornton wrote some lines of gratitude to his patrons, reciting them after goutily playing his final role, that of Sir Christopher Curry in *Inkle and Yarico* :

> Brought by respect, by strong attatchment led
> Tonight, these well known boards again to tread:
> Nor gout, nor pain, can keep me from your view,
> When I reflect how much I owe to you.
> Time has been, now many seasons o'er,
> (That happens time that can return no more,)
> When, in the comic or the tragic part,
> I've felt your plaudits, grateful to my heart;
> When warm with zeal, and brac'd with tragic rage
> I've shown the raving passions of the page;
> Or through the spirit of the comic scene,
> A thousand and a thousand times have been.
> In Belcour, Ranger, and in hunger sharp,
> In various scenes have trac'd the drama's art.
> But now the power - the acting power is past,
> Leaving one glow - one only glow at last -
> A grateful glow, that kindles at the heart -
> That feels an impulse it would fain impart;
> Pure in its nature, to its feelings true;
> That swells with thanks - with grateful thanks to you.[11]

Early in his career Thornton had become renowned for these rhymed addresses; possibly it was this skill which encouraged the townspeople of Reading to send to him prologues and epilogues in advance of the opening of the theatre of 1788. Whilst he tendered his thanks, Thornton seems not to have used the offerings.[12]

Thornton's Family

Thornton's parents appear to have had no connection with the theatre. However, in marrying Elizabeth Pritchard he joined a theatrical family which was to serve his company in good stead. Elizabeth's father David was a country manager and her mother (possibly a Miss Caulfield before marriage) a performer.[13] In addition to Elizabeth, the Pritchards had a son, David, and a daughter, Hannah Henrietta, who married, in turn, James Shafto Robertson (a name sometimes interchanged with Robinson), William Perkin Taylor and Benjamin Wrench.[14]

Mrs Elizabeth Thornton was widely commended for her charm as a person and for her skill on the stage. Everard draws a picture of her on board the leaking ship in which the family attempted to get from Brighton to Portsmouth when Thornton was about to take up the post of prompter there:

> When I got below, into what may be supposed the cabin, it was indeed an awful sight to see Mrs Thornton with her young family about her, up to her knees in water, with a child upon each.[15]

To this good sense and calm could be added the maternal charms of the woman, so warmly commended by Ann Holbrook.[16]

From her days at Portsmouth Mrs Thornton undertook character roles: there were her personations of Mrs Gadabout in *The Lying Valet*, the Nurse in *Romeo and Juliet*, Diana Trapes in *The Beggar's Opera* (in reversed productions of this she played Filch), Audrey the Shepherdess in *As You Like It* and Mrs Grubb in *Cross Purposes*. But there were pretty young heroines in her repertoire, such as Kate Hardcastle (*She Stoops to Conquer*), Perdita (*Perdita and Florizel*), Tilburnia in *The Critic* and respectable townswomen such as Mistress Quickley (*The Merry Wives of Windsor*). Old women and hags were obviously a joy to Mrs Thornton: she was to be found on stage as one of the Witches (a role usually played by male comedians in the company on the Georgian stage) in *Macbeth*, the Ballad Woman in *Harlequin's Revels* and an Old Woman in *Linco's Travels*. Already she was attempting roles which many an older actress normally took, such as Mrs Candour in *The School for Scandal* and Miss Prue in *Love for Love*.[17]

A benefit night gives us an idea of an actress's range. At Chelmsford in 1798 Mrs Thornton chose for her benefit *The Heir at Law*, in which she took the role of Ciceley Homespun and her son-in-law, Hatton, that of Zekiel Homespun, partnered by Mrs Thornton's daughter who played Caroline. Between plays the beneficiary's attractive voice was put to good use in the song 'Moss Roses'.[18] Even if she did not appear in a play, Mrs Thornton would sing or recite: an instance is at the benefit for Gibbon, a mason, at Gosport in the following year when Mrs Thornton spoke in the character of a mason's wife the specially written epilogue entitled '*No French Invasion*'. As the performance was under masonic patronage, Mrs Thornton was quick to seek the approval of the audience.[19]

Elizabeth Thornton normally gained plaudits for her roles; her voice, her lightness and vivacity and her range of parts in which she transformed herself were all commended. She herself appeared to be all-virtue and after a performance at Andover as a courtesan in George Lillo's domestic tragedy *George Barnwell* the *Monthly Mirror* morally opined, 'We would rather not again see the Manager's lady in such character as Millwood'.[20] Throughout her life Elizabeth Thornton played a vital role on and back stage and her death after a short illness in March 1816 must have left her husband sorely bereft. A single sentence in the Reading newspaper sums up her attainments: 'In her professional pursuits and all the relations of life she was deservedly esteemed'.[21]

The Thorntons had several boys and at least three girls. One of the daughters married Edward Barnett, an actor and later the inheritor of the Thornton circuit; another married William Thomas P Hatton, an actor, and the third married Robert Henry Kelham, the owner of a printing business and circulating library in Chelmsford.[22]

Edward Barnett was born *c*.1770, the son of two performers at the Portsmouth Theatre; Thornton would have worked with them when he was prompter there. Little is known of his youth; he is reputed to have studied for the stage under the Kembles, probably Roger and Sarah, and to have performed opposite John Philip Kemble in *The Stranger*. Later he married one of Thornton's actress daughters who unfortunately died very young, before 1820.[23] This may, of course, have been in childbirth which accounted for many deaths. The two sons of the marriage, Richard and James, whilst still children sometimes appeared on the stage. Later Richard became the leader of the orchestra at Guildford.[24] In 1825 Edward Barnett remarried; his second wife was another actress, Frances Wolfe, who outlived him. Barnett and Frances were eventually buried at Ryde on the Isle of Wight.[25]

Barnett's relationship with the company was not an exclusive one. Some of the time he was performing in London at the Lyceum, just off the Strand, the Haymarket and at Covent Garden, excursions which drew public censure from Thornton: he complained in the *Chelmsford Chronicle* of the 'secession' of his son-in-law at the time of one of his Lyceum engagements.[26] His strengths lay in his ability to sing as well as to act. As a mason, he drew his brethren to the playhouse. Surely it was he who, at Reading, commissioned Varma, a local musician on the staff of the Opera House, London, and the Paris Conservatoire, to compose a musical piece, *Freemasonry*, to honour the visit of the masons to the Reading theatre?[27] Barnett also seems to have been an able administrator. When Thornton divided his company into three sections he was left in charge of one of these, although Thornton appears to have kept a hand on the reins, travelling to see the work of the sections guided by both Barnett and Hatton.[28] After Thornton's death Barnett kept the circuit in operation until the middle of the nineteenth century, an amazing achievement at a time when playhouses were in the grip of a recession.

Barnett appears to have been a bit-part player, gaining roles, however small, wherever he could, although these were more substantial in Thornton's company; for example, in *Timour the Tartar* he played Timour's hesitant father, Oglon, at Guildford in 1814; and the following year at Gosport, for his benefit, he staged *The School for Friends*.[29] At the Lyceum in 1815 he played Isaac in *The Maid and the Magpie*, but for most of his London appearances he is simply named as a company member.[30] He had a 'rich stage face', commended on a number of occasions.[31]

Another of the Thorntons' daughters married William Thomas P. Hatton and, like her sister, died young, leaving Hatton in 1792 to marry at Lyme Regis Ann Hinds when he was playing there in Henry Lee's company. Ann was a member of Thornton's company; William predeceased her.[32] Hatton gained his experience of the stage in Thornton's theatres, other provincial playhouses and several of those in London. There were appearances at Weymouth in 1800 where the Duke of Kent appreciated his performances.[33] He played in Fulham at the White Hart Theatre, at Drury Lane (with a first appearance in 1801 as Will Steady in *The Purse*) and at the Haymarket Theatre, where, during the 1803 season, Hatton was mentioned as a member of the company although his appearances were so slight that his roles were not nominated.[34] He went on from here to play a season in Edinburgh.[35] In Thornton's company he wrote and performed songs and duets for various occasions: one of these was a 'loyal duet' on the visit of the Yeomanry Cavalry to the Chelmsford Theatre.[36] This range of experience served him in good stead and he proficiently superintended one of the three sections of Thornton's company.[37] His real interest lay in staging spectacular productions involving large casts, sumptuous costumes and decor as elaborate as could be fitted into country theatres.

The Duke of Kent, on becoming Governor of Gibraltar ('the old Cock of the Rock'), gave him a grant to take an actors' company to its garrison theatre for a season in the autumn of 1802.[38] Realising that no company had played on the Rock for twenty-seven years, Harris and Lewis of Covent Garden had attempted unsuccessfully to obtain a similar permission.

In 1805 Hatton was invited by John Bernard to play in America. He saw Hatton as the 'accurate representative of lowlife, equally happy in the blustering boldness or swaggering gayety of the bully, or in the heartless villainy or savage triumph of the ruffian'.[39] This stock casting Hatton rejected and decided to join Alexandre Placide at the playhouse in Charleston, South Carolina, where there was a promise of roles in high tragedy. After performing one evening in 1807 Hatton, feeling hot and possibly running a temperature from yellow fever, decided to sleep on the verandah of his house. He caught a chill from which he died.

The Company and Its Roles

In London and the provinces Hatton took such roles as Hotspur (*Henry IV*), the Spanish conquistador Pizarro in Sheridan's play of the same name, Charles the Wrestler (*As You Like It*), Malvoglio (*The Tale of Mystery*) and Glenalvon in *Douglas*. In lighter plays he was to be seen as Gazy (*Peeping Tom*), Serjeant Dub (*Love Laughs at Locksmiths*), Dr Hellebore (*The Mock Doctor*) and Will Steady (*The Purse*). Some of these roles he took to South Carolina, adding to them Osmond, the heavy villain of *The Castle Spectre*, Scaramouche in *Don Juan*, the title role in Macbeth and Sir Abel Handy in *Speed the Plough*.[40] What did he make of these? Henry Lee, in whose company Hatton acted at Lyme in 1792, noted: 'Mr H. was a clever actor in his line, of a bustling spirit; could do anything - tragedy or comedy; but he was rather unsteady in his conduct'.[41] Much the same point is made in the *Thespian Dictionary*: 'he pays great regard to character and dress, and is a serviceable and meritorious actor, but colours rather too coarsely'. There were betterments earlier than 1805; a correspondent in the *Reading Mercury* noted that the actor was 'much improved since we last saw him, and gave the very difficult character of Orsino (*Alfonso*) in a masterly manner and in the scene with his son drew repeated bursts of applause from his auditors'.[42] James Winston commended Hatton, remarking that he was surprised that one with abilities 'certainly above mediocrity' spent so long in 'such a company' as Thornton's.[43]

In 1810 Hatton's son - reputed to be good in pantomime - was playing in the company of the Salisbury Comedians, managed by Thomas Collins, in Chichester and later his name appears on London playbills; and a Miss Hatton was to be seen as Harriot (*The Jealous Wife*) in Thornton's company at Gosport in 1816, possibly a daughter of the above actor. Her strengths and weaknesses were singled out by a reviewer:

> ...this young lady is very pretty, and acted with much feeling,
> but unfortunately she knew not what to do with her arms,
> which fault may be easily remedied. But we admired her much
> more in a dance after the play.[44]

As well as their daughters, the Thorntons had at least two sons who intermittently helped on stage. They attended Gosport Academy - 'where young gentlemen are educated for the navy and army, public offices and the university' - under the principalship of Dr William Burney; here they performed in the 'Playroom' at Cold Harbour. *Richard III* followed by *The Village Lawyer* with scenery 'mostly prepared at home' gives an idea of the kind of evening to be enjoyed here.[45] The elder of the sons, H[enry?] Thornton, ended his school days by acting the role of Polydorus in a rewrite of Richard Glover's epic about Leonidas, recast by Roberdeau, one of the masters, as *Thermopylæ*. A successful presentation, the handsome costumes and striking stage pictures were praised.[46] The young Thornton spoke the epilogue in which mention was made of his future career:

> But now life's drama calls, to act my part
> On its great stage: Adieu the mimic art!
> Now, roughly cast for Naval-war's stern Play
> To urge thro' danger's paths my valorous way;
> To guide Britannia's vengeance on her foes;
> To purchase death, or honour-earn'd repose![47]

Notices about the lad fade during the Napoleonic Wars. Possibly he had purchased death too soon.

A word should be said about the Pritchard side of the family. The two most colourful members of this were David (Elizabeth's brother) and Hannah Henrietta (Elizabeth's sister). David enjoyed a provincial career but seems not to have acted in London. He had a neat figure, was a competent singer and dancer and was eminently suitable for roles in light comedy but these abilities were combined with a restless disposition and a fiery temper.[48] More complex roles could pose difficulties as the remarks on his portrayal of Goldfinch (a witless young man of fashion) in *The Road to Ruin* and Young Wilding in *The Lyar* suggest:

> A brother [i.e. a brother-in-law] we believe, of the Manager's
> [Thornton] appeared... who, although by no means successful in
> those arduous characters, has since given great satisfaction in
> parts of less consequence.[49]

By the early 1790s David had married an actress and the pair were described as 'an acquisition to any theatre, those of the metropolis not excepted'.[50] Possibly it was the couple's daughter who appeared on the American stage in the nineteenth century.[51]

The three marriages of Hannah Henrietta Pritchard are apt to obscure her acting ability. Tate Wilkinson, in whose company she performed in 1785, remarked on her suitability in the breeches title role of *The Irish Widow*:

> Her figure in the small clothes was neat to a degree of perfec-
> tion; and her deportment, spirits and conception of that part
> was, I think, the best I had then or have since seen.[52]

Yet she was able to present in the title role of *Isabella* a mature, tragic heroine with an impact that reduced her audience to terror:

> ...she appears really deathly white, her hair disarrayed and her
> clothes in real disorder. Her laughter and certain tones of her
> voice are really horrible and excite unpleasant repulsive feelings.[53]

After her marriage to Robinson, Hannah married William Perkins Taylor, the manager of the Nottingham circuit, and finally Benjamin Wrench, a member of the company.[54] Hannah enjoyed wide experience of playing in the provinces, appearing at Bath, Derby and Plymouth as well as with the York company. She progressed to both Covent Garden and Drury Lane.[55] Descriptions of her visit to the Chelmsford Theatre in 1792 suggest the anticipated star quality she brought with her. The notices expressed that she was 'late of Drury Lane' and that she would appear in *Percy, Elwina, The Irish Widow* (her old standby) and *Inkle and Yarico*. Her brother and sister appeared alongside her.[56]

Other Members of the Regular Company

Other personnel in addition to members of the family were required to maintain the company. Although Thornton was occasionally helped by Hatton and Barnett, both men were absent for long periods of time and at least twice it became necessary for the manager to enter into a partnership. In neither instance was this a lasting arrangement. George Davenport and his wife Mary Ann were members of the Covent Garden company who regularly played the provinces during the summer recess. Soon after the beginning of the century they spent several seasons at Windsor and Thornton, probably admiring at close quarters the acumen of Davenport, in 1804 joined forces with him, briefly announcing the arrangement (the *Thespian Dictionary* mentions a 'new arrangement' occurring in 1803) through the *Chelmsford Chronicle*.[57] After that next to nothing is heard of the Thornton-Davenport connection. Possibly Davenport's appointment as secretary to the Covent Garden Theatrical Fund, a charity for impecunious past actors of the theatre, left him no time for other administrative activities.[58]

The second of Thornton's attempts to find a partner was a financial disaster. In 1816, recently bereft of his wife and left without Barnett's help - he was appearing at the Lyceum Theatre - he chose one Edward Dawson, seemingly an inhabitant of Chelmsford or one of the nearby Essex villages, to take on the joint management of the company.[59] His name appears on none of the playbills, although as early as 1795 a Mrs Dawson crops up in a newspaper advertisement; possibly, unlike Davenport, Dawson was not an actor.[60] The Chelmsford season passed uneventfully but shortly before it ended a plaintive note appeared in the newspaper: Dawson had abandoned the company, decamping with the actors' salaries. The final night was to be a benefit for the players: so little is known of Dawson that there is a touch of irony in the play chosen for this event, *The Stranger*.[61] The thief's name is not to be found in the records of criminal proceedings at Chelmsford. Presumably unpunished, he escaped enriched.

The musicians formed a small, tightly knit section of the company, although unfortunately very little is known about them. Unlike the actors, some of them seem to have had a base in the town in which a theatre was situated where they earned a living by teaching and performing, providing an orchestra during the theatre season. Such orchestras were small. At Windsor there were only six players in the pit of the 1793 playhouse.[62]

William Ivers was one of the violinists and his daughter as a child sometimes played opposite one of the Thornton boys whose age she matched.[63] Richard Binfield, who played the violin, flute and piano and occasionally acted, retired from the company in 1799, planning to settle in Reading where he would teach and play at the assemblies. To this he added the post of organist at St Lawrence's Church and furthermore established a Music Warehouse on the corner of Cross Street and Friar Street from which words of songs rendered in the theatre could be bought. The trienniel music festival in the town was founded by him. His wife was the keeper of the box office. Hannah, their daughter, was an actress and singer who at the age of five played Little Bob in *The Poor Sailor*. She is possibly the Miss Binfield of Friar Street who appears in 1841 in one of the town directories listed as a 'Professor of Music' alongside Bilson Binfield of Baker Street.[64] Benjamin Webster, possibly still a teenager, was a violinist at the Croydon Theatre where the gallery audience pelted the orchestra with the pastry from the mutton pies sold as refreshments.[65] John Sale was a Windsor musician who, assisted by his family, gave concerts in the Town Hall and appears to have undertaken secretarial work for Thornton: one of the Lord Chamberlain's licences for performances at this theatre is addressed to him.[66] There was Vosper at Gosport who conducted the band at the theatre and gave concerts, accompanying his songs on the piano. His arm and head were injured when, returning to the town from Titchfield, his horse bolted and upset the gig.[67] On somewhat rare occasions the band was augmented with amateur musicians; an instance is at the benefit of Davis, the leader of the band at Reading in 1816, when extras from the town played for the performances of *The Wheel of Fortune* and *The Miller and His Men*.[68]

Most members of the stage company were employed to act and maybe, according to their abilities, to sing and dance as well. However Mr and Mrs Ratchford specialised in dancing, for the most part only taking on minor speaking roles. Sometimes the pair appeared together, as at

Gosport for their benefit when they put on *The Highland Reel* but later Mrs Ratchford danced in Thomas Collins' theatres during the summer months - one of her specialities was the hornpipe - and Ratchford teamed with his daughter.[69] It is likely that Ratchford was also a dancing master in London - during the winter months he often appeared at Covent Garden and the Haymarket - and in this connection he would play a violin, or a smaller version known as a 'kit'.[70] This may account for his role as the music master in *Catherine and Petruchio*.[71]

A few of the acting members of the company gained a limited fame, progressing for short seasons to the London patent houses or to the Haymarket Theatre but the majority of them spent long periods playing in Thornton's theatres or passing from one provincial troupe to another. Let us look briefly at several with a known history.

The Benson family has already been mentioned when dealing with the Windsor Theatre. Benson played minor roles at various London theatres, including Drury Lane, but for several summer seasons during the 1780s he appeared at Waldron's Windsor theatre and as early as 1785 he and his wife were appearing at Thornton's Newbury theatre. His operatic farce *Britain's Glory or A Trip to Portsmouth* with music by Samuel Arnold was produced several times by Thornton on the south coast. Benson's wife and one of their daughters were members of Thornton's company as well. The irrational claims which Benson made about his ownership of the Windsor theatre, loans notwithstanding, may be explained in part by the brain fever which prompted him to kill himself at the age of thirty-one by jumping from an upper storey of a house in Covent Garden.[72]

Several members of the company turned their hand to writing songs, especially comic ones, as these were required. Hatton's work has been mentioned. Bristow may stand representative for the others: at his and his wife's benefit in Gosport he sang his own composition 'The Wonderful Bell Ringing Portsmouth Ghost'.[73]

Also connected with the Windsor Theatre were James Mudie and his wife who succeeded Thornton. The new manager had been an officer in the forces. His wife, it was claimed in the *Monthly Mirror*, had 'a deficiency of teeth in her lower jaw' which created a hiss as she spoke. The paper went on to give a criticism of Mrs Mudie as Mrs Haller in *The Stranger* summarising her capability as unsuited to the London theatres although 'useful and respectable in a Country Company'.[74] For a brief period the fame of their daughter outshone that of her parents. An infant phenomenon, she had appeared the previous year at both the patent theatres in London as Peggy in David Garrick's rewrite of *The Country Wife* under the title *The*

Country Girl. In spite of Garrick's attempts to make unexceptionable William Wycherley's text, the inappropriateness of a five year old child tackling the role caused Thomas Holcroft to register an objection in his journal the *Theatrical Recorder.*[75] John Philip Kemble claimed that this phenomenon was no child but had been an innkeeper at Tadcaster when he was an actor with the York company.[76] Another child prodigy of Thornton's company was Mary Ann Ivers, at sixteen to become Mrs Orger, who started her stage life at the age of six as one of the infants in *The Children of the Wood*, playing the role until she grew too large for the robins to cover her with leaves when lost and asleep.[77]

Elizabeth Richards 'improved herself' in Thornton's company with the result that by the early 1790s she was taking many of the leading roles. She married John Edwin whom she met at Lord Barrymore's private theatricals at Wargrave when the actresses of Thornton's company joined his lordship's army friends on the stage. Subsequently, enticed by a generous salary, she entered the company of John Boles Watson and from there progressed to the Bath theatre which she made her home.[78]

Ralph Wewitzer.
(Ashmolean Museum, University of Oxford)

66

The Company and Its Roles

Having played in both Covent Garden and Drury Lane, Ralph Wewitzer and his wife joined Thornton at Chelmsford in 1792. They were on a provincial tour at the Birmingham Theatre when the building caught fire and so were forced to seek work elsewhere. Wewitzer specialised in the portrayal of French, German and Jewish elderly men.[79] 'There is no actor on the stage,' wrote Leigh Hunt, 'who approaches his foreign accent and manner, and his characters are generally so uninteresting in the author and so totally dependant on his acting for their effect, that if he has any fault in this style it is the universal and equal humour which he gives to everything foreign.'[80]

Burton was an actor with a wide experience of country theatres. He suffered badly from nerves which tended to deprive him of speech, so that at one stage of his career he was forced to perform in dumb show. However he was playing at Thornton's company in Chelmsford during 1795, joining in songs with Mrs Pritchard.[81]

Too fat to dance when the play required and sometimes too fat to act, Daniel Egerton played in the company during 1807, certainly at Oxford and Gosport, bringing his first wife with him. Stephen Kemble appears to be the link between Egerton and the manager, for Kemble often starred for a few nights at Thornton's invitation. Egerton took emotionally heavy, tragic characters, giving merely a reading of the role rather than a performance.[82] Mrs Egerton played Lady Randolph to William Henry West Betty's Norval (*Douglas*).[83]

Thornton was not above poaching actors when he felt that they would serve his theatres well. Stanwix, one of Thomas Collins' actors playing at the Portsmouth Theatre, was filched when Thornton was residing in nearby Gosport. His tenor voice was pleasant, causing Collins to complain justifiably, 'at present we can do very little in the singing way' and he also had the advantage of membership of the masons.[84] At his benefit night in Chelmsford a contingent of the Lodge of Good Fellowship appeared on stage with Stanwix to back his songs.[85] Towards the end of his career Thornton managed to inveigle one Gilbert, also a member of the Portsmouth Theatre, to join his own Gosport company.[86] At other times Thornton seems to have hired a performer from the Portsmouth Theatre to play at Gosport as in the case of Mrs Brereton who in 1809 played the title role of Adelgitha and later in the evening gave a patriotic address as Britannia.[87]

Many other names of performers are, of course, listed on the bills but next to nothing is known of their progress apart from some of their roles. One wonders about the lives of the Simpsons, the Saunders, the Cliffords,

Rawling in his transvestite clothes, Stanley a 'captain' of the company, Miss Cranford, Thompson who took on Fawcett's characters, Hargrave with his mellow voice and graceful action and a passing Miss Herbert amongst a host of others.[88] Even more shadowy are the amateurs who occasionally performed: Captain Harcourt, a 'young gentleman in the neighbourhood of Reading', played in *The Chapter of Accidents* and anonymously, in *Hit or Miss*, a 'Gentleman of Chelmsford' took the part of Dick Cypher.[89] Sometimes an amateur was allowed to take a major role: at Oxford an anonymous young man played Richard III. Perhaps to allay criticism Thornton assured his patrons that the lad would be found 'entirely perfect and respectable'.[90] Another time Thornton hired Watmore, the landlord of the Three Tuns in Windsor, to play Abel Drugger in *The Alchemist*.[91] Occasionally an amateur would pay a fee for the privilege of performing in the company. Thornton is hardly likely to have advertised this fact; a fictional example is Ramble in Thomas Mozeen's novel *Young Scarron* who is allowed to join Bob Loveplay's group for a subscription of £20.[92]

The Scene Painters

Again, few facts are known about the scene painters. A diminutive fellow, 'Little' Harvey, was the scenic constructor and painter to the company and appears to have travelled from one theatre to another. For example in 1795 he was in Reading designing new scenes for *Henry VI*.[93] Six years later there was a refurbishment of the interior of the house and Harvey decorated this as well as producing scenes for *The Point of Honour*.[94] He also travelled to Chelmsford in 1799 where he was assisted by Griffiths, an artist of the town who had created the scenes for *The Castle Spectre* in the previous year, earning a benefit in consequence.[95] Unfortunately Harvey met with an unspecified accident at the Gosport Theatre and his condition was so serious it was feared he would die. Luckily the town housed a dedicated doctor who tended him until he recovered and then sent him on a convalescence, paid for by a benefit night.[96] In addition to painting the scenes there were occasions when Harvey was seen as a performer; in *Pizarro* is an instance.[97]

There were two travelling artists whose home base appears to have been at Windsor. They were decorating and making scenes for the Chelmsford Theatre in 1797 and after the front extention to the Windsor Theatre the building was 'elegantly ornamented' by them. They remained anonymous.[98]

Sometimes local artists were employed on a temporary basis; one was William Johnson who worked at the theatre at Chelmsford prior to Harvey. He was well known to local people, warmly commended for his scenes and allotted a benefit performance. The money-making ploy summed up by the term 'pit converted to boxes' was operated. Temporarily the pit would have been divided by ropes or chains into 'boxes' and box prices charged. Some claimed that Johnson 'did not merit the benefit he received' but Thornton registered in the newspaper his satisfaction.[99]

In Berkshire Tobias Young appears to have worked jointly as scenic designer and painter to Lord Barrymore, to whom he was articled for 'a term of years', and to Thornton at the Reading Theatre.[100] Young was a native of Southampton and gained his reputation through local landscape painting, such as his New Forest subjects, and at the Royal Academy exhibitions. At Reading in 1788 he painted a transparency portrait of David Garrick and, standing in front of the portrait, recited a monody on the actor written by Sheridan. On another occasion he recited a description of a sea-storm.[101] The following year was a busy one; he began work with Lord Barrymore at his private theatre at Wargrave, was scene painter at the King's Opera House in the Haymarket and undertook commissions for Thornton at Reading. For his benefit performance in October at Reading Young created a set of scenes, complete with pillars, which produced the 'most striking and astonishing effect'.[102] After creating elaborate settings for Barrymore's production of *Don Juan* in 1791 Young redesigned them for the Reading theatre which lacked the depth of stage to obtain the required vista; nevertheless the settings were 'rich and most elegant'.[103] For the following week he created a series of 'correct views' for the Reading production of the farce *Nootka Sound*; they showed views of an English ship at anchor in the West Indies, landscapes of the surrounding countryside and a spread of the Spanish and English camps complete with flags and banners.[104] The show was made up of songs, sold at the theatre in book form, and disconnected dialogue; the whole production was devised by James Byrn, ballet master at Covent Garden where it was staged the previous year.[105] The idea of 'correct views' is an interesting one: does the correctness refer to a topographical precision or to a close approximation to the settings of the first London production?

Emmanuel was also employed by both Thornton and Lord Barrymore. Possibly Thornton introduced Emmanuel to Lord Petre of Thorndon Hall, Essex - his company played at the private theatre of both men - and the artist was commissioned to fit up a theatre at Thorndon in 1792.[106] Also in 1792 Thornton staged *Robinson Crusoe* at Chelmsford with 'correct Views of the

69

Island' by Emmanuel.[107] As Johnson was the regular artist at Chelmsford at this time, here is an indication that Emmanuel's scenes were taken on tour.

Occasionally artists who worked for another manager would be engaged for short periods by Thornton. William Cave is an example. With a wide range of talents including mural painting, gilding ecclesiastical carvings and book illustration (Richard Wavell's *History of Winchester* amongst others), he had produced scenes for the Winchester Theatre under Collins' management. Thornton employed him to paint a number of scenes for the new theatre at Gosport in 1796. A classical drop cloth won especial commendation: it portrayed a 'grand view of ruins, now actually existing at Rome; the frontispiece coloured with the royal diadem of England supported by two figures of Fame'.[108] Much the same arrangement was made in 1806 when Kirby of the Royal Circus decorated the Windsor Theatre after minor alterations and created some scenes.[109]

Sometimes the scene painter is little more than a name. A mist hides the personalities of two Croydon artists, Banks and Shields, who were the scene painters in 1800.[110] One is left wondering if the first named is Thomas Banks the Drury Lane artist, who undertook humble country tasks such as painting the scenery for Richardson's travelling theatre.[111]

In addition to professional artists, people who enjoyed the theatrical ambience also helped with scenery. At Andover, for example, Buckland, a local carpenter and handyman employed by the rector of the nearby village of Fyfield, made the scenes and they were painted by Gilbert White, the incumbent's son.[112]

Occasionally a performer-artist took the stage. Thomas Frederick Luppino, both an actor and a dancer, arrived in Gosport and on his benefit night displayed his own scenes for *One O'Clock*.[113]

Throughout Thornton's management the policy was for new scenes to be extolled and the painters credited but when the management passed to Bronsdorph and Jones a change was evident. That most of the scenes in *Don Giovanni* had been seen before and applauded was not an advertising tactic worth pursuing.[114]

Visitors of Distinction

In addition to the regular company there were the visits of performers who had made names for themselves on the stages of the patent theatres and the Haymarket. These would play for any length of time from a couple of nights to a week or longer.

A person who encouraged Thornton throughout his career, from the opening of his Reading playhouse until her retirement, was Dorothy Jordan. The repertoire she played at Reading was to stay with her, although augmented, throughout much of her life. She played Peggy in *The Country Girl*, Portia in *The Merchant of Venice*, one of her transvestite roles, Sir Harry Wildair, in *The Constant Couple* and Priscilla Tomboy in *The Romp*. She then left Reading to prepare for her visit to the Cheltenham theatre where she would play before the royal family on the occasion of George III's visit to the spa to take the purgative waters.[115] During her liaison with the Duke of Clarence Jordan took on many engagements at the London patent theatres as well as some provincial tours but the income proved insufficient for the Duke's needs and after his break with the actress she was forced to undertake tiring journeys in order to earn enough to support herself and her FitzClarence children. During November 1812 Mrs Jordan played at Collins' theatre in Portsmouth as well as at Thornton's in Gosport. At Portsmouth where, amongst other characters, she played Lady Teazle (*The School for Scandal*) and Hoyden (*A Trip to Scarborough*), coarse remarks were shouted at her from the auditorium in spite of Collins employing the peace officers of the borough to keep order.[116] The audience no doubt were influenced by the caricatures of Jordan and Clarence by such cartoonists as James Gillray; there was, too, something unbecoming about a woman in her fifties playing the roles she had adopted years previously.[117] However, there were compensations in her artistry. Five years earlier a theatrical correspondent who saw her play at Windsor had claimed that 'there is always something bewitching in her acting which since the secession of Miss Farren [the successor to the original Lady Teazle of Frances Abington] makes even her Lady Teazle more bearable than any other'.[118] All would seem to have gone well at Gosport where she appeared in *Scandal* and *The Sleep Walker*, enjoying a respite from the former unpleasantness by her stay with the clerical son of Bishop Brownlow North of Winchester.[119] A prolonged period away from home took her on to Southampton, Salisbury and eventually Bath.[120] In the September of 1813 Jordan played at Ryde and the following month appeared at both Reading and Newbury.[121] Here, more appropriately, she took on the role of Widow Cheerly in *The Soldier's Daughter*.[122] At Gilder's Square the actor Robert Dyer saw her perform three of her roles, Violante, Hoyden and Nell:

> She was then in her decline but fascinating in decay. I believe this was nearly her last appearance on the stage.[123]

Andover in November was Jordan's next stop where she spent some pleasant days with friends as well as performing.[124] Her first visit to Oxford took place during the autumn of 1815 when she played in Thornton's rackets court theatre at Christ Church offering to full houses such roles as Lady Teazle, the Widow Cheerly, Letitia Hardy (*The Belle's Stratagem*) and Violante.[125] Obviously just as Jordan had helped Thornton in playing at his Reading Theatre during the first season, so he, in her displacement, was a comfort and means of earning her family's keep.

Dorothy Jordon.
(Author's collection)

There is a sadness in the visits of William Henry West Betty to Thornton's theatres, for in them we see the gradual decline of a one-time child prodigy. He appeared, much trumpeted, at Windsor and Gosport at the end of 1804 and the following year Thornton took, for him, the unprecedented step of presenting the young man at a theatre outside his own circuit, that at Winchester belonging to Thomas Collins. This was one of the busiest times of Betty's childhood career in which he had appeared at the London patent houses as well as making extended tours. At the age

of thirteen, his first appearance was as Richard III and then another lust-
ful, middle-aged villain, Earl Osmund in *The Castle Spectre*. More suit-
ably he played Young Norval in *Douglas*, a role on which his early reputation rested and still popular to the extent that one hundred people were
unable to gain admittance.[126]   In 1807, the year before he went to
Cambridge University, Betty appeared in Oxford. Aged sixteen, the first
dew of the actor had evaporated but nevertheless not all of his audiences
could crowd into the theatre.   He played Young Norval with Daniel
Egerton supporting as Glenalvon. It was a performance which by that
time drew a mixed reception. Three years earlier 'Justus' in the *Monthly
Mirror* had balanced his strengths and weaknesses:

> To say nothing of the infantine figure, the affected hollow,
> though, at times, screaming voice of this young man, his merit in
> this part is considerable. The burst of youthful ardour was forcibly
> depicted, and this is the prominent feature of the piece. His dis-
> crimination is totally defective; the humble, though ardent-mind-
> ed peasant Norval, was more impetuous than Douglas, instigating
> his mother to be permitted to 'head the vassals of his house'.[127]

After the performance Betty 'supped with a party of the very first
respect' and at the end of his stay he dined in Magdalene College.[128] Betty
played under the patronage of the Duke of Norfolk for three nights at
Arundel in December drawing, it was claimed, an audience from a twenty mile radius, not all of whom could get into the small theatre.[129]
Thornton advertised that he had received a letter from the manager of
the Margate Theatre, prior to Betty's 1807 visit: there, over nine nights,
the box office receipts topped £900 and Betty's benefit night was
'upwards of £100'.[130] Laying claim to Betty's popularity, Thornton
increased the box prices by one shilling and the pit and gallery by six-
pence at the Oxford Theatre for his visit in the same year.[131]

Immediately before a resurrection engagement at Covent Garden in
1812, Betty acted at Gosport for a few nights. Then twenty-one years old,
Norval, the shepherd lad, was repeated together with Selim in *Barbarossa*
and Osman in *Zara*.[132] The theatre accommodation seems to have been
large enough for all who attended; the attractions of childhood had
deserted Betty and Lord Byron, who saw him perform three months earlier, described him to Lord Holland: 'His figure is fat, his features flat, his
voice unmanageable, his action ungraceful....'[133] To be fair to Thornton,
although Betty's career was virtually finished in London, he made many
provincial appearances until 1824 when at the Southampton Theatre he
announced his retirement from the stage.[134]

Edward Cape Everard was an actor who appeared from time to time with Thornton's performers, blurring the distinction between company member and visitor. He offers an example of Thornton's belief in truly working those whom he temporarily engaged. Everard seems to have played for the first time in the company at Reading in 1788 taking the part of Sparkish (*The Country Girl*) in which Jordan was also appearing.[135] He was eclipsed by her. The following year he appeared at the India Arms in Gosport during the spring. Later with Thornton at Horsham, Everard was caught by the limits of the sixty day regulation. One of the magistrates, Ellis, who had issued the licence was insistent that Thornton should not overrun his time. Thornton decided that the benefit nights, not counted in the total of licet performing nights for some reason, would take place and Mrs and Miss Cornelys arranged for John Palmer to join them and their daughter with the recompense of a following benefit of his own. Few turned up to see the Cornelys family, with the result that the two actresses refused to help Everard with his production of *The Merchant of Venice*. Substitutes were found from the section of the company playing at Dorking, Palmer arrived again, this time to assist Everard and the performance began, played to a good house by a cast assembled in the nick of time. Unfortunately Ellis also arrived during the evening. The entertainment was abandoned but luckily Everard had received his receipts in time. It was Palmer who suffered financially.[136] Invited to Reading at the end of the year, Everard's experience as a dancer was demonstrated alongside Thomas West, temporarily a member of the company, for whose benefit he appeared and also on another night in a dwarf dance. Complications beset Everard's next benefit. He decided to present *The Farmer* in which he had originated the role of Jemmy Jumps together with *Much Ado about Nothing* in which he played Dogberry, assisted by Thornton as Claudio and Mrs Thornton as Beatrice.[137] On the afternoon of the benefit Everard was delivering tickets when he was told that, two hours before starting time, a crowd large enough to fill the theatre was waiting at the doors. Threats to break them down encouraged Everard to let in the populace but no one was ready to take the entrance money. Everard had to appeal in the newspaper for reimbursement. Even so, the beneficiary reckoned that he had lost twelve pounds. In January 1790 Everard went with the company to Henley, repeating his role of Sparkish.[138] The following year saw him back again for a couple of weeks at Reading.[139]

In 1795 Thornton's treatment of Everard became even more frenetic when he rushed him around five counties in as many weeks, getting him to play at Cowes, Arundel, Reading, Guildford, and Chelmsford for six nights a week with travel on Sundays.[140] The volley of coach journeys was about to start again. Everard joined the company at Windsor in July until

Thornton moved him to Chelmsford where he shared a benefit with Mrs Dawson acting in *The Deserted Daughter* and *The Farmer* between which he danced, sang and gave recitations. By September he was back in Windsor only to be moved on to Weybridge. With a section of the company playing in Reading as well, a benefit was held out to Everard to play in Berkshire and then to return to Weybridge for another. Thornton arranged that during Everard's absence from Weybridge a Reading actor should fill in for him. The ploy did not work. A highly popular actor at Reading, only Everard would do and so the two actors again exchanged theatres. By this time Everard had lost the benefit in Reading; that in Weybridge, Thornton informed him, was to be shared with two other performers. The coach did not arrive in the latter town until seven in the evening, leaving Everard no time to call upon his supporters there, amongst whom were numbered the Duke of York at Oatlands House. As he dressed for the role of Shylock, he determined to leave the company.[141]

Yet Everard returned. In the early months of 1796 Thornton opened his theatre at Cowes and Everard was to be seen in the opening play of the season, *The Busy Body*. By seven o'clock there was a 'tolerable house' but only four actors had been able to make their way across the Solent. To dissuade Thornton from cancelling the evening's entertainment Everard offered to play both Sir Francis Gripe and his son Charles. In spite of his optimism, difficulties arose when the two characters appeared on stage together: 'I was in this point unavoidably deficient [wrote Everard]; save that I was told that the metamorphosis was not perceivable'.[142] Relations between actor and manager grew tense over the length of time Everard took to change from his between-plays dancing dress to his after-piece costume. Everard charged Thornton with paying him a guinea a week for acting but expecting him to dance for nothing but insults. Thornton declined to pay any extra fee and so the two parted for the last time.[143]

Another dancer who performed on Thornton's stages was the earlier mentioned Thomas West, teaming on several occasions with Everard in such divertisements as a double hornpipe. He choreographed many of his own dances; one at Reading was entitled *Cymon and Iphigenia*. There was an interest here in acting, too. He was to be found playing the part of Abel Drugger in *The Tobacconist*, a cut-down of *The Alchemist*, in the manner of David Garrick.[144]

Thornton encouraged comedians to visit his company. Foremost among these was John Quick of Covent Garden, a favourite with George III.[145] When the king attended the opening night of the purpose-built Windsor Theatre it was his wish that Quick should take the role of Scrub in *The Beaux' Stratagem*. Unusually, the king chose the pieces for Quick's benefit night at

Windsor too, asking for *Wild Oats* and *The Recruiting Sergeant.*[146] Quick visited the Chelmsford Theatre in the following year, playing the role of Tony Lumpkin (*She Stoops to Conquer*) which he had originated some twenty years earlier, a personification which did not escape censure:

> ...these young masters have lately found in him a very imperfect
> representative. There are, however, parts exclusive of old men
> in which he can be seen with satisfaction.[147]

He arrived at Gosport in 1799 and immediately followed this by a visit to nearby Portsmouth - a place he had used in his younger days as a seaside retreat - this time introducing his audiences to Lovegold in *The Miser.*[148] Further flying visits were to the Newbury Theatre in 1802 to play Old Doiley in *Who's the Dupe* and in 1810 during the Race Week.[149]

Another comedian who appeared in several of Thornton's theatres in the latter part of his professional life was Joseph Shepherd Munden.

John Quick.
(National Portrait Gallery, London)

Never one to stay for long whilst touring, he came to Gosport in December 1812 for a couple of days. After a provincial appreticeship, Munden spent over twenty years at Covent Garden where he originated the role of Old Downton in *The Road to Ruin*. This characterisation he brought to Gosport and Reading in September 1814. Later he performed in Oxford.[150] Thornton wrote of Munden in glowing terms: his skill demonstrated a 'profound science in the histrionic art [which] puts all competition at total defiance,' a sentiment with which Charles Lamb would have agreed.

It is obviously impossible to mention all the visiting performers, nevertheless the roll over the years shows an impressive awareness of the principal actors of the London theatres and an ability to induce them to venture into the country: selective mention may be made of John Palmer, Thomas Ryder, Mr and Mrs Noke of the Haymarket, Stephen Kemble and his wife the former Miss Satchell, John Bannister, Isabella Mattocks, Anna Maria Crouch, Michael Kelly, George Frederick Cooke, Charles Incledon, John Richer, John Fawcett and his wife, Miss Booth, Sarah Smith - later Mrs Bartley - and James Raymond.

In addition to this list, a number of performers arrived who were not actors in the accepted sense. One of these was the Chevaliere D'Eon who gave an Assault D'Armes at Reading in June 1796. Her uniform (throughout her life and possibly due to a number of transvestite disguises as well as a physical malformation, doubt was expressed about the gender of D'Eon) was described in the newspaper advertisement: 'Madame D'Eon will appear in the same Uniform which she wore at the time when she served as Captain of Dragoons and Aid de Campe to Mareschal Duc de Broglio in Germany'.[151] In these exhibitions D'Eon was assisted by an actress and former student, [Mary?] Bateman.[152] Before coming to Reading the fencer had appeared in Bath and Oxford and after this engagement with Thornton moved on to Southampton where she was badly injured during a display.[153] Again, Thornton saddled his artists with matinée performances as well as in the evening.

In the year of its invention, 1802, Thornton presented the *Phantasmagoria* at a number of his theatres, including Reading, Newbury and Gosport. The machine was a projection device, using a lamp and a slide. The slide mount was on a rachet with the result that the image could gradually be enlarged or shrink to a pinpoint of light.[154] Signor Moritz (advertised as 'from Italy') developed a number of portraits into a programme of 'Optical and Magical Illusions' and popularised this on Thornton's circuit.[155] At Reading the representations, an indication of people who commanded a popular interest, consisted of the Prince of Wales and the Duke of York, the form of Louis XVI which changed, by a merging of images, into a skeleton, Nelson and Shakespeare, Kemble in the role of Octavian (*The Mountaineers*), Dorothy Jordan, Martha Gunn, the Bleeding Nun from *The Monk*, the ghost scene in *Hamlet* and eventually concluded with a portrait of the King.[156] Thornton was so taken with this device that he wrote a rhymed address to accompany the showings. Moritz augmented his presentation, assisted by his eight year old son, by balancing musket and bayonet points on his head, two coach wheels on his teeth and an egg on the point of a straw.[157]

One is struck by the size of the company, which grew as Thornton progressed through his years of management and the complexity of keeping an operation running which could be divided into as many as three sections, each playing simultaneously in a different theatre. The range of visitors, too, is wide, even at a time when managers made every attempt to provide as many different and well-known faces as possible. Generally Thornton was recognised as a manager who succeeded in doing this but it could be an expensive ploy and at times individual theatres were not large enough to recoup the costs through the box office. In his first season at the Reading Theatre Thornton had spent extravagantly in bringing stars to the town and Everard's stricture was justified: '...had he confined himself only to a decent company [the audience] would have been perfectly satisfied and he some hundreds of pounds the gainer, but if a man will mount his hobby, let him pay for it'.[158] Only with experience did Thornton learn to find a just mean and, as we have seen he did with Everard, learn to make the most of a visitor by taking him the rounds of several theatres.

1. British Library: Burney Collection of Playbills, 1, King's Lynn Theatre, 1774, 937 f 2.
2. Lincoln Central Library: Playbill collection.
3. British Library: Playbill collection, 426, Portsmouth, 1781-2.
4. Birmingham Central Library: Playbill collection, 1783.
5. G W Stone and C Beecher Hogan, *The London Stage* (Carbondale, 1968), part 5, 3.1687. Winston, *Tourist*, p.31. Everard, *Memoirs*, pp 149-152.
6. The story of the shirts was recast into verse with slight variations by Egan in *The Life of an Actor* , p.83:
   So absorbed was Old T. in his various pursuits,
   That at morn he'd march forth in last night's russet boots;
   Indeed, some thought his brain had a crack,
   For once his dear wife had six shirts for him made,
   When return'd from his journey she thought them mislaid,
   But, behold, they were all - on his back!
7. Walter Alexander Donaldson, *Recollections of an Actor* (1865), p.113.
8. *Biography of the British Stage*, pp 204-5.
9. *Tourist*, p.18.
10. *Reading Mercury*, 18 July 1791 and 12 August 1793.
11. *Chelmsford Chronicle*, 29 August 1817.

12. *Reading Mercury*, 12 May 1788.
13. *Thespian Dictionary*. Highfill, *et al, Biographical Dictionary*, 12.169.
14. Lillian Arvilla Hall, *Catalogue of Dramatic Portraits in the Theatre Collection of Harvard College Library* (Cambridge, Mass., 1931), 4.145-7. *Thespian Dictionary*. I can trace no familial connection between Elizabeth Pritchard and Hannah Pritchard (1711-1768), the Drury Lane actress.
15. Everard, *Memoirs*, p.103.
16. Ann Catherine Holbrook, *The Dramatist* (1809), p.25.
17. see note 4.
18. Chelmsford Central Library: playbill, 24 August 1798.
19. *Reading Mercury*, 16 September 1799.
20. *Monthly Mirror*, 17 (1804), 206. George Lillo, *George Barnwell or The London Merchant* (1731).
21. *Reading Mercury*, 18 March 1816.
22. see note 4. Lee, *Memoirs* , p.136. Highfill, *et al, Biographical Dictionary*, 7. 176. *Universal British Directory* (1793), pp 513 and 515. Essex Record Office, Chelmsford: 'Transcripts of Monumental Inscriptions in the Churches of... Chelmsford', manuscript, T/P72/1.
23. John Coleman, *Fifty Years of an Actor's Life* (1904), p.490.
24. Guildford Institute: Playbill collection, Guildford, 30 July 1834.
25. *Berkshire Chronicle*, 26 February 1870. *Hampshire Telegraph*, 8 August 1825.
26. *Chelmsford Chronicle*, 5 July 1816.
27. *Reading Mercury*, 3, 10, 17, 24 September 1810.
28. *Reading Mercury*, 9 October 1815.
29. Guildford Muniment Room: Playbill collection, 17 June 1814, G7118. *Hampshire Telegraph*, 3 July 1815.
30. Ralph Wewitzer, *A Brief Dramatic Chronology of Actors, etc., on the London Stage* (1817), p.23.
31. *Monthly Mirror*, 24 (1807), 291.
32. Highfill, et al. *Biographical Dictionary*, 7. 176 *Gentleman's Magazine*, 15, new series (1841), 557. Lee, *Memoirs*, p.136.
33. *Hampshire Telegraph*, 19 July 1802.
34. Charles Beecher Hogan, *Shakespeare in the Theatre, 1701-1800* (Oxford, 1957), 2.722. Harvard Theatre Collection, Winston's manuscript notebook, TS1335.211. *The Times*, 25 November 1801. *Morning Chronicle*, 22 July 1803.
The White Hart Theatre, a barn adjoining the tavern, was situated on the corner of Parson's Green and Ackmar Road; the manager's name was Duckworth.
35. *Reading Mercury*, 21 November 1803.
36. *Chelmsford Chronicle*, 6 July 1798.
37. *Hampshire Telegraph*, 7 June 1802.
38. Philip Dennis, *Gibraltar and its People* (Newton Abbot, 1990), p.33. *Hampshire Telegraph*, 19 July 1802.
39. John Bernard, *Retrospections of America, 1797-1811* (New York, 1887), p.311.
40. Theatre Museum: Haymarket Theatre file. *Thespian Dictionary*. Richard Phillip Sodder, 'The Theatre Management of Alexandre Placide in Charleston, 1794-1812', Louisiana State University, 1983, PhD dissertation, p.629.
41. Lee, *Memoirs*, p.136.
42. *Reading Mercury*, 30 August 1802.
43. Winston, *Tourist*, p.10.
44. *Theatrical Inquisitor*, 3 (1813), 125. *Hampshire Chronicle*, 9 July 1810. Lee, *Memoirs*, p.136.
45. *The Ancient and Modern History of Portsmouth, Portsea, Gosport and their Environs* (nd), p.94. *Hampshire Telegraph*, 26 June 1803, 16 April 1804.
46. *Hampshire Chronicle*, 22 April 1805.
47. Thomas Holcroft, *Theatrical Recorder* (1805), p.450.
48. *Thespian Dictionary*.
49. *Thespian Magazine*, 1 (1793), 255
50. *Thespian Magazine*, 1 (1793), 177.
51. Highfill, *et al.*, *Biographical Dictionary*, 12. 169-70

52. Tate Wilkinson, cited in Hodgkinson and Pogson, *Manchester Theatre*, p.104.
53. C G Kuttner cited in Hodgkinson and Pogson, *Manchester Theatre*, p.111.
54. S[ybil] R[osenfeld], 'The Theatrical Notebooks of T H Wilson Manly', *Theatre Notebook*, 7 (1952-3), 2. *Thespian Dictionary.*
55. Highfill, *et al*, *Biographical Dictionary*, 14. 386-8.
56. *Chelmsford Chronicle*, 24 August 1792.
57. *Chelmsford Chronicle*, 22 June 1804. *Thespian Dictionary*. Winston, *Tourist*, p.18.
58. Highfill, *et al.*, *Biographical Dictionary*, 4. 190-1.
59. *Chelmsford Chronicle*, 5 July 1816. Essex Record Office: Petition for a Sixty Day Licence, 16 July 1816. Q/SB6 444/27.
60. *Chelmsford Chronicle*, 17 August 1795.
61. *Chelmsford Chronicle*, 4 October 1816.
62. Knight, *Varieties*, p.72.
63. Berkshire Record Office, Reading: playbill, Newbury, 20 November 1798.
64. *Reading Mercury*, 16 September 1799 and 1 April 1805. *Chelmsford Chronicle*, 24 August 1798 and 9 August 1799. *Rusher's Reading Guide and Berkshire Directory 1817* (Reading, 1817), p.2. *Fernyhough's Reading Directory 1841* (Reading, 1841), p.7.
65. Croydon Central Library: Anderson, manuscript notes.
66. *Thespian Magazine*, 3 (1794), 34 . Public Record Office, Chancery Lane: Theatre Licence, Lord Chamberlain's Papers, LCS/163.
67. *Portsmouth Telegraph*, 25 August 1799. *Hampshire Telegraph*, 18 December 1815.
68. *Reading Mercury*, 30 December 1816.
69. Bodleian Library: John Johnson Collection, playbill, 19 October 1812. Highfill, *et al.*, 12. 257-8. *Jackson's Oxford Journal*, 29 August 1803. *Portsmouth Gazette*, 5 May 1800.
70. *Grove's Dictionary of Music and Musicians*, ed Eric Blom (1954), 4. 769.
71. Hereford Public Library: scrapbook of Kemble and Siddons Papers, playbill, 15 June 1801.
72. *Thespian Dictionary*. Highfill, *et al* , *Biographical Dictionary*, 2. 44-7. *Reading Mercury*, 5 September 1785.
Britain's Glory was staged at the Haymarket Theatre in August 1794.
73. *Portsmouth Telegraph*, 19 May 1800.
74. *Monthly Mirror*, 20 (1805), 310
75. *Theatrical Recorder*, pp 408-410. Reviews praising the performances of the child are to be found in the *Monthly Mirror*, 20 (1805), 120 and 21 (1806), 349
76. Lou Warwick, *Theatre Unroyal* (1974), p.50.
77. *Biography of the British Stage*, p.203.
78. Oxberry, *Dramatic Biography*, pp 201-2. *Thespian Dictionary*. C Baron Wilson, *Our Actresses* (1844), p.105.
79. *Thespian Dictionary*. Thomas Gilliland, *The Dramatic Mirror* (1808), p.1011.
80. Leigh Hunt, *Critical Essays on the Performers of the London Stage* (1807), pp 116-7.
81. *Thespian Dictionary*. *Chelmsford Chronicle*, 14 August 1795.
82. *Hampshire Telegraph*, 12 and 19 October 1807. William Oxberry, *Dramatic Biography and Histrionic Anecdotes*, (1825-7), 3. 256-9. Stephen and Lee, *DNB* 3, 569.
83. *Jackson's Oxford Journal*, 25 July, 26 September 1807.
84. *Hampshire Chronicle*, 21 January 1797.
85. *Chelmsford Chronicle*, 11 and 18 August 1797.
86. *Hampshire Telegraph*, 18 December 1815. British Library: Playbills, 269, Gosport, 31 July 1815.
87. *Hamsphire Telegraph*, 1 May 1809.
88. *Sussex Weekly Advertiser*, 5 and 12 December 1791. *Monthly Mirror*, 17 (1804), 205
89. *Reading Mercury*, 27 June and 4 July 1791. *Chelmsford Chronicle*, 13 September 1816.
90. *Jackson's Oxford Journal*, 3 October 1807.
91. *Reading Mercury*, 13 August 1798.
92. Thomas Mozeen, *Young Scarron* (1752), p.21.
93. *Reading Mercury*, 19 October 1795.
94. *Reading Mercury*, 24 August 1801.

95. *Chelmsford Chronicle*, 24 August 1798 and 19 July 1799.
96. *Hampshire Telegraph*, 7 June 1802.
97. *Chelmsford Chronicle*, 26 July 1799.
98. *Chelmsford Chronicle*, 7 July 1797 and *Reading Mercury*, 13 August 1798.
99. *Chelmsford Chronicle*, 31 August and 7 September 1792.
100. Samuel Redgrave, *A Dictionary of Artists of the English School* (1874), p.471.
101. *Reading Mercury*, 4 August 1788.
102. *Reading Mercury*, 12 October 1789.
103. British Library: Burney Collection, unidentified clipping. *Reading Mercury*, 23 May 1791.
104. *Reading Mercury*, 30 May 1791.
105. Allardyce Nicoll, *A History of English Drama, 1660-1900* (Cambridge, 1955), 3. 338. Dougald MacMillan, ed, *Catalogue of the Larpent Plays in the Huntington Library* (San Marino, 1939), p.145.
106. Anthony Pasquin [pseud], *The Life of the Earl of Barrymore* (1793), p.15. *Thespian Magazine*, 1 (1793), 181.
107. *Chelmsford Chronicle*, 17 August 1792.
108. *Hampshire Chronicle*, 26 November 1796. Turner, 'A Notable Family of Artists', *Proceedings of the Hampshire Field Club*, 22 (1961), 30-33.
109. *Reading Mercury*, 4 August 1806.
110. *Chelmsford Chronicle*, 6 July 1792. *Monthly Mirror*, 10 (Oct 1800), 260.
111. Egan, *Life of an Actor*, p.195.
112. Bodleian Library: Diary of the Revd Henry White, entries for 4, 8, 15 February, 1 and 12 March 1788, Diaries 42111-2.
113. *Portsmouth Gazette*, 14 October 1811. Verbal information from Derek Forbes.
114. British Library: Playbill collection, 299. 54.
115. *Reading Mercury*, 16, 23 and 30 June, 1788. Tomalin, *Mrs Jordan's Profession*, pp 79-88, *passim*.
116. *Portsmouth Telegraph*, 23 and 30 November 1812.
117. A selection of the caricatures is given in *Mrs Jordan. The Duchess of Drury Lane* (1995), catalogue to an exhibition held at Kenwood House in 1995.
118. *Monthly Mirror*, 24 (Oct 1807), 276
119. A Aspinall, *Mrs Jordan and her Family* (1951), p.243
120. Tomalin, *Mrs Jordan's Profession*, p.264.
121. Eric Jones-Evans, 'The Royal Theatre, Ryde' *Hampshire County Magazine* (February 1975), p.55.
122. *Reading Mercury*, 4 October 1813.
123. Robert Dyer, *Nine Years of an Actor's Life* (1833), p.8.
124. Aspinall, *Mrs Jordan*, p.255.
125. *Jackson's Oxford Journal*, 26 August and 2 September 1815. Paul Ranger, 'The Theatres of Oxford: Forty Years of Family Management', *Oxoniensia*, 54 (1989), 393-8.
126. *Hampshire Telegraph*, 31 December 1804. *Hampshire Chronicle*, 1 April 1805.
127. *Monthly Mirror*, 18 (August 1804), 132. Playfair, *Prodigy*, pp 139-141.
128. *Jackson's Oxford Journal*, 26 September and 3 October 1807.
129. *Reading Mercury*, 14 and 21 December 1807.
130. *Hampshire Telegraph*, 23 November 1807.
131. *Jackson's Oxford Journal*, 26 September 1807. *Theatrical Inquisitor*, 1 (1812-3), 98-100.
132. *Hampshire Telegraph*, 28 September and 5 October 1812.
133. George Gordon Byron, *Byron's Letters and Journals*, ed Leslie A Marchand (1973), 2. 192.
134. *The Drama*, 6 (1824), 306.
135. *Reading Mercury*, 16 June 1788.
136. Everard, *Memoirs*, p.136.
137. *Reading Mercury*, 23 November and 21 December 1789.
138. Everard, *Memoirs*, p.138. *Reading Mercury*, 30 November 1789 and 25 January 1790.
139. *Reading Mercury*, 27 June and 4 July 1791.
140. Everard, *Memoirs*, pp146.
141. Everard, *Memoirs*, pp152-5.
142. Everard, *Memoirs*, p.157.

143. Everard, *Memoirs*, pp156-8.
144. *Reading Mercury*, 19 and 26 October 1789.
145. John Taylor, *Records of My Life* (1832), 1.425.
146. *Thespian Magazine*, 2 (1793), 260.
147. *Thespian Dictionary. Chelmsford Chronicle*, 18 and 25 July 1794.
148. *Portsmouth Gazette*, 11 March and 1 April 1799.
149. *Reading Mercury*, 6 December 1802 and 13 August 1810.
150. *Hampshire Telegraph*, 28 December 1812. *Reading Mercury*, 5 September 1814.
151. *Reading Mercury*, 25 July 1796. Cynthia Cox, *The Enigma of the Age. The Strange Story of the Chevalier d'Eon* (1966), p.116.
152. J Buchan Telfer, *The Strange Career of the Chevalier D'Eon de Beaumont* (1885), p.325.
153. M Coryn, *The Chevalier D'Eon, 1728-1810* (1832), p.224.
154. A working reproduction of the phantasmagoria may be seen in the Musuem of the Moving Image on the South Bank, London.
155. *Reading Mercury*, 29 November 1802.
156. *Reading Mercury*, 16 December 1802.
157. *Hampshire Telegraph*, 25 October 1802.
158. Everard, *Memoirs* p.135.

Stephen Kemble as Falstaff.
(Author's collection)

CHAPTER 6
PLAYS AND PRODUCTIONS

The repertoire of a Georgian theatre company often appears to be chosen on an *ad hoc* basis but each company offered distinctive work. In Thornton's theatres light musical plays tended to predominate. However, there was a spread of interests and the overall choice consisted of the plays of William Shakespeare and Richard Sheridan, gothic plays, sentimental dramas, after-pieces and operettas, documentation past and present, plays of local appeal, heroic dramas, the 'old dramas' and plays centring on and requiring the help of animals.[1]

The Plays of William Shakespeare

William Shakespeare's plays, usually in an edited version, gained in popularity on the Georgian stage. Certainly those in which a flaw fractured the integrity of a strong central figure, as in *Macbeth*, *Othello* and *Hamlet*, were frequently given. At the start of his management of the Reading theatre Thornton had invited his friends of the strolling days, Stephen Kemble and his wife - both of Covent Garden - to play in *Hamlet* the title role and Ophelia. Spasmodic performances of the play were given until 1815; just before Thornton's retirement, Mrs Hill, a regular member of the company, played in breeches the male principal for her benefit.[2] Macbeth and his wife were popular roles for the benefit nights of married couples: an instance is the presentation of the Bartleys of Covent Garden making a guest appearance at Reading, also in 1815.[3] *Romeo and Juliet* was augmented at Newbury in 1797 by an impressive torchlight funeral procession, common to eighteenth-century productions, to the tomb of the Capulets, requiring the services of some of the amateurs of the town. The role of Juliet was taken by Thornton's daughter, the Nurse by his wife and Mercutio was played by Hatton, very much a family affair.[4]

Of the history plays, *Henry IV* was a favourite, with a production focus on Falstaff.[5] The play was presented in Reading in 1792 and ten years later at Gosport with Stephen Kemble playing the knight. A writer for the *Hampshire Telegraph* acknowledged his talent: '...his style of acting - his figure [Kemble was extremely corpulent], aided by a just discrimination, has given him a decided superiority over his competitors'.[6]

A few of the comedies remained more or less in their original form and of these *The Merchant of Venice* was popular, especially with Jordan playing Portia to Everard's Shylock at the end of a visit to Reading in 1788. Here was a rare chance to see her at Belmont, for at about this time Jordan decided she would fare better if she concentrated on a more robust kind of comedy.[7] Some rewritten versions of the comedies were staged at Thornton's theatres, one of which was David Garrick's cut-down of *The Taming of the Shrew*. That the play revolved around a partnership made it useful material for a married couple to perform as the Stanleys found at Chelmsford in 1815.[8] Mrs Powell of Drury Lane took the role of Catharine at Gosport on a visit in March 1809 when it must have done well as Thornton chose the piece two months later for his own benefit.[9]

Sometimes part of a play was extrapolated as a vehicle for the children of the company: *The Enchanted Island* is a case in point. A seventeenth-century version of *The Tempest,* it was further doctored for the younger Thorntons and Hattons to perform at the opening of the Reading Theatre.[10]

The Plays of Richard Sheridan

Richard Sheridan's *The School for Scandal* was a comedy often revived by Thornton during his career. It was presented during the first season of the Reading Theatre with Jordan's Lady Teazle and spasmodically put on until the year of his retirement when it was seen at Chelmsford.[11] Thornton was still manager, although Green of the Bath Theatre had been entrusted with forming a company, which he did, requesting Mrs Davison, née Duncan, of Drury Lane to take the role of Lady Teazle. She was highly experienced in this, having performed it at the Lane in 1804, 1805 and opposite Macready's Joseph in 1819 at Covent Garden.[12] Oxford saw the comedy on the stage of the Merton College rackets court, followed a couple of weeks later by *The Rivals*, playing to such acclaim that 'as many as could be received within the Court, retired for want of room'.[13]

Sheridan's play with the stongest drawing power on Thornton's circuit was his story of the Spanish conquest of the Incas in South America, *Pizarro*.

The play contained a number of spectacular set pieces, massed groups of soldiers, priestesses, mourners and the strongly drawn parallel between the invading Spaniard, Pizarro, and Napoleon mustering his forces on the further side of the Channel to attack the south coast of England. Only three months after the play was first seen at Drury Lane Hatton, deputising for Thornton, drew up the proscenium curtain on a production at Chelmsford.[14] To delight his audiences, the acting manager seems to have pinned his faith on 'splendid scenery, dresses and decoration'.[15] A firm of costumiers, Brooks and Heath, made exact replicas of the London costumes as a speculation to hire or sell to minor and provincial companies. Thornton arranged that this firm should visit Chelmsford and take on the responsibility of dressing the company. An idea of the sumptuous appearance is indicated in the £42 cost of the outfit for Ataliba, King of Quito. As well as directing the piece, Hatton took the part of Rolla; the company also included Mrs Thornton and a couple of the children, the Binfield family and Benjamin Wrench.[16] With such large set-piece scenes as the Temple of the Sun with its Peruvian architecture and the Valley of the Torrent with a gushing waterfall straddled by a rickety wooden bridge on which Rolla was fatally injured by shots from the Spanish muskets, an incompleted decor set back the production by a few days. At Chelmsford the scenic designers for the production were 'Little' Harvey, helped by Griffiths, a local artist.[17]

Few performances were given in Chelmsford as the costumes were required at the Windsor Theatre where the royal family was expected to attend but before the move from Essex was made, Thornton arrived to see several of the shows. One is left slightly in doubt whether the players in Chelmsford journeyed to Windsor or only their dresses.[18] Oxford was the September venue for the production where the company was augmented by that of Reading.[19] Here performances started a week late and the newspaper advertisements gave the impression that new costumes and scenery were in the process of preparation. The exigencies of transporting heavy and bulky materials so long a distance may have taxed the company's resources.[20] The rackets court of Merton, larger than most of Thornton's conventional theatre buildings, allowed £150 to be taken at the box office for a single performance. Even so, the building was not capacious enough for the crowds and on the final night seven hundred disconsolate people wandered along Merton Street unable to get in. From Oxford it played for a few single days at the Reading Theatre. A prognostication that 'it would fill the house in every part' proved to be true.[21]

Actors from Thomas Collins' theatre in Portsmouth, prior to their own production of *Pizarro*, took the ferry one evening to see Hatton's offering at Gosport which opened in mid-January, 1800. Collins planned to take the role of the Spanish ecclesiastic Las Casas; however, once this production opened at the Portsmouth Theatre he seems to have substituted that of Rolla, the popular young hero. Then fifty-six and suffering from a carcinoma of the face, Collins could not possibly escape censure: 'Mr Collins must be sensible that his age and stature were entirely inadequate to the appropriate representation of the Peruvian leader who is in the prime of manhood and possessing the most athletic energies'.[22] By March the Gosport Theatre was still full, supported sometimes by parties sailing from Portsmouth who arrived, in spite of a production conveniently located in their own town, to sample the wares of Thornton's company, finding it 'strange and mortifying that so small a town as Gosport should always boast of a better company'.[23] There were, of course, disappointments. On one occasion it was discovered that the Gosport Pizarro, had 'evidently made too free with the bottle that evening' and the piece lost its full effect.[24] By the end of March either Hatton or Thornton treated the company to a puff in the newspaper: 'This little theatre is become the fashionable resort of the inhabitants of Portsmouth and Portsea; indeed from the very excellent manner in which the New Pieces have been brought forward as well as the number of very good Actors the manager has taken such pains to select for his winter campaign little else could have been expected'.[25] Waiting until Thornton's run of *Pizarro* had finished, Collins fired a damp salvo from Portsmouth: 'The performance of *Pizarro* at our theatre would do credit to a Metropolitan theatre'.[26]

Gothic Plays

Plays of terror were a highly acceptable form of entertainment on the Georgian stage and Thornton provided his audiences with opportunities to enjoy them. Many were set in ruined gothic castles, a location reflected in the titles. In 1791 rumour had it that Thornton's company was to leave Horsham after an unsuccessful start to the season; denying this, the manager employed a cluster of castle-dramas to whet the appetite of the townsfolk:

> The fact is the Generalissimo is making every necessary preparation, vigorously to besiege *Belgrade, The Castle of Andalusia, The Haunted Tower,* etc. etc. and for that purpose is in daily expectation of reinforcements to join the Captains Cornelys, Stanley, Rawling, Hatton, etc.[27]

86

Plays and Productions

The most renowned of the castle plays was that of Matthew Gregory Lewis, *The Castle Spectre*, with its setting in the then remote town of Conway. It appeared for the first time on the stage of Drury Lane in 1797 and by March 1798 Thornton had translated castle and ghost to Gosport in competition with Thomas Collins' production of the same play at Portsmouth.[28] After Gosport the company travelled to Chelmsford where Griffiths painted the scenes for the production.[29] In the autumn the play was in preparation at Reading and the following year (1799) Hatton was directing it, again at Chelmsford. A success, the receipts of one performance came to £42 and £10 worth of prospective audience was turned away from the full playhouse.[30] When the play was staged at Oxford in 1802 the audience was promised that the production would display the 'original' scenes and dresses, possibly referring to a copy of the Greenwoods' scenery used

The oratory scene from The Castle Spectre *by Matthew Gregory Lewis.*
(The Bodleian Library, University of Oxford)

during the first season at Drury Lane.[31] Sporadic performances held the stage: an example is that of 23 October 1811 when members of the company at Gosport, without any star billing, performed the play as a prelude to a series of dances by William West, ballet master of Covent Garden.[32] After the success of *The Castle Spectre* Lewis wrote a string of gothic dramas. A popular example is *Alfonso*, staged at Reading in 1803 with a final scene consisting of the city of Burgos devoured by flames.[33]

A further famous castle was that of Blue Beard, the wife-slayer. George Colman the Younger's play was staged at Chelmsford in 1798 and 1799 with scenes by Harvey and Griffiths. It proved to be a 'great success', with most of the boxes booked in advance. No half-price was offered because of the expense of mounting a show employing many elaborate scenes and mechanics. Possibly it was this use of spectacle which prompted Hatton to choose the melodrama for his benefit.[34]

In William Dimond's play *The Foundling of the Forest* the first act takes place in a forest, an elaborate cut wood illuminated by flashes of lightning. Both grove and storm were to become part of the gothic apparatus. A key melodrama, the piece was played at Reading in 1810, chosen by Mrs Thornton for her benefit night.[35] Forests were also employed in Thomas Holcroft's *A Tale of Mystery*, made the more terrifying by the banditti who haunted the terrain, depriving Francisco, after an attack on him, of the power of speech. Performances were given in Newbury and Reading during 1804.[36] The brigand gangs rapidly assumed a romantic aura, explored in some detail in *The Miller and his Men*, a study of Grindoff, miller by day and banditti captain by night. Isaac Pocock wrote the piece in 1813; the play was in production at Reading in September 1814 but thereafter it was rarely performed on the Thornton circuit. The conclusion consisted of an expensive 'blow-up' in which Rosina ignited kegs of gunpowder resulting in the disintegration of the mill and the spectacle of many of the banditti hurtled by the blast into the air. In the Reading production the scenery was produced by Melville.[37]

Ann Radcliffe's novel *The Italian* was dramatised as *The Italian Monk* by James Boaden in 1797 and was performed at Gosport in 1798. It then disappeared from Thornton's repertoire, an interesting comment on the reception of a workmanlike play based on a highly popular novel.[38] Was it not to the taste of the naval personnel who principally attended the theatre? But nor was it tried in other theatres.

William Reeve's adaptation of the Don Juan legend was part ballet, part songs and choruses and part scenic wonders. At a cost of £500 Thornton staged this spectacle at Windsor in 1795 and then moved to Chelmsford two of its notable machines, the 'Equestrian Horse' and the 'View of the Infernal Regions'. A highlight was a 'shower of fire', disappointingly not in working order for the first Chelmsford performance.[39]

Sentimental Dramas

A successful sentimental drama was one in which the playwright 'interested the passions in the cause of virtue, and endeavoured to correct the vices and follies of a dissolute age, at the very moment when he is administering to its pleasures'.[40]

Richard Cumberland's *The West Indian*, with the sentimental character of Belcour, the naïve man moving in a world of urban sophistication, was presented with regularity on the circuit, especially in the latter part of the eighteenth century.[41] A further Cumberland play in this genre is *Inkle and Yarico*, the story of a Polynesian girl who, jilted by her white lover on his return to England, becomes crazed with grief. The play was given at the opening night of the Chelmsford theatre in 1790 and repeated in the town two years later. Yarico's journey from sedate elegance to madness caused a lady in one of the boxes to faint.[42] This was the play (mentioned earlier) which Thornton, taking the role of Inkle's father, Sir Christopher Curry, chose as his farewell to the circuit.[43] *The Road to Ruin* by Thomas Holcroft was a vehicle to display the talents of Thornton's family during the early years; the manager found it an 'elegant comedy'. At Chelmsford and Reading, Thornton played Old Dornton, his wife the Widow Warren and one of their daughters the feather-brained Sophia.[44] Elizabeth Inchbald's *Lovers' Vows* proved enormously popular in 1799 at Chelmsford at a time when the works of Kotzebue, the originator of the piece, were admired.[45]

These few plays indicate that, from a wide range of possible choices, only a few titles were regularly mounted and this well-established nucleus was staged in the provinces throughout the first half of the nineteenth century by many other companies in addition to Thornton's.

Afterpieces

An afterpiece is difficult to define: it may be written with that function in mind, or it may be a truncated version of an existing full length play. Many of the afterpieces were in the form of operettas, presented with fewer songs than the term now suggests.

Visiting players to Thornton's theatres enjoyed the chance to perform in *Love in a Village*, an admired musical written in 1762 by Isaac Bickerstaffe with music by Thomas Arne.[46] In the opening season of the Reading Theatre Charles Bannister of Drury Lane played Hawthorne to full houses. The piece was repeated on the visit of Anna Maria Crouch in the same season who took the role of Rosetta.[47] She returned in 1799 to play the same, bringing with her Michael Kelly, her singing teacher, who played Young Meadows.[48] Charles Incledon, who had begun his career at the Southampton Theatre under Thomas Collins, played Meadows at Reading in 1803.[49]

Of the other afterpieces presented, a brief mention may be made of *The Flitch of Bacon* (based on the tradition of the Dunmow flitch given each year to the most happily married couple in the village near Chelmsford) performed in 1793 at the Windsor Theatre with a Captain Wilson taking part.[50] Barnett was praised for his performance at Croydon in *The School for Friends* in 1807 although only one pair of breeches and no shoes were in evidence in the costume department.[51] *The Heir at Law* , with Bannister as Dr Pangloss, provided a gallery of rustic characters for Reading audiences in 1810.[52] *The Soldier's Daughter* gave Dorothy Jordan an afterpiece role when she came to the Gosport Theatre in 1812 following her break with the Duke of Clarence.[53] She took the role of the Widow Cheerly, a portrait which captivated Pitt Lennox:

> Mrs Jordan's widow was all that vivacity and sensibility could
> make it. To this the house ever gave their testimony in loudest
> applause. The enthusiasm with which they seized the following
> words can scarcely be adequately described. 'It is said of me
> that I have a felicity in raising the spirits and creating good
> humour where ever I am'.[54]

Pantomimes were sometimes presented as afterpieces. Two in which the scenery was of obvious importance were *The Magic Cavern* and *Robinson Crusoe*. In the first of these, staged at Gosport, Harvey had created the magic cavern, Pantaloon's house, an illuminated bridge and the Palace of the Fairies of the Lake, the latter containing water.[55] Thornton was silent about the decor for *Robinson Crusoe*, given several times at Oxford; this may have been an austerity production, defying the *raison d'être* for the show.[56]

Documentation Present and Past

Stage presentations gave audiences an insight into current events whether they were battles at sea, adventures and discoveries or state ceremonial. Thornton was eager to keep up with this trend although slight expense was involved. Only infrequently were they in the form of a drama with continuous dialogue; more often the theme was explored through a variety of media such as paintings, processions, dances, songs and musical interludes, with the result that the pieces were rarely set in print.

The French Revolution and the ensuing Napoleonic wars provided many sequences which could be exploited. Benson, in 1791 at Windsor, created a large canvas based on a succession of recent events for his benefit night. The plight of the French royal family was his theme, brought to the stage by a series of paintings by Hodgkins and Milbourne which revealed Louis XVI and Marie Antoinette leaving Paris, their recognition by the Post Master, the return to Paris under arrest, the decrees of the National Assembly and so through to the end of the sad story.[57]

A Gosport writer took up the Napoleonic thread and the role of his fellow townsmen in the downfall of the tyrant in *The Battle of Waterloo*, this time a musical spectacle given in 1816. The piece ran for a number of evenings locally with a twenty-two year old actor playing the part of Napoleon and then transferred to Reading with Barnett tackling the role of Prince Blucher who led the Prussian army.[58] One is again left with the impression that in order to preserve fluidity of presentation gauzes, panoramas and large roughly-painted canvases were used.[59]

British colonial activity formed the basis for a number of shows in which the contribution of the theatre painter was an important factor. Emmanuel created in 1792 a transparent drop curtain for *Tippoo Sahib,* one of William Reeve's musical entertainments with unpublished dialogue by Mark Lonsdale based on a highly serious event which had occurred earlier in the year in India.[60] Tippu, Sultan of Mysore, had ravaged the territory of the Raja of Travancore and was promptly attacked in retaliation by the Governor General, Lord Cornwallis, who defeated the sultan. Tippu was forced to cede half of his dominions to the governor, a punishment summed up pictorially in the removal by Cornwallis of the sultan's three sons.[61] The rideau was exhibited at Chelmsford and Croydon. A correspondent in the *Thespian Magazine* disparaged the figure drawing: '...the painter has certainly obeyed the commandment in not making any thing in the likeness of heaven and earth'.[62]

Under Hatton's direction *British Bravery or Taking the Island of Trinidad*, although described as a pantomime, turned the Newbury stage into a living newspaper in 1797. The plot hinged on the action of Sir Ralph Abercromby, commander in chief of the British forces in the West Indies, in implementing the policy of forcibly taking the French-held islands, which included Trinidad. A series of paintings told the story. The absence of a published record of the play suggests that again this was a locally made entertainment, reliant more on image than text.[63]

Home affairs struck a different note. In 1789 a temporary abatement of the porphyria from which the king had been suffering induced the monarch to insist that the court attend St Paul's Cathedral in procession for a service of thanksgiving. This event, shown in truncated form on the Reading stage six months after the actuality, brought before the house 'the carriages of His Majesty, the Prince of Wales, the Dukes of York, Cumberland and Gloucester, city and other state coaches, Horse Guards, Officers of the Police... and the Lord Mayor'. One can only imagine that this was a panorama put to use again, with or without a gauze, which gradually revealed the participants.[64]

A spirit of documentation often gave inner life to a conventional dialogue play. The plot itself might have been based on a historical event, obvious from an advertisement for *The Countess of Salisbury*, a play by Hall Hartson, 'founded on historical fact and revised, altered and corrected by a gentleman in the neighbourhood of Gosport' where a revival was staged.[65] Verisimilitude would have been advanced if the promise that the play would be dressed 'in the Habits of the Times' were successfully kept.

A documentary of a different kind was John O'Keeffe's play *Wild Oats*, the picaresque adventures of a troupe of wandering players making their way through Berkshire and Hampshire. Thornton brought the piece to Chelmsford in 1796. The comparison of the plight of the players easily thrown off balance by the vicissitudes of society and romance and the stability of the established theatres in which the play was presented was an ironic touch.[66] When the piece was presented at Thornton's theatres in the two home counties, then an extra documentary dimension was created.

Lastly, current events, in which there was a present reality, could be highlighted by raising the intensity of a section of a play written some years earlier. At Reading in 1797 the battle between the English and Spanish fleets shown at the end of Sheridan's burlesque *The Critic* (written in 1779) was, for example, a serious call to recognise the parallel to Admiral Duncan's encounter with the Dutch fleet, thus highlighting the needs of the widows and orphans of those who had died in the engagement.[67]

Plays of local appeal

Thornton's repertoire is not strongly represented by plays making reference to the specific localities in which the playhouses were situated but several are worth mentioning. Windsor, with its castle and historic significance was an obvious setting and Stephen Kemble, on a visit to its farmyard theatre in 1787, staged a composite entertainment of songs and poetry, *The Day*, which terminated with a transparency of 'the Order of the Garter' - does this refer to a crest? or to a representation of the ceremony? - illuminated by a display of fireworks. Windsor and the Garter Knights were synonymous.[68] For a later Windsor benefit the ingenious Benson chose to stage the 'new comedy' *All Alive at Windsor*.[69] It is likely, as the play was neither performed in London nor published, that this was an improvisation created especially for Windsor.

An interlude at the Gosport Theatre was titled *The Pretty Girl of Gosport*. A clutch of plays telling of a pretty girl from various towns had been written. This was unpublished and may have been a barely disguised plagiarism. Other nautical entertainments which were popular locally were *The Embarkation* and *The Naval Pillar*. The theme of the first of these was founded on an expedition to Holland which set sail from Deal in 1799. *The Naval Pillar* was one of Dibdin's slight musical offerings.[70]

Songs referring to a locality could more easily be composed. For his wife's benefit at Gosport Bristow composed the song 'The Wonderful Bell-Ringing Portsmouth Ghost' and reference has already been made to songs in honour of the masons.[71]

Heroic dramas

Only two representative examples of heroic dramas are mentioned here as they were not a strong feature of Thornton's repertoire. It is noteworthy that women played an increasingly important part, to the extent that in the second example Euphrasia is the heroic character of the piece. The light-hearted Bristow uncharacteristically put on *The Stranger* at Newbury in 1798 for his benefit.[72] The play tells of the 'erring heart' of a wife who would 'return to her sanctuary', the love and fidelity of her husband. Bristow is likely to have had in mind John Palmer who performed the title role at Liverpool earlier in the year and died of a seizure in the course of a performance.[73] Bristow's own characterisation would serve as a reminder and possibly documentation of the event. The Thornton children and Barnett helped with this benefit. After so serious a commemo-

93

ration Bristow performed a series of acrobatics and went on to demonstrate the 'animation, life and death of Harlequin'.

Why would *The Grecian Daughter* have been performed in Chelmsford, Newbury and Reading, leaving no recorded performances at other locations? Arthur Murphy's static drama, popularised by Sarah Siddons, contained many fine sentiments but the audience had to wait until the final act before it witnesed excitement in the form of the stabbing of the Roman usurper-tyrant Dionysius by Euphrasia, the heroine of the tragedy. In several instances the play was the choice of the actress playing the heroine: thus at Newbury the audience saw Mrs Johnson aided by Thornton as her ailing father Evander and at Reading the Barnetts, having played a series of related roles such as Macbeth and his wife, undertook the father and daughter roles; at Chelmsford a visiting actress, Mrs Powell, the 'principal tragic actress of Drury Lane', Thornton advertised, took on Euphrasia. Wherein the spectators' interest lay in this heavy, literary work is puzzling.[74]

The 'Old Dramas'

The country repertoire, as much as that of the patent theatres, contained a corpus of plays written in the eighteenth century, or earlier, which held the stage over many years. They were mainly dramas rather than comedies and they offered an earnestness of moral outlook that contrasted oddly with the myriad soufflés staged in the early years of the nineteenth century. The earliest of these was *A New Way to Pay Old Debts* by Philip Massinger, then awaiting its resuscitation by Edmund Kean, but chosen by Saville, an established member of Thornton's early company, for his benefit in 1789. The ensuing house was so thin that a letter was inserted in the newspaper suggesting that Thornton should allow the actor a further benefit which he did in the following month.[75] For the rest of the manager's professional life the play lay under wraps.

Nicholas Rowe's *Jane Shore*, a much used subject, was a contrasting she-tragedy and although written as early as 1714 the play was still acceptable entertainment by Thornton's day. Mrs Edwin, paying an extended visit to the company at Gosport, chose the play in 1807.[76] Thornton seems to have doubted its drawing power, for the next performance was in 1809, chosen yet again by a visitor, Mrs Powell.[77] By 1816 however Thornton was near enough to his retirement to relax the managerial veto and the play was put on in Reading by the company.[78]

The death of Young Norval in Douglas *by John Home.*
(Author's collection)

More popular by far was the Revd John Home's tragedy *Douglas*. Although Betty appeared as Young Norval on his visits to Thornton's theatres, this was in reality a workaday company piece and as such it was staged in the Reading Theatre in 1791.[79] The popularity of several of the speeches which teenage reciters memorised made it an admirable choice by the boarding school at Writtle, requesting a performance at

Chelmsford.[80] One suspects that the play was often staged with simplicity for when a spectacular was in preparation *Douglas* was mounted in the preceding busy week, an indication, too, that the text was part of every actor's stock in trade.[81]

Amongst the older plays comedy was not entirely neglected and one that prospered was *The Suspicious Husband*, written in 1747 by Bishop Benjamin Hoadley, the story of a guardian's jealous protection from which Jacintha eventually escapes with the help of a rope ladder. Lively scenes and sprightly conversation gave, it was claimed, 'the care-tired mind a few hours of dissipation'.[82] As early as the first season of the Reading Theatre the play was staged and was also used during that of the new Windsor Theatre, although Waldron had earlier introduced it to audiences in the Peascod Street theatre.[83] The last recorded Thornton production of the comedy was in 1806 at Reading.[84]

Animal Dramas

From the beginning of the nineteenth century the fashion for dramas with animal actors, established in London, spread to the provinces.[85] In 1815 at Gosport *The Dog of Montargis or The Forest of Bondy* (Thornton used the titles indiscriminately) was staged in which a visiting hound, Tyger (owned by J Walter Jones of the New Royal Circus), appeared to display his 'extraordinary powers of amazing sagacity' by bringing down the murderer of his master.[86]

A single horse had earlier made a minor incursion in a production of *1588* bearing Mrs Thornton as Queen Elizabeth.[87] Thornton progressed to engage the horse-troop of James West and Robert Woolford which had recently gained Andrew Ducrow, the great horseman and acrobat then making a career break from Astley's Amphitheatre, to appear at some of his playhouses during 1814. They opened in February at Gosport, staging the main offering of *Timour the Tartar* with its horse processions, combats and attacks, for two weeks to full houses. March saw them in Newbury where a spectator wrote in the newspaper:

> ...having witnessed the Equestrian Performances in London, we
> had no idea they could have been given with any possible effect
> in a provincial theatre. - It is really astonishing to see them go
> through the self-same manoeuvres with the self-same effect as if
> they had a larger space for action, indeed the smallness of the
> scale so far from lessening our delight increases our wonder and

THE CELEBRATED COMPANY OF

EQUESTRIANS,

With their wonderful and astonishing

Stud of HORSES

Having been received in Timour the Tartar, with universal bursts of acclamation and reiterated shouts of applause, has induced the revival of the grand dramatic romance of

BLUE BEARD,

Which will be performed for TWO NIGHTS ONLY, viz. FRIDAY and SATURDAY.

THEATRE GUILDFORD,

On FRIDAY the 17th day of JUNE 1814,

Will be presented the comic dramatic piece, called

LOVER'S QUARRELS,

Or, like Master like Man.

| Don Carlos | Mr. GREEN, | Lopez | Mr. FAWCETT, | Sancho | Mr. OWEN, |
| Donna Leonora | ——— | Mrs FAWCETT, | Jacintha | ——— | Mrs CROOK. |

END OF THE PLAY,

The incurable, elegant, and wonderful Performance of the celebrated

MR. DUCROW

ON THE TIGHT ROPE.

Clown to the Rope ——— ——— Mr. CAMPBELL

To conclude with the grand and brilliant Spectacle of

BLUE BEARD

Or, Female Curiosity.

As acted at the new Theatre Royal Covent Garden and acted upwards of 100 Nights with unbounded applause.

Abomelique (Blue Beard)	A.	Mr. FAWCETT,	Selim	———	Mr. COBHAM,
Ibrahim	— Mr OWEN,	Hassan — Mr. HATTON,	Shacabac	———	Mr. BARNETT,
Saphia	———			Messrs. GREEN, STANLEY, PLUMMER, &c.
Irene	Mrs. CROOK,	Beda	Mrs. OWEN,	Fatima	Mrs. WEST.

IN WHICH THE

EQUESTRIAN TROOP,

With their beautiful, sagacious and intrepid

STUD OF HORSES,

Will go through the whole of their surprising, and really wonderful Evolutions and Manœuvres.

A Grand Procession

Over the Mountains, BLUE BEARD mounted on his Hanoverian Charger, preceded by his Cavalry, Military Band, &c.

SELIM commencing the Spah's Cavalry, with the Preparations for the

Attack on Blue Beard's Castle.

THE BLUE CHAMBER,

To conclude with the Storming of Blue Beard's Castle, by Cavalry and Infantry. The Combats between the Knights—The various Deaths of Horses, and the

Final Overthrow of Blue Beard,

In the course of which, those beautiful Horses will exhibit many new and astonishing Feats of Courage, Intrepidity and Sagacity.

Boxes 3s. Pit 2s. Gallery 1s.—Nothing under full price can possibly be taken.

The Theatre will continue open every Evening.

Doors to be opened at Six, and to begin precisely at Seven o'Clock.

Tickets to be had, and Places for the Boxes, may be taken at the Theatre each Morning from Ten till Two.

Russells Printers, Guildford.

Playbill, Guildford Theatre.
(Guildford Museum)

97

admiration. The piece is well got up at all points, and we are
highly gratified in saying the indefatigable zeal and artistry
evinced in the conduct of the concern has experienced its merit-
ed reward of favour, support and approbation.[88]

Further performances ensued at Reading followed by *Blue Beard* also
with its inserted equine interludes.[89]

Thornton attempted to present the hippodramas again in 1815 in the
rackets court of Christ Church. Samuel Russell was completing a successful
season at Thornton's original home in the Merton College court where a
bevy of stars had been engaged; in front of the stage an amphitheatre, safe
for feats of equitation, had been built and Makeen and his stud invited to
perform interludes after the presentation of *The Dog of Montargis*.[90]
Thornton's visitors were well enough known, Jordan, Munden and Miss
Booth, but animals were the draw and Thornton, without the safety of an
amphitheatre, again engaged West and Woolford's troop of horse to perform on the stage itself alongside the actors. The animals had been appearing in London, Bath and Bristol, and would give *Timour the Tartar* in
Oxford.[91] Thornton's players were up in arms at the dangers inherent in the
situation and attempted, an hour before the performance, to come to special terms with their manager or not appear. He instantly sacked the Oxford
actors and decided to cut his losses by closing the theatre at Reading, where
audiences were thin because of the cancellation of the races, so releasing
the players there to stand in for the former employees at Oxford.[92]

Benefit Performances

Benefit performances were popular amongst actors not only for the
extra income they provided but also because the choice of plays and roles
were in the hands of the performers; thus they had the chance to assume
characters which otherwise might not have been available to them.
Mention has already been made in passing of benefits and so only an
example of a run of benefits at the Gosport Theatre is given.

Stanwix, on 15 May 1797, received a benefit; he relied on the bills of the
day rather than the theatre's newspaper advertisements to announce the
plays chosen. After the company, the members of the manager's family
received their benefits: Pritchard was given his on 20 May, and again the
titles are not mentioned in the newspaper. Both of these performances were
supported by the Gosport and Alverstoke Volunteers. Finally the manager's
night arrived when he staged *The Will* and gave a rhymed address.[93]

In addition to the actors, various other members of the company received a benefit night. Thompson, a resident of Gosport who acted as the hairdresser to the theatre, gained a benefit in 1816 as did Mr Davis, the leader of the orchestra, at which he played a piano concerto by T E Bell.[94] Burton, the comic in the company, had recently been bereaved of his wife and his colleagues presented for his benefit *Speed the Plough*. A poem, *The Pleasures of Belief*, written by the widower, was on sale at the printing office, price 1/6d.[95] Individual benefits were often acknowledged in the newspaper and could be fulsome, as was Barnett's: 'he cannot omit this opportunity of offering his warmest acknowledgements for the liberal indulgence he has invariably received, which is indelibly impressed on his heart, and will ever be borne in his mind with the liveliest recollection of fervent gratitude'.[96]

Thornton was a supporter of worthy causes and many received a benefit from his theatres. Mention has been made of his concern for the injuries of sailors serving under Admiral Duncan during 1797. At Gosport the recipients were the 'injured and widows of the battle on October 11'. Much ceremony was made of these evenings supporting the common good: *The Cure for the Heart Ache* with the suitable nautical addition of *The Benevolent Tar* were performed, an address was given by the manager and the whole company sang the National Anthem and *Rule Britannia* three times. The receipts were £64. 12. 6d.[97] A similar benefit for British prisoners of war was heralded by a rhetorical flourish in the newspaper in 1811:

> Mr Thornton, feeling the strong call of humanity upon all classes
> of society, to assist, as far as possible, the general and most praise-
> worthy contributions now in agitation for giving relief to our brave
> Countrymen suffering in foreign bondage, with much pleasure
> dedicates his theatre to the cause, for an Evening's performance.[98]

At other times benefit money might be donated 'to the poor', more particularly to the 'dispensary for the poor' or, at Oxford, 'to a large family in the greatest distress'.[99]

Acquiring the Text

As late as 1832 David Osbaldiston gave evidence to the Select Committee on Dramatic Literature that provincial managers were in the habit of pirating works currently appearing on the London stages.[100] It is difficult to tell whether Thornton was guilty of this practice, although there is Winston's information that approximations of the text of the play were spoken. A performance of 'a new comedy' - not yet learned by the company - at Andover serves as an example. Thornton was shocked to see one of the audience with a copy of the play in his hand and in order to wrest the book from him he pretended that the prompt copy had been mislaid. The patron kindly offered his own book.[101] A possible indication of plagarism would be the speed with which a play was staged after a London presentation had opened. On 24 May 1799 Sheridan's *Pizarro* opened at Drury Lane; but this was not in rehearsal in a Thornton theatre - Chelmsford - until 27 July with a first night, in spite of incomplete settings, on 1 August; this must be tempered by the fact that the piece was under the directorship of Hatton who, with his London connections, may have more easily gained a copy than Thornton would.[102]

Further examples are a couple of George Colman's plays. In January 1798 his *Blue Beard* was staged at Drury Lane and in July found its way on to the Chelmsford stage, leaving seven months in which to get hold of the text, rehearse a piece which was an elaborate spectacle and produce scenes and dresses, none of which were likely to have been in stock.[103] Another money-spinner by Colman, *John Bull*, was first staged in March 1803 and during its run of forty-seven nights at Covent Garden the play-wright made £1200.[104] Obviously, the script would not be given up light-ly. By June however, Thornton staged the play at Windsor and then went on to show it at Chelmsford in August and Reading in September.[105] Colman the Younger was manager at this time of the Haymarket Theatre and possibly Hatton's and the Barnetts' occasional appearances there may have expedited the loan of the text.

The normal procedure was for Thornton to buy a script. Thomas Morton's *Speed the Plough* was bought from the management of Covent Garden for the Gosport production in 1800.[106] Thomas Harris, manager of the patent house, sometimes sent a copy of a new play to a number of country managers with a view to their purchasing it.[107] On another occasion Thornton bought the scripts of *The Purse* and *Frightened to Death* from the manager of Drury Lane for performance at Chelmsford.[108] These plays were subsequently performed at some of Thornton's other theatres and it was his custom to assure patrons that he was 'in possession of all the new and popular pieces brought out at the London theatres'.[109]

Afterword

There is a light-hearted adventurousness in Thornton's repertoire. It reflects not only those plays he feels will sell well but also the many-sided talents of his company. Sometimes he is more astute in his selections than actors making a choice for their benefits. There is only a slight variation between the plays presented at one theatre (say the Windsor with its visitors attached to the court) and at another (such as Reading, a mercantile town). What does make a difference to the repertoire is the choice of aristocrats or groups of people requesting specific plays, but more about these when considering the audiences on the circuit.

1. For contextualisation of these plays see Robertson Davies, 'Playwrights and plays' in *The Revels History of Drama in English*, ed Clifford Leech and T W Craik, 6 (1975), 147-269, *passim*.
2. *Reading Mercury*, 2 June 1788. *Hampshire Telegraph*, 3 July 1815.
3. *Reading Mercury*, 21 August and 4 September 1815.
4. Berkshire Record Office, Reading: Playbill collection, Newbury, 3 April 1797.
5. *Reading Mercury*, 27 August 1792.
6. *Hampshire Telegraph*, 8 November 1802. *Monthly Mirror*, 24 (1807), 227-230.
7. *Reading Mercury*, 23 and 30 June 1788. Tomalin, *Mrs Jordan's Profession*, pp 28-55 *passim*.
8. *Chelmsford Chronicle*, 18 August 1815. Robertson Davies, 'Playwrights and Plays' in *The Revels History of Drama in English*, 6.150n.
9. *Hampshire Telegraph*, 13 March and 15 May 1809.
10. *Reading Mercury*, 12 May 1788.
11. *Reading Mercury*, 12 May 1788. *Chelmsford Chronicle*, 18 July 1817.
Dorothy Jordan's Reading performance was by way of an exploration; at Drury Lane she was not to play Teazle until 1797, following Frances Abington and Elizabeth Farren who had had previously 'owned' the role.
12. Wilson, *Our Actresses*, p.176. Hall, *Dramatic Portraits*, 1.53. Stephen and Lee, *DNB*, 5. 628.
13. *Jackson's Oxford Journal*, 24 August and 14 September 1799.
14. *Chelmsford Chronicle*, 26 July 1799.
15. *Jackson's Oxford Journal*, 14 September 1799.
16. Bodleian Library: John Johnson Collection, Chelmsford playbill, 5 April 1800. *Chelmsford Chronicle*, 26 July and 2 August 1799.
17. *Chelmsford Chronicle*, 26 July 1799.
18. *Chelmsford Chronicle*, 12 July 1799.
19. *Reading Mercury*, 16 September 1799.
20. *Jackson's Oxford Journal*, 14 and 21 September 1799.
21. *Reading Mercury*, 30 September 1799.
22. *Portsmouth Telegraph*, 17 and 24 February 1800. *Hampshire Chronicle*, 7 December 1807.
23. *Portsmouth Telegraph*, 10 March 1800.
24. *Portsmouth Telegraph*, 17 March 1800.
25. *Portsmouth Telegraph*, 31 March 1800.
26. *Portsmouth Gazette*, 24 April 1800.
27. *Sussex Weekly Advertiser*, 5 December 1791.
28. *Portsmouth Gazette*, 12 March 1798.
29. *Chelmsford Chronicle*, 24 August 1798.
30. *Chelmsford Chronicle*, 5, 12 July and 30 August 1799.

31. Sybil Rosenfeld and Edward Croft Murray, 'A Checklist of Scene Painters working in Great Britain and Ireland in the Eighteenth Century', *Theatre Notebook*, 19 (1964), 59. *Reading Mercury*, 14 August 1802.
Both father and son were named Thomas Greenwood; the senior died shortly before the play was staged so the greater part of the scenes were designed by the son.
32. Author's collection: playbill, Gosport, 23 October 1811.
33. *Reading Mercury*, 12 September 1803.
34. *Chelmsford Chronicle*, 3 August 1798, 12 and 19 July 1799.
35. *Reading Mercury*, 24 September 1810.
36. *Reading Mercury*, 2 January and 17 September 1804. The play, written in 1802, was delayed by continuing runs of *Pizarro* and the introduction of the Phantasmagoria.
37. British Library: Playbill collection, 299, 26 September 1814. *Reading Mercury*, 26 September 1814.
38. *Portsmouth Gazette*, 16 April 1798.
39. *Chelmsford Chronicle*, 31 July and 7 August 1795.
40. John Hawksworth writing of the plays of Richard Cumberland in the *Gentleman's Magazine*, 42 (1772), 81.
41. For several examples see *Chelmsford Chronicle*, 15 July 1790; *Reading Mercury*, 30 May 1791; *Portsmouth Gazette*, 8 April 1799.
42. *Chelmsford Chronicle*, 2 July 1790 and 24 August 1792.
43. For advertisements of a couple of performances see *Chelmsford Chronicle*, 22 and 29 August 1817 (at Chelmsford) and *Reading Mercury*, 14 April 1817 (at Newbury)
44. *Chelmsford Chronicle*, 6 July 1792. *Reading Mercury*, 27 August 1792.
45. *Chelmsford Chronicle*, 5 July 1799. Thornton advertised that the work was a translation; it was based on *Das Kind der Liebe* by August Friedrich Ferdinand Von Kotzebue and first performed in 1798. The play figures in Jane Austen's *Mansfield Park*.
46. The play was given at the Lyric Theatre, Hammersmith, as late as 1928; see Robertson Davies, 'Playwrights and Plays' in *The Revels History*, 6. 162n.
47. *Reading Mercury*, 19 May and 21 July 1788
48. *Reading Mercury*, 23 September 1799. Michael Kelly, *Solo Recital*, ed Herbert van Thal (1972), p.160.
49. *Reading Mercury*, 31 January 1803.
50. *Reading Mercury*, 16 September 1793.
51. *Monthly Mirror*, 24 (1807), 291
52. *Reading Mercury*, 3 September 1810.
53. *Hampshire Telegraph*, 23 November 1812. Brian Fothergill, *Mrs Jordan* (1965), pp 255 and 259.
54. William Pitt Lennox, *Plays, Players and Playhouses* (1881), 1. 52.
55. This unpublished pantomime was written by Ralph Wewitzer - the former manager of the Windsor theatre, which may account for Thornton staging the piece - and Frederick Pilon with music by William Shield.
56. *Hampshire Telegraph*, 9 October 1809. *Jackson's Oxford Journal*, 14 September 1799 and 21 August 1802.
57. *Reading Mercury*, 12 September 1791.
Henry Hodgkins and C Milbourne were two artists at Covent Garden. In the 1780s the latter worked at the Portsmouth Theatre. Hodgkins, an Irishman, was noted for the speed with which he painted, finishing a scene in a single day. See John O'Keeffe, *Recollections of the Life of John O'Keeffe* (1826), 2. 40 and Rosenfeld and Croft Murray, 'Check List of Scene Painters', *Theatre Notebook*, 19, 42-3 and 20, 136.
58. British Library: Playbill Collection, 299, Gosport playbill, 11 April 1816. *Hampshire Telegraph*, 22 January 1816.
59. An entertainment with the same title was staged at the Royalty Theatre, London; possibly it was the piece which originated in Gosport. See Nicoll, *English Drama,*, 4. 431.
60. *Tippoo Sahib or British Valour in India* was first mounted at Covent Garden in June 1791.

Plays and Productions

See Nicoll, *English Drama*, 3. 345.

William Reeve, 1757-1815, was composer to Covent Garden Theatre and later proprietor of Sadler's Wells. See *Grove's Dictionary*, 7. 87-8.

61. *Encyclopaedia Britannica* (1911), 26. 1005 and (1985), 11. 792.

62. *Thespian Magazine*, 1 (1793), 176. *Chelmsford Chronicle*, 24 August 1792.

63. Berkshire County Record Office, Reading: Newbury playbill, 3 April 1797.

64. *Reading Mercury*, 30 November 1789. A similar procession which should have been held at the Shakespeare Jubilee celebrations at Stratford but was rained off was built into a play, *The Jubilee*, and transmuted to the stage of Drury Lane by David Garrick. Thornton gave the entertainment an occasional airing; see David Garrick, *Three Plays by David Garrick*, ed Elizabeth P Stein (1926), pp 55-113 and Johanne M Stochholme, *Garrick's Folly* (1964), pp 143-174.

65. *Portsmouth Telegraph*, 29 March 1802.

66. *Chelmsford Chronicle*, 22 June 1796.

67. *Reading Mercury*, 6 November 1797.

68. *Reading Mercury*, 24 September 1787. Kemble had mounted a piece with the same title at the Haymarket the previous year for two performances, although in his version no mention was made of the Garter ceremony.

69. *Reading Mercury*, 3 and 17 September 1792.

70. *Portsmouth Telegraph*, 24 March, 26 April 1800. *The Embarkation* was written by Andrew Franklin, with music by William Reeve; *The Naval Pillar* had been presented the previous year at Covent Garden.

71. *Portsmouth Telegraph*, 19 May 1800.

72. Berkshire Record Office, Reading: Newbury poster, 20 November 1798. The original German play by Kotzebue was translated by Benjamin Thompson.

73. A description is given by Whitfield in the *Monthly Mirror*, 6 (1798), 67-9.

74. *Reading Mercury*, 21 March 1803, 11 September 1815. *Chelmsford Chronicle*, 16 June 1809. Comedies and farces were more to the liking of Arthur Murphy, a prolific writer, journalist and lawyer who in literary retirement was appointed Recorder of Sudbury. This proximity to Thornton's birthplace may have kindled in the manager a sympathy for him.

75. *Reading Mercury*, 23 and 30 November 1789.

76. *Hampshire Telegraph*, 19 October 1807.

77. *Chelmsford Chronicle*, 4 August 1809.

78. *Reading Mercury*, 23 December 1816.

79. *Reading Mercury*, 23 May 1791.

80. *Chelmsford Chronicle*, 1 August 1794.

81. eg *Chelmsford Chronicle*, 12 July 1799.

82. [Isaac Reed], *Biographia Dramatica* (1782), 3. 311.

83. *Reading Mercury*, 4 September 1786, 1 September 1788. *Thespian Magazine*, 2 (1793), 313.

84. *Reading Mercury*, 22 September 1806.

85. William Pitt Lennox, *My Recollections from 1806-1873* (1874), 1. 168.

86. *Portsmouth Gazette*, 6 March 1815; *Reading Mercury*, 18 November 1816 and 24 March 1817. Further presentations were given at Reading and Newbury. The play had been written the previous year by William Barrymore based on Pixérécourt's *Le Chien de Montargis ou La Forêt de Bondy*.

87. *Hampshire Telegraph*, 10 February 1806.

88. *Hampshire Telegraph*, 7 February 1814. *Reading Mercury*, 21 February and 7 March 1814. A H Saxon, *The Life and Art of Andrew Ducrow* (Hamden, Conn, 1978), pp 65-7.

89. *Reading Mercury*, 21 February, 21 and 28 March 1814.

90. *Jackson's Oxford Journal*, 17 and 24 June and 16 July 1815.

91. Saxon, *Ducrow*, p.70.

92. *Jackson's Oxford Journal*, 23 September 1815. *Reading Mercury*, 21 August, 11 and 25 September 1815.

93. *Portsmouth Gazette*, 8, 15 and 22 May 1797.

94. *Hampshire Telegraph*, 26 January and 4 November 1816.

95. *Reading Mercury,* 9 August 1813.

96. *Hampshire Telegraph,* 4 December 1815.

97. *Portsmouth Gazette,* 30 October 1797. *Chelmsford Chronicle,* 24 November 1797.

98. *Hampshire Telegraph,* 25 March 1811.

99. *Reading Mercury,* 19 February 1787 and 4 October 1802. *Jackson's Oxford Journal,* 26 September 1807.

100. *The Report of the Select Committee on Dramatic Literature* (1832), pp 126 and 223.

101. Winston, *Tourist,* p.9.

102. *The London Stage,* part 5, p.2177. *Chelmsford Chronicle,* 26 July and 2 August 1799.

103. *Chelmsford Chronicle,* 27 July 1798.

104. Richard Brinsley Peake, *Memoirs of the Colman Family* (1841), 2. 413.

105. *Reading Mercury,* 6 June 1803. *Monthly Mirror,* 16 (1803), 134. *Reading Mercury,* 5 September 1803.

106. *Portsmouth Telegraph,* 21 April 1800

107. Wilkinson, *Patentee,* 3. 33.

108. *Chelmsford Chronicle,* 27 July 1798. Theatre Museum: provincial files, Chelmsford; the copy is signed by Henry Thornton of Chelmsford and Edward Barnett of the Theatre, Ryde.

109. *Salisbury Journal,* 11 April 1803.

CHAPTER 7
STANDARDS

The Manager

A yardstick for evaluating the standards of the work which Thornton's company mounted is difficult to determine. To compare like with like one would have to look at Thornton's productions against a background of similar companies performing in the same areas. This may be done as Thornton was often preceded by other managers and their companies. His idiosyncratic approach to his work has already been commented on. That managers had their eccentricities was expected; that these would interfere with the standard of the work was not. Beneath Thornton's singularity was an astute business sense, shown in the acquisition and consolidation of the circuit, as well as an actor who, although dispensing with accuracy in his rendering of the text, created a series of lively and boldly drawn characters in spite of the limitations of gout, professional worries and, at the end of his career, overwork and bereavement.

Several actors, temporarily in the company, testified to the man's success. Whilst Thornton was chief of a band of strollers, Bernard judged him to be 'tolerably well informed' and 'very gentlemanly in his manners', two rare virtues in the Georgian theatre world.[1] Some years later Everard took up this concept of Thornton as a man of knowledge gained through his early education, his management of the strollers, his success as an actor in Whitley's company, his time as a prompter at Portsmouth and his return to management: 'Mr Thornton had commenced manager and had met with the success which his knowledge and diligence well deserved'.[2] Diligent Thornton was and he expected his actors to be so too. From the Chelmsford newspaper it appears that Thornton worked his actors with a longer week than other companies enjoyed - nightly performances except Saturday - and established the convention of daily matinées during the races; but in this Thornton expected no more than he himself was diligently prepared to give.[3]

The Company

The company was as good as the actors it contained at any given time. Thornton appears from the start of his management to have kept his sights on the foremost provincial companies, attempting to emulate their high standards, as his words about the Newbury Theatre shortly after the opening of the building show: 'The young ladies lately engaged at the... theatre as comic dancers, 'tis said are very capital, and their performance truly admirable'. With such additions he hoped the troupe would vie 'with the very first country companies'.[4] There is a humility in his public acknowledgement that the goal had not been reached to date.

During the first season at Chelmsford in 1792 the extended Thornton family provided most of the company, including Thornton and his wife, David Pritchard and his parents, Mrs Robinson and Hatton and his wife; the latter pair were judged to be 'far above mediocrity'. Beyond the family circle Cornelys, the 'veteran of provincial playhouses', was commendable but others were wanting: Mills needed assurance and the remaining actors were 'but so so'.[5] However, the following year for the Windsor season Thornton picked up several additions, including David Williamson of Covent Garden, Maymes of Drury Lane, John Simpson from Dublin and Miss S T Herbert from Bath. This injection of talent raised the players to the 'best company Windsor ever could boast', presumably a knock at the companies of Berkley Baker and Francis Waldron.[6] The same kind of comparison had also been made at Henley five years earlier: '...the striking abilities of the performers were so directly opposite to the companies (if they may be called so) we have heretofor been accustomed to....'[7]

But the problem remained. Whilst the company gave value for money, it could not compare with those at Bath and Bristol, for its overall standard was uneven. At Andover eleven years later Hargrave was commended for his vocal powers which a critic recognised would be improved by experience, although Thompson possessed talent enough to gain a place in 'our first provincial theatre', words revealing that Thornton's company still had not reached that standard.[8]

The point was reiterated when a Mr T Jameson, looking at the supporting company for Betty's performance of Young Norval in *Douglas* at Gosport, singled out Mrs Hardy who took the role of Lady Randolph. Her figure, voice and 'every other stage requisite' should ensure that she gained a more exalted situation in a superior company.[9]

In the eyes of many of the townspeople in the locations of the playhouses the tone of the company was highly acceptable and this would appear of greater importance than sparkle in a performance. An unidentified remark refers to the company at Croydon after one of Thornton's early visits in 1794: 'Mr Thornton is an honest worthy man and his company are regarded as better fed, clothed and washed, and consequently more sober, clean and perfect than any other circuitous troop in the Kingdom'.[10] Above all the company was respectable and diligent, virtues Thornton possessed. In Reading the private conduct of the actors was reckoned to 'conciliate the respect of the town-people who no doubt will liberally reward them at their approaching benefits'.[11] At Windsor, too, this was to become its own reward.[12] One could assume that the visits of the royal family to the theatre there were in themselves an indication that the company offered an acceptable standard. During the summer of 1793 and the ensuing winter season the royal party made seven visits to the theatre per season.[13] But was the royal family too easily pleased? The king in 1793 commanded *The Child of Nature* and *The Padlock* at the Windsor Theatre; the description of the productions in the *Thespian Magazine* suggests a rough and ready interpretation of the text in which belief could hardly be suspended:

> In the first place the disguise of Leander was no disguise at all; for the 'strolling drummer' should certainly have a garment to hide the leg supposed to have been lost (and which, by the by, should have been supplied by a wooden one) as well as the silk stockings and pink shoe strings which Mr Hardinge chose to appear in; but the outward covering reached no further than decency itself would dictate. In the next place we listened in vain for the dulcet notes of 'the sweet guitar', which was not once struck with the thumb of Leander, who received, unheeding, the order from Mungo to play another tune, ere he had yet gratified his auditors with any. Lastly Ursula and Leonora crowding together to one bit of a casement, from which each was obliged to recede when the other spoke, completed this absurd scene.[14]

An easy-going acceptance was maintained by the king and his family, reflecting the probability of double expectations, one for the London patent theatres and a completely different standard for that in Windsor. There was certainly never any mention of a desire to replace Thornton, as Smith had been replaced at Weybridge, or to set up a well-endowed and more professional playhouse. But it was the Windsor residents who were disappointed and as late as 1807, the year after the theatre had passed out of Thornton's hands, 'A Townsman' ended his letter to the *Monthly Mirror*: 'But the manager [Mudie] ought to consider it not the attraction of a single London performer (or a star as they are called) that will please a Windsor audience: no - they expect a good company, and then he may expect good houses'.[15]

There were complaints about Thornton's company from different quarters. James Winston carped throughout *The Theatric Tourist* about its deficiencies. When dealing with the Newbury Theatre he claimed: 'Like most of Thornton's theatrical towns, were we to trace the drama in this place, it would only be to enumerate a catalogue of strolling companies of the most inferior order'.[16] Time and again, examples are not given and Winston's writing is imprecise. Shortages, whether of men, voices or clothing were picked up by other writers. On acquiring the Windsor theatre Thornton was hampered by the lack of singers available, especially when he attempted to stage an operetta such as *Rosina*:

> Of the vocal corps we cannot boast - the lady in *William*, was however, not below mediocrity: her voice is pleasing but a want of judgement is easily discernable, which is only attainable by strict attention.[17]

The following year it was not the voices of singers but that of the Windsor prompter which was too much in evidence.[18]

Occasionally a single actor rather than the company was criticised. At Chelmsford in 1792 a mysterious stricture was made about a young man who 'by his attention to his occupation, might render himself a material acquisition in a theatrical performance'; through his neglect at the time he was jeopardising a 'very good subsistance'.[19]

'P' in the *Theatrical Inquisitor*, writing of the supporting cast for the visit of Miss Smith ('forced smile and the rolling eye') to Gosport in 1813, damned with faint praise the presentation of *The Jealous Wife*:

> A Mr Johnson performed the part of Lord Trinket, a personage not unlike Mr Jones of Covent Garden. We should be happy to mention the other actors, but really, we have forgotten their names. We must say, we never witnessed the subordinate parts in a country theatre sustained so well. The Lady Freelove of the evening was remarkable for nothing but an affected whine, a nasal twang, which gave us sensations not the most pleasing.... There was one gross absurdity in the play, which might be easily removed, but which, we believe, never will; we allude to the ridiculous manner in which the maid servants are dressed: Lady F's waiting woman made her appearance in white kid gloves, and in a dress more elegant than that of Harriot; this stupid custom cannot be sufficiently reprehended.[20]

Gosport was somewhat unfortunate; even Hatton could have an off-night there. On one occasion when playing Barbarossa he reached the scene in which Zapphira was approached with romance in mind, only to discover that his words were not. Pitt Lennox described the incident:

[He] appealed to the prompter in vain. Another moment and
that sibilation 'so unpleasant to the actor's ear' would have driv-
en him from the stage, when, seeing the gallery crowded with
sailors, and regardless of the anachronism, he exclaimed with
tragic energy:

> Did not I
> By that brave knight, Sir Sidney Smith, assisted,
> And in conjunction with the gallant Nelson,
> Drive Bonaparte to his fierce marauders
> From Egypt's shore?

Three cheers from the jolly tars rewarded this impromptu
interpolation.[21]

An absence of able bodied men could be an embarrassment as at
Reading in 1793. *The Road to Ruin* was given but numbers of scenes
were omitted because of the shortage. David Pritchard appeared as
Goldfinch, unfortunately 'by no means successful' although in minor
roles he had given total satisfaction. Again comes the comparison of the
Thornton company with those judged superior: 'The Representatives of
Mr Dornton and Silky merit the first commendation; their performance
would have been a credit to a Royal Theatre'.[22]

Two reviews of this production when staged at Newbury may be compared. The first writer found the company sloppy in its professional
approach:

> ...they have performed (or rather mangled) *The Road to Ruin*
> - a Mr Pritchard was the Goldfinch; but by no means 'the sort': a
> child of eleven or twelve years old played Sophia; and a man of
> the wrong side of fifty personated young Dornton, the parts of
> Old Dornton and Sulky, were however, well supported by
> Messers White and Saunders, the latter was really admirable...[23]

In contrast Pritchard gained an accolade from a second critic. After
giving information on the changes made to strengthen the company,
Pritchard was singled out:

> Mr Thornton with his usual taste and assiduity, finding novelty
> attracting, has brought forward most of the recent popular
> pieces that have been acted at the London Theatres, particularly
> *The Road to Ruin*. Pritchard, in Goldfinch, discovered great
> judgement and discrimination of character....

The Visitors

That Thornton was able to attract to his playhouses visiting artistes of quality is an indication of the approval with which he was regarded by members of the theatre profession. Writers of topographical books which mushroomed in the early years of the nineteenth century also used lists of visitors as an indication of the success of the playhouse within their own locality as in this work, published in Guildford in 1845, by which time the Barnetts were maintaining the company:

> Many artistes, now duly appreciated, and enrolled in the annals of histrionic fame, appeared here, when the cloud of obscurity veiled their merits from the public eye. Mrs Orger (then Miss Ivers) made her debut under Mr Thornton, its manager; whilst the ill-fated Mrs Jordan performed almost her last character on this stage. The pathos of Paton and Pearman (we ask pardon for the alliteration) and the magnificent tones of Braham, Incledon, and Phillips, have also, at different times, added their powers of enchantment to the ordinary attractions of a provincial company.
>
> Here appeared Miss Foote in her own charming Miss Rosalind, and Master Betty in the hey-day of his career; Bartley, Farren, Harley, Meadows, Yates and Bannister, each in himself a host, have occasionally 'starred it' at Guildford; and many other popular comedians have been connected with the company....[24]

The Puff

In using newspaper copy as evidence of evaluations of plays, one has to be careful. It was Thornton's custom to write much of this material himself, in fact at Chelmsford he was charged for copy as well as for advertisements.[25] But the accounts are not valueless. They give an indication of the aspirations of the manager in staging various plays and in engaging visiting performers and at times show a perceptive honesty in recognising an artistic shortfall.

Standards

1. Bernard, *Retrospections*, p.43.
2. Everard, *Memoirs*, p.135.
3. *Chelmsford Chronicle*, 26 July 1793 and 23 July 1802.
4. *Reading Mercury*, 29 October 1787.
5. *Thespian Magazine*, 1 (1792), 156
6. *Thespian Magazine*, 2 (1793), 226. Hare, *Theatre Royal, Bath*, p.224.
7. *Reading Mercury*, 12 February 1787
8. *Monthly Mirror*, 17 (1804), 206.
9. *Monthly Mirror*, 24 (1807), 450.
10. Theatre Museum: Peter Davey manuscript notebooks, 6, Croydon Theatre.
11. *Thespian Magazine*, 2 (1793), 255.
12. *Thespian Magazine*, 2 (1793), 261.
13. *Thespian Magazine*, 2 (1793), 260 and 3 (1794), 33.
14. *Thespian Magazine*, 3 (1794), 33.
15. *Monthly Mirror*, new series, 2 (1807), 222.
16. Winston, *Tourist*, p.30
17. *Thespian Magazine*, 1 (1792), 155. *Rosina* was written by Frances Brooke with music by William Shield and was alleged to be based on the *Book of Ruth*. From its first performance at Covent Garden in December 1782 the role of William was played by a woman. See Nicoll, *English Drama*, 3.206, 240 and 378.
18. *Thespian Magazine*, 3 (1794), 33.
19. *Chelmsford Chronicle*, 17 August 1792.
20. *Theatrical Inquisitor*, 3 (1813), 125.
21. Lennox, *Celebrities*, 2. 136.
22. *Thespian Magazine*, 1 (1793), 255.
23. *Thespian Magazine*, 1 (1793), 176.
24. Russell, *Guildford:*, ed Laurence, p.188.
25. The Essex Chronicle Office, Westway, Chelmsford: file copies. On tendering the invoice, the advertisement and copy is crossed through and a marginal note of the fee made.

Under Two Managers

CHAPTER 8
EVERYDAY PRACTICALITIES

The Actors' Salaries and Responsibilities

Each member of Thornton's company received a salary. According to Walter Donaldson the 'old managers', including Thornton, normally paid their actors one guinea per week. Boots, shoes, buckles, stockings, hats, feathers, swords, canes, wigs, gloves and military costumes were supplied by the actor; performers who sang had to provide parts of their songs for the orchestra. Thomas Collins, Thornton's south coast rival, in 1805 was paying members of his company from 18/- to £1. 11. 6d. If anything Thornton was probably a little more generous as there were several defections from Collins' company to Thornton's.[1] This salary was augmented by a benefit performance and usually every actor received one at each of the locations where a stop was made for a season. After the expenses of the evening (such as the cost of lighting the house, salaries etc.) the box-office takings were given to the beneficiary.

Maintaining the Premises

Any building used constantly by the public needs regular maintenance; if the sparsity of news about refurbishment is an indication of how infrequently this was seen to, then Thornton's theatres must often have become shabby and disintegrating. The impression is gained that unless there was a structural addition, then any improvements were little more than surface decoration.

As one of the earliest theatres to be built and one that remained on the circuit through two generations of management, the Reading theatre often needed attention. In 1793 repairs were undertaken, possibly to the roof as there was an assurance that the building had been aired.[2] A sale of the Wargrave theatre of the bankrupt Lord Barrymore had been held at Christie's Auction House in October 1792 when Thornton bought 'sashes and frames, doors, dressings and enrichments each side of the stage, with the entablature drapery and columns [the latter were probably wooden and painted to resemble stone]' for £4.10/-. Possibly the opportunity was taken in 1793 to position these in the Reading theatre.[3]

In the refurbishment or rebuilding of 1801 Thornton availed himself of the opportunity to build stage boxes in which 4/- per seat was charged.[4] By 1808 Thornton advertised that the theatre has been repaired and fitted up; the latter phrase may refer to the interior furnishing, such as the construction of the boxes, the facades, the stage, rather than the outer brick shell.[5] During 1814 Woolford and West's equestrian troop took part in the plays which undoubtedly was partly responsible for the need for further paint and decoration.[6]

The improvements at the Windsor Theatre were structural rather than decorative. In 1798, five years after the opening of the purpose-built theatre, the neighbouring houses were transformed into an elegant royal entrance, allowing a suite of rooms for hospitality; these, a Windsor correspondent claimed, were 'highly approved by their Majesties'.[7] Thornton conceived the happy plan of hanging the front of the theatre with lamps and illuminated transparencies at an expense of £50 on the visit of the royal family. This was Thornton's practice at Gosport too, where the King's Arms, the theatre tavern, and the private passage into the building were illuminated in celebration of victories at sea.[8] Further alterations, but unexemplified, were made to the Windsor Theatre in 1806. This was the occasion when Kirby, a member of Thornton's company who sporadically played at the Royal Circus, designed some scenes and decorated the fabric.[9]

Immediately before the Margravine of Anspach, who lived at nearby Benham, desired a play at Newbury, material alterations were made to the building, a hint of the extent to which Thornton was prepared to accommodate his royal and aristocratic patrons.[10] An attractive addition was made to the Chelmsford Theatre a year after a programme of redecoration: a month before his retirement Thornton installed some 'elegant chandeliers'. At the same time alterations to the boxes were considered a great improvement. Would that it were known what these consisted of.[11]

Lighting

There were few occasions in which it was necessary for Thornton to give his audiences any information or warning about the theatre lighting. However, several instances are on record. At Croydon the town was without gas until 1830 and so suspended around the edge of the auditorium were cut glass chandeliers holding wax candles. Oil-lamp footlights and side lights were used on the stage.[12]

When Moritz or Lunardi brought the *Phantasmagoria* to Thornton's theatres the manager, perhaps as a safety precaution, warned his audiences in advance that for a successful projection to be made all of the lights in the theatre would have to be extinguished. In an auditorium lit by candles - and maintained throughout the normal performances - this could be a tedious business. A further warning was given that no doors would be opened for latecomers.[13]

Whether by candles or oil lamps lighting could be dangerous. In 1808 oil footlights set fire to one of the proscenium doors at the Arundel Theatre. As well as indicating a fire hazard, the incident also highlights the smallness of this particular theatre.[14]

Heating

A building, often cheaply constructed, and one that was only open sporadically, posed problems in the winter. Few heating appliances were to be found in playhouses. Thornton seemed to distinguish between stoves and fires when he advertiseed warmth and comfort. For a mid-winter lecture in 1814 at Newbury there was a promise that the place would be 'made perfectly warm by a powerful stove', implying only one for the whole theatre. Reading held out a brighter prospect in March twenty years earlier: 'The theatre will be rendered exceedingly warm by stoves, and being well enclosed'.[15] The latter part of the sentence presumably refers to the passages which ran around the outside of the auditorium leading to pit and boxes. Additional heat came from the oil lamps and candles burning as well as a human output of warmth from audience and actors. Also at Reading in 1803 Thornton advertised: 'Good Fires constantly kept in the theatre'.[16] The enquirer is left asking whether these stoves and fires are synonymous with some kind of brazier, highly dangerous in an interior made principally of wood, or whether 'fires' refers to some kind of fireplace and 'stoves' to a permanent appliance. It is amazing that with primitive lighting and heating fire razed so few country theatres.

The Sectionalisation of the Company and Sub-Managers

One unified company made its way around the Thornton circuit in the 1780s and there was little sense of pattern in the choice of location for seasons of varying length. As the number of theatres grew, so it became desirable to make use of them with greater frequency. The first division of the company was made in 1792. From July through to September a contingent played at Chelmsford and from August through to September a further phalanx entertained audiences at Reading, from whence it made brief forays to Windsor. The Chelmsford season continued later than the Reading and by the beginning of October the complete company moved to Croydon. Both Hatton and Thornton, who played Captain Absolute in *The Rivals*, were at Chelmsford until mid-August, when Thornton moved on to an unsuccessful brief season at Windsor. Thomas Cowslade, printer of the *Reading Mercury*, announced, 'We are happy to hear that our old manager, Thornton,... is likely to pay us a visit', in honour of the Race Week. So it was that towards the end of August, Thornton was to be seen playing Harry Dornton in *The Road to Ruin*.[17] Thus Thornton not only performed but also kept a watching brief as manager on the two sections at three of the theatres, an indication of his energy. The company divided again in 1797 when a season opened at Chelmsford on 11 July carrying through to after 25 August. A further section played at an unidentified ad hoc theatre in Arundel and then went on to establish itself at Weybridge in a new theatre from 7 August. Their ways joined by 4 September at Reading. Hatton and Mrs Thornton played at Arundel but which of the two was nominally in charge is difficult to say; at some locations Mrs Thornton had been referred to as the manager whilst at Gosport Hatton was decidedly the driving force behind the mounting of productions.[18] Thornton was in Chelmsford for the beginning of the season and then transferred to Weybridge - performances commanded by the Duchess of York were not to be neglected - leaving Mrs Thornton to return to Chelmsford. Thus, not only convenience but also expediency dictated where the senior members of the family were to play.[19]

When Thornton leased the rackets court in Oxford from 1799 only the period of the summer vacation was available to him for his season with the result that part of the company regularly played there in the latter weeks of July and during August, leaving the other section to perform often in Reading, coincident with the race week, and sometimes Chelmsford.[20] Playing time at Oxford was gradually extended to mid-

September by his last visit in 1815.[21] At Reading and Chelmsford in 1799 Hatton was in charge directing a series of spectacles which included *Laugh When You Can, Pizarro* and *Blue Beard.*[22]

On a number of occasions a section of the company wintered at Gosport, an engagement which could begin as early as September with other performers based in Newbury and sometimes Reading.[23] By 1815 a considerable time in the summer too was spent in Gosport. The acquisition of the Ryde theatre in 1813 presented its own challenges for this became the southernmost of the circuit. It was then expedient to hold a season here during the summer and to leave other performers to entertain at Reading and Newbury.[24]

There were several rare occasions when Thornton divided the company into three contingents. Let us take one example, the summer of 1815, when divisions honoured the usual arrangements at Oxford and Gosport and additional actors performed at Chelmsford and then went on to Reading and Newbury. For example on one day, 28 August, *Romeo and Juliet* was presented at Gosport, *James, King of England* at Chelmsford and *The School for Scandal* at Oxford.[25] Advertisements give little indication of who might be in charge at Chelmsford and Gosport, nor is Thornton listed to appear on stage at either of these places; however, at Oxford, with the theatre refurbished and a line-up of visitors, which included Dorothy Jordan, it is highly likely that the manager would have been on hand.

Sectionalisation of the company posed obvious organisational difficulties for Thornton in ensuring that scenes and costumes, where they were to be moved, were present on time at the right theatre. Moreover, there were the logistics of moving not only the bulk of company members, but also individual visiting performers.

Lodgings for the Company

For much of the time both the rank and file of the company and the Thornton family were away from home - if a Georgian actor had a place which could be thought of as home - with the need to arrange lodgings. Many of the company as well as some of the visiting stars stayed with shopkeepers, living above the premises. An indication of their addresses is given in the newspaper advertisements and on playbills in which the public are advised where to buy tickets for benefit performances. Thus we find Miss Kelly from the Lyceum staying in Gosport with Mr Smith the chemist in North Cross Street, Messers Kirby and Yarnold lodging in Newbury with Mr Garratt the sadler, Mr and Mrs Aickin staying with Partlet the butcher in Arundel and Coughdon staying with Mr Parker the butcher of Fisher Row, Reading.[26] The advantage of this arrangement was the availability of a shop assistant to sell tickets for an actor's benefit when the performer was away from the premises. Landladies in private houses also took in lodgers, actors amongst them, and as examples mention may be made of Stanwix staying with Mrs Warner opposite the Half Moon in Chelmsford and Miss Booth staying at Mr Taylor's in Holywell Street, Oxford.[27] Visiting stars at the theatres sometimes preferred to stay at an inn. Thus Wrench on his visit to Oxford put up at the Bull in St Aldates, the hostelry which stood in front of the theatre building and the Chevaliere D'Eon found the Angel Inn at Reading convenient.[28]

The Thornton family enjoyed some advantages. In Chelmsford their position was the same as that of company members and they chose to stay with Mr Cooke the cabinet maker of Back Street and then at two provision shops, with John Guy, a butcher in New Street, and later with Shuttleworth the Grocer.[29] Thornton's son-in-law, Robert Henry Kelham, resided at his father's business in the town and often sold tickets for the theatre; nevertheless the Thorntons elected to stay at other addresses.[30] However, in Reading the house adjoining the theatre was annexed and here the Crockfords - box-keepers to the theatre - lived and both the Thorntons and the Hattons appear to have lodged temporarily with them or used some of the rooms in the tenement.[31] The Barnetts preferred to make their own arrangements, often staying with Mrs Ledger in Chain Lane.[32] Whilst in Oxford, the Thorntons often stayed with Mr Isaac who resided in the High Street.[33]

Rehearsals

James Winston gives the impression that Thornton, with his lines uncommitted to memory, could not have rehearsed adequately the plays in which he took part. That some of the company's productions were highly commended by critics and audience alike undermines this supposition.[34] Of course, the rehearsal process on the Georgian stage differed from that of today's theatres. Rehearsals could consist of decisions on which side of the stage an actor should make his entrances and exits and words were simply spoken, with no attempt at realism or passion. The eighteenth century habit of standing in a line across the front of the proscenium and delivering words as much to the audience as to other characters cut the need for much plotting of movement and similar business.[35]

Sometimes a play was presented which demanded the careful direction of massed crowds, processions and the use of stage machinery. One such was *Pizarro*. Hatton advertised as early as 26 July 1799 that this was in rehearsal at Chelmsford - he gave the cast list - and would be presented five nights after the announcement appeared. Although this was principally a ploy to whip up expectations so brief a preparation was an unrealistic forecast and the first night had to be delayed until 5 August.[36] A slightly later advertisement mentioned on 16 September 1799 that rehearsals were under way in both Reading and Oxford.[37] During this season the sectionalised company was performing in both towns and rehearsals would presumably have progressed independently. The thrust of this and a following announcement concerned the scenes and costumes together with notes of their cost and the promise that the production would be 'the most superb spectacle that was ever exhibited in a country town'. This selectivity represents the facets of the show on which Hatton spent much time after leaving Essex and the dialogue passages spoken between two or three characters

Benjamin Wrench.
(Ashmolean Museum, University of Oxford)

would have held less importance for him. Indeed, these were often rehearsed privately by actors: Benjamin Wrench, for example, mentions working with his wife's help on the role of Francis (*The Stranger*) over a two week period.[38] Nevertheless, the many supers needed drilling and moments in *Pizarro* such as the shooting of Rolla on the rickety bridge straddling the Valley of the Torrent needed practice and precision. On the advertised opening night the piece was ready to be presented in Reading but not Oxford where it had to be delayed for a week.[39]

Later revivals of *Pizarro*, because of the obvious shortage of rehearsal time, leave one wondering whether the full spectacle was presented. At the Race Week in Chelmsford, a busy and crowded time because of the matinées, one year after the first presentation Raymond arrived to play Rolla in a 'most noble and spirited performance'. The same problem arises with Raymond's visit to Chelmsford in 1816 to play Rolla: how was this elaborate production re-mounted, especially so soon after Mrs Thornton's death which must have taken up much of Thornton's attention?[40]

Time and space for rehearsals was at a premium and one wonders when and where these took place. It was customary in some companies to rehearse in the empty theatre on several of the free evenings during the week. For example, John O'Keeffe mentions a 'night rehearsal' and a 'trial of scenery', possibly a parallel either with a technical or a dress rehearsal on today's stage.[41] Thornton had, however, cut the free time to a single night each week during many seasons, leaving only the mornings and afternoons of working days, a time normally used for rehearsing the standard repertoire ready for immediately impending performances. Luckily most of the company's seasons were long, encouraging expansiveness, but some time was needed for travel on occasions such as the forays from Chelmsford to Ongar and from Windsor to Andover.[42] The problems of time and space were exacerbated when two sections had to rehearse plays independently and then join forces in presenting them at the next station as a single entity. Occasionally, too, Thornton advertised, as at Newbury, before the opening of a new season that he had procured texts of the latest plays and would present 'as much variety as time will permit'.[43] Unfortunately very few of the Newbury titles were advertised in the newspaper and so the veracity of the claim remains unproven but again the problem of time is raised.

It is difficult to calculate the exact length of days during which a play was rehearsed. On 3 August 1792 Thornton informed newspaper readers in Chelmsford that *Robinson Crusoe* was in rehearsal; these preparations were probably advertised as soon as they began. The play opened on 19 August. Thus there was slightly over two weeks not only to rehearse the new piece, but also to prepare new scenery - this was hardly the play in which stock pieces could be used - and costumes. Additionally there were the other plays in the repertoire, usually changing nightly, to run through if they had not been given for a while. Such preparations took place at a time heavily laden with performances. A couple of years later at Chelmsford patrons were advised on 1 August that two plays were in rehearsal, *The Mountaineers* and *The Sicilian Romance*. The

Mountaineers was performed on Monday 18 August, only once as this was the manager's benefit and thereby the last night of the season, with the scenes and machines completed over the preceding weekend. One of the intricacies demanded was a working drawbridge by means of which the characters passed from the castle of Bulcazin Muley to his gardens.[44] The first night date of *The Sicilian Romance* is not given in the newspaper but it seems it would have been one evening between 9 and 17 August. Thus, as Wrench suggests when writing of personal preparation, company rehearsals would seem to have been often over a two week period.

There is a rare indication that the manager used rehearsal periods for timing individual plays and computing from these the length of the evening's offerings: at Reading it was estimated *The Follies of a Day* and *Seeing is Believing*, interspersed by a comic song and a recitation, beginning at 7.00 pm would end by 10.30 pm.[45]

Advertising

Although unsophisticated, there were several ways of advertising a play open to Thornton. One was to deliver playbills to shops, coffee houses and taverns for display; these could also be pasted up in public places. A reason for the number of bills which have survived to the present in good condition is that they were also used as programmes for the evening's entertainment. Some bills in use at the Windsor Theatre on nights when the court attended were printed on silk and those for the royal family laid on the backs of the chairs they were to occupy. An example is a bill for 28 June 1800 when Quick, Barnett, Mrs St Leger and Mrs Mills performed in *The Beaux' Stratagem*. Silk notwithstanding, all of the usual information such as prices and sellers of box places are given.[46]

Local newspapers were a further means of giving advance information; however, use depended on the circulation of these. At Reading and Chelmsford Thornton was able to use the *Reading Mercury* (edited by Thomas Cowslade from the beginning of Thornton's managership of the theatre until 1798, when his mother-in-law, Anna Maria Smart, took an interest in this side of the business) and the *Chelmsford Chronicle* of which William Clacher was proprietor and editor from 1777 to 1797.[47] Until 1815 the gross charge for an advertisement in the *Mercury* was 5/- which then increased to 7/-. *Jackson's Oxford* Journal covered the central area of the city but Thornton used this infrequently. At some of his theatrical bases newspapers published some miles away offered the chance to advertise: thus at Windsor Thornton relied on the *Reading Mercury*, at Andover on the *Salisbury Journal*, at Arundel on the *Hampshire Telegraph* and the *West Sussex Advertiser* and at Gosport, for a while, on the Winchester publication, the *Hampshire Chronicle*. Some of his important theatres were not covered by a publication: Guildford is a case in point.

The *Monthly Mirror* and the *Theatrical Inquisitor* were two London journals which published reviews of plays in country theatres and Thornton's houses benefitted from these; for the most part the reviews were a just balance of praise and critical remark.

As many of the towns in which Thornton had decided to build a theatre were on coaching routes the natural reaction of people interested in the play was to seek out the playhouse, whatever the bill of fare. In diaries and letters one comes across references to instantaneous decisions to go to the playhouse: 'We went to Chelmsford,' noted John Hanson of Bromley Hall, 'where we went to the play at night, saw *The Belle's Stratagem* and *Catherine and Petruchio* and proceeded next morning to Kelvedon'.[48]

Accidents and Illness

Actors were as prone to accident and illness during Thornton's management as they are now. Then playhouse buildings, mainly wooden constructions lit by candles and oil lamps, offered additional hazards. During winter rehearsals the stage could be bitterly cold but conversely the fire which damaged much of Fore and Back Streets, Chelmsford, on 19 March 1808 came perilously near to the theatre and it was the gap between a row of burning houses and Clacher's property which saved it.[49]

On stage people were vulnerable, too. The details of Harvey's accident at Gosport have already been given; this was an extreme case. Properties which did not function adequately were a more common cause of accidents. Mrs Powell visited the Croydon Theatre in 1810, a matter of months before the end of Thornton's management here. Whilst she was playing the title role in *Adelgitha*, the dagger with which the maiden attacked the Roman tyrant, Dionysius, was turned on her and she was almost fatally stabbed. It was discovered that, instead of having a retractable blade, this was no property but a real dagger.[50]

Illness could be an expensive business for a manager and the general trend for an actor was to appear, come what may, at performance time. However, a spirit of laxity might creep into a company. Thornton decided to expose this at Gosport. In the same issue of the newspaper in which he wrote of Harvey's accident he also let his patrons know that recently he had spent nearly £100 in salaries 'to performers who were unable through illness to attend to their professional duties in the Theatre'.[51]

The indispositions of well-known visitors could also be a managerial hazard. In 1817 Junius Brutus Booth the Elder should have appeared at Reading but at the last minute sent a letter crying off. Habitual intemperance together with an unbalanced streak made the actor an unreliable engagement, especially at Christmas time, and the cause of lost revenue for Thornton. The manager displayed Booth's letter in the box office.[52]

Lastly, there were the promised visiting stars who were unable to play because of unexpected protractions of the London seasons. In 1815 the Oxford season should have begun on 8 July but Thornton apologised that the theatre was still in the process of being got ready and a delay to the 10th was proposed; however, the Oxford paper informed that the London patent houses had extended their season by several days.[53]

Letting the theatres

It was in the interests of the manager to let the theatre building between visits when he could; however this was rarely to another theatre company. A few of the lettings Thornton made will illustrate the entertainments offered by those who leased the properties.

A widowed mother of four, Mrs M'George, gave a lecture on heads (a popular subject at the time) at the Chelmsford Theatre in October 1799. She augmented this by her singing. Unfortunately the wet weather had caused flooding in the town with the result that the attendance was thin.[54]

Two lecturers in astronomy gave separate series at the Reading Theatre in April 1805. The first to arrive was Lloyd. He had been seen ten years earlier on the Isle of Wight in Newport and at Gosport.[55] Now he was to present a series of three lectures for which he charged 8/- or 3/6d each, expensive when compared with a theatrical performance and possibly for this reason Lloyd later altered the charges to 3/-, 2/- and 1/-. His subject was illustrated with a Dioastrodoxon, or transparent orrery, 21 feet in diameter.[56] A 6d syllabus was available. Hot on his heels came Walker (no stranger either to Thornton's theatres) also using a transparent orrery known as the Eidouranion.[57] The following month a letter from Lloyd appeared in the newspaper claiming that Walker was a mere tailor from Birmingham and in no position to construct an orrery, whereas he,

Lloyd, had lectured in astronomy for the past twenty years. By way of reinforcement another letter appeared in the columns a couple of weeks later praising the diction and clarity of Lloyd's address and recommending the sessions to children and students.[58] Walker was obviously impervious to the attack: he turned up at Chelmsford in 1812 to entertain with his orrery, still charging the usual theatre prices and accompanied by a musician on the celestina.[59] Eighteen months later the prickly Lloyd, having in the meantime lectured in London at the Haymarket Theatre, was to be heard at Reading again, still defending his orrery: 'The public will not confound this splendid View of the Heavens with any *Minor Exhibition* of a similar description, no other person in the Kingdom being in possession of an arrangement so voluminous, perspicious and liberal'.[60] Taking a cue from Walker, Lloyd also was accompanied by a celestina, 'whose dulcet tones infinitely excel in melody'.[61] However, Lloyd received a highly critical reception. A correspondent for the *Theatrical Inquisitor* heard him at Portsmouth:

> ...with all due deference to the person's abilities, we still have a
> strong notion that Mr L. (on account of the divers blunders
> which he made in his delivery) understands very little of the
> subject on which he professes to treat.[62]

Bird, a lecturer from Abingdon, made a virtue of his self-taught status on his visit to the Reading playhouse in 1817: he, too, sported a transparent orrery, gave a set of three lectures, charged the usual theatre seat prices but allowed half price to both servants and children.[63]

Another who used Thornton's theatres at Arundel and Gosport as well as Collins's south coast buildings was Lee Sugg the ventriloquist.[64] The Gosport Theatre also offered a roof to Cartwright's Musical and Philosophical Exhibition in 1800; demonstrations were given at this of Irish and Scottish airs, musical glasses and the Pyrotechnia or Philosophical Fireworks.[65]

Recitals were always popular at theatres. On a Saturday night in 1794 Charles Claggett gave a recital on the Aiuton or even-handed organ and Johann Backofen, noted as a harpist, clarinet and basset-horn player, gave a recital of instrumental and vocal music on a Wednesday in 1804.[66] A 'numerous and polite audience' of Gosport people listened during the summer recess of 1806 to the songs of Charles Incledon, supported by George Bartley of Drury Lane, a 'plump young man with a thin voice', who gave recitations.[67] A concert was provided by several members of the Margate company who, breaking their journey to Norwich, stopped overnight at Chelmsford in order to perform at the theatre.[68]

One man shows were also highly popular. Two examples: John Bannister gave a lively performance of his *Budget* to a crowded house at Newbury in 1809, impersonating a host of characters, and earlier at Chelmsford Charles Dibdin, about to retire from the stage, 'received a bumper' when he presented his entertainment of recitations and songs, *The Frisk*, in 1802.[69]

It is noteworthy that whether an entertainment or a lecture was offered the usual theatre prices were generally in operation. This could be an indication of the rent Thornton asked, assuming that the sum was based on the charges for a benefit production. However, there was much of social value and interest, even when the company was not in residence, in these occasional functionings of the theatre. If the playhouse was not providing entertainment, then another use would be found for the building, as in the erstwhile mentioned honey store at Andover or the auction rooms the Chelmsford building became.[70]

1. Walter Donaldson, *Fifty Years of Greenroom Gossip* (1881), p.113. Winston, *Tourist*, p.56.
2. *Reading Mercury*, 11 February 1793.
3. Christie, Mason and Woods Ltd, London: Archive department, *A Catalogue of all the Valuable Materials of the Theatre and Several Erections at Wargrave* (1792), p 9, interleaved with manuscript sale notes and accounts. *Reading Mercury*, 24 September and 8 October 1792.
4. *Reading Mercury*, 24 August 1801. Winston, *Tourist*, p.18.
5. *Reading Mercury*, 13 August 1808.
6. *Reading Mercury*, 21 February and 22 August 1814.
7. *Reading Mercury*, 13 August 1798.
8. *Hampshire Telegraph*, 3 May 1802.
9. *Reading Mercury*, 4 August 1806.
10. *Reading Mercury*, 27 November 1809.
11. *Chelmsford Chronicle*, 18 July 1817.
12. Croydon Central Library: Page, 'Recollections'. British Library: Playbill collection, 276, Croydon, 30 March 1830.
13. *Portsmouth Telegraph*, 5 April 1802.
14. *The World's Fair*, 1 November 1958, snippet by 'Southdown'.
15. *Reading Mercury*, 3 January 1814 and 24 March 1794.
16. *Reading Mercury*, 7 February 1803.
17. *Chelmsford Chronicle*, 17 August 1792, *Reading Mercury*, 20 and 27 August 1792. *Thespian Magazine*, 1 (1792), 103.
18. *Monthly Mirror*, 17 (1804), 206.
19. Arundel Museum: Playbill collection, 18 July 1797. *Chelmsford Chronicle*, 7 July and 4 August 1797.
20. *Reading Mercury*, 26 August 1799.
21. *Jackson's Oxford Journal*, 23 September 1815.
22. *Reading Mercury*, 26 August, 9, 16 and 23 September, 1799. *Chelmsford Chronicle*, 19 and 26 July, 30 August 1799.
23. eg *Hampshire Telegraph*, 13 December 1802. *Reading Mercury*, 13 December 1802.
24. *Hampshire Telegraph*, 28 June 1813. *Chelmsford Chronicle*, 25 June 1813.

25. British Library: Playbill collection, 269. *Chelmsford Chronicle*, 25 August 1815. *Jackson's Oxford Journal*, 26 August 1815.

26. *Hampshire Telegraph*, 7 October 1811. Newbury District Museum: playbill, Newbury, 31 January 1817. *Reading Mercury*, 14 December 1789. Arundel Museum: Playbill collection, 18 July 1797.

27. *Chelmsford Chronicle*, 11 August 1797. *Jackson's Oxford Journal*, 9 September 1815.

28. *Jackson's Oxford Journal*, 9 September 1815. *Reading Mercury*, 25 July 1796.

29. *Chelmsford Chronicle*, 28 October 1796 and 23 June 1809.

30. *Chelmsford Chronicle*, 5 July 1799 and 26 July 1805. County Record Office, Chelmsford: 'Transcript of Monumental Inscriptions in the Churches of Chelmsford', T/P72/1. Chelmsford Central Library: Playbill collection, 24 August 1798.

31. *Reading Mercury*, 1 September 1788, 27 August 1798 and 30 September 1799.

32. *Reading Mercury*, 25 September 1809.

33. Cheltenham Museum and Art Gallery: Playbill collection, 28 August 1807.

34. Winston, *Tourist*, p.9.

35. The mechanics of this practice is demonstrated in such a painting as Thomas Parkinson, 'The Highwayman Scene in *She Stoops to Conquer*' (1773), Robertson Davies Collection, illustrated in Iain Mackintosh, ed, *Royal Opera House Retrospective 1732-1982* (1982), p.132.

36. *Chelmsford Chronicle*, 26 July and 2 August 1799.

37. *Reading Mercury*, 16 September 1799.

38. Oxberry, *Dramatic Biography*, 4.147.

39. *Reading Mercury*, 16 September 1799. *Jackson's Oxford Journal*, 21 September 1799.

40. *Monthly Mirror*, 10 (1800), 114 *Chelmsford Chronicle*, 8 August 1800, 5 July and 13 September 1816.

41. O'Keeffe, *Recollections* , 1. 375.

42. *Chelmsford Chronicle*, 17 September 1790. *Salisbury Journal*, 11 April 1803.

43. *Reading Mercury*, 16 November 1807.

44. George Colman the Younger, *The Mountaineers* (1794), p.3.

45. *Reading Mercury*, 14 December 1789.

46. Theatre Royal, Windsor: Playbill collection.

47. University of Reading: K G Burton, 'The Early Newspaper Press in Berkshire (1723-1855)', thesis submitted in 1954 for the award of MA and subsequently privately printed. *Essex Chronicle*, 15 April 1938, 'A Tour in 1776'.

48. Cited by A F J Brown, *Essex People 1750-1900* (Chelmsford 1972), p.53.

49. [Robert Jasper Peck], *Narrative of the Late deplorable Fire at Chelmsford, Essex* (1808), *frontis.*

50. *Monthly Mirror*, new series, 7 (1810), 70.

51. *Hampshire Telegraph*, 7 June 1802.

52. British Library: Playbill collection, 299, 26 December 1817.

53. *Jackson's Oxford Journal*, 8 July 1815.

54. *Chelmsford Chronicle*, 4 October 1799.

55. *Portsmouth Gazette*, 18 May 1795.

56. An orrery was 'a curious machine for representing the motions or phases of the heavenly bodies'. It was invented by George Graham and named in honour of the first Earl of Orrery. See: *The Encyclopaedia Britannica* (1797), p.517.

57. He visited Gosport, for example, in 1800: see *Portsmouth Gazette*, 4 August 1800.

58. *Reading Mercury*, 19 April - 20 May 1805.

59. *Chelmsford Chronicle*, 5 June 1812.

60. *Reading Mercury*, 31 January 1814.

61. *Hampshire Telegraph*, 9 August 1813. The celestina is a keyboard instrument 'in which the sound is produced by the friction of a continuous band of rosined silk upon catgut or wire strings'. See: *Groves Dictionary*, 2. 137.

62. *Theatrical Inquisitor*, 3 (1813), 125.

63. *Reading Mercury*, 12 May 1817.

64. *Portsmouth Gazette*, 29 June and 6 July 1801. Lee Sugg originated from London but from

boyhod he performed at provincial theatres. See: W A Donaldson, *Fifty Years of an Actor's Life* (1858), p.41.

65. *Portsmouth Telegraph*, 27 October 1800.

66 *Chelmsford Chronicle*, 17 October 1794 and 16 November 1804.

Charles Claggett originated from Waterford. As well as conducting several orchestras of repute he invented various instruments. The aiuton was an 'ever-tuned organ, an instrument without pipes, strings, glasses or bells , which will never require to be retuned in any climate'. Claggett's musical instruments were kept at his house in Greek Street, Soho, which he termed the Musical Museum. Johann Backofen, who was born in Durlach in 1768 travelled extensively giving concerts. He became court musician at Gotha and then Darmstadt. See: *Grove's Dictionary* , 1. 341 and 2. 312-3 and the *Reading Mercury*, 10 March 1794.

67. *Hampshire Telegraph*, 23 June 1806.

Tate Wilkinson, for whom Incledon worked, wrote of him: 'To enumerate his merits as a singer, they are so universally known, admired and allowed as to render it needless; but I think he will die like the swan tuning delightful music'. See: Tate Wilkinson, *Patentee*, 4, 168.

William Hazlitt on Bartley cited in W Davenport Adams, *A Dictionary of the Drama* (1904), 2.119.

68. *Chelmsford Chronicle*, 15 June 1814.

69. *Reading Mercury*, 4, 11 and 18 June 1802. *Chelmsford Chronicle*, 4 September 1809.

John Adolphus, the biographer of John Bannister, described the *Budget* as 'a vehicle for animated description, exhilarating monologue, song, both unmixed, and interspersed with prose, anecdotes serious and burlesque, sentiment and bagatelle, broad laugh, generous feeling, and moral instruction'. See: John Adolphus, *Memoirs of John Bannister* (1839), 2. 174.

70. Local information.

Under Two Managers

CHAPTER 9
AUDIENCES

Inhibitions

Each of the various towns in which Thornton set up a theatre provided him with a distinctive audience. That at Reading was no exception; indeed, it was the most strongly delineated of any on the circuit. John Man, the town historian, discerned its chief characteristics:

> There has lately been erected here [in Reading] a neat little theatre where a very respectable company perform (I had almost said to empty benches) for a few weeks in the autumn, but certain it is they meet with very little encouragement from the inhabitants, but this is partly owing to the bigotry of the Methodists, and in part to the immoderate thirst for gain that pervades every class of shopkeepers, making them regret the loss of every shilling that by any other means is prevented from finding its way into their tills. Thus the sons of Thespis are almost banished from a town whose inhabitants might certainly benefit from their exhibitions if they were encouraged here as they are among the most polished nations of Europe.[1]

Reading was a town strong in nonconformity - with six chapels catering for a third of the townspeople - and Anglican evangelicalism. As Man pointed out, a militancy was adopted against the playhouse and its performers. It was, however, his stricture against the mercantile outlook which stung both the pro and anti-theatre groups.[2] Thornton regarded Man's words as unwarranted. He urged large audiences to attend during the ensuing week

> as completely to wipe off the stigma which has been thrown upon it in a late publication, which states that for want of Theatrical Performances being properly encouraged here as they are among the most polished nations of Europe, the people

are deprived of the improvement which is certainly to be obtained from witnessing the exhibition of moral pieces.[3]

The Revd Henry Gauntlett, non-resident curate of Nettlebed and Pishill, who, two years earlier had founded in Reading a society for encouraging Sunday observance and suppressing vice, rapidly composed, on behalf of the town's evangelicals, a reply to Man. Under the *nom-de-plume* 'Defector' argument ricocheted:

> For what is the stage? I reply, The nursery of vice and crime. To this you will probably retort, and exclaim - 'The school of morality and virtue!' But let us proceed to argument. If the stage be the school of morality and virtue, how has it happened that the most immoral, dissolute and vicious of mankind, have always been its firmest supporters and its warmest admirers? How comes it to pass, that those whose lives contradict almost every injunction of the decalogue, should be charmed with the beauty of virtue in the theatre?[4]

The Revd Henry Gauntlett.
(Reading Local Studies Library)

In the face of this invective the quiet mocking of the Revd Richard Graves of Bath in his earlier *The Spiritual Quixote* scarcely seems satirical in tone. Captain Gordon, the actors' enemy, expostulates:

> 'Players, I believe, are considered by your laws as vagabonds; and, I have been told, are excommunicated by some ancient Canons of the Church, and yet are permitted to stroll about, and corrupt the morals, and introduce an habit of dissipation, in almost every little borough and market town in England'.[5]

Other Reading clergy who preached and wrote intermittently against the stage were the Hon and Revd William Cadogan of St Giles' Church and the Revd William Marsh of St Lawrence's. As if defusing a bomb before the inevitable explosion took place, William Mavor in his work on Berkshire, written the year previous to the controversy, noted that an 'air of gentility is thrown over [Reading], and there is an elegant sociability in the manners of the inhabitants, which is irresistibly attractive to strangers'.[6] Twenty years after the publications, Mary Russell Mitford in *Belford Regis* looked back to the beginning of the century and remembered the Friar Street theatre and its depleted audiences:

> The public amusements of the town... were limited to an annual
> visit by a respectable company of actors, the theatre being very
> well conducted and exceedingly ill attended, to tri-ennial concerts
> rather better patronised, to almost weekly incursions of itinerant
> lecturers on all the arts and sciences and from prodigies of every
> kind whether three year old fiddlers or learned dogs.[7]

Four years before Gauntlett was writing in Reading, the Revd John Styles of Newport, Isle of Wight, was composing a tract inveighing against the theatre on the Isle of Wight, as much directed against Thornton's work in Cowes as any other town. It is of interest as he considers not only the actors as degenerate but also the audience, including the prostitutes whom he suggests attended, as depraved:

> ...it is here that vice lifts up its head with undaunted courage;
> that the most licentious and abandoned females endeavour, by
> meretricious ornament, and every art which lascivious wanton-
> ness can invent, to allure the young and inconsiderate, who,
> with passions enkindled by what is passing on the Stage, are
> thrown off their guard, and thus fatally prepared to fall the vic-
> tims of seduction. The avenues to the Theatre, the box-lobby,
> and many of the most conspicuous places in it, are filled with
> women of this description.[8]

Whether Styles had any particular section of the community in mind, he does not say. A possibility would be the ship builders who, since the beginning of the French Revolution, worked in Cowes and would form a large body of men, many of whom lived without domestic comforts.[9] In the north of England Tate Wilkinson had described the voices of those proclaiming against the playhouse as 'darning an old ruffle' and the final effect became worse.[10] The Independents serve as an example. They were not averse to buying a theatre building when it closed: in Gosport the playhouse became the Old Congregational Sunday School under the pastorship of the Revd Mr

Macconell and at Windsor from 1814 the theatre building was used as a Congregational Chapel.[11] Mention has already been made of the Weybridge Theatre which between seasons was used as a Methodist chapel.

The inhibitions on school boys and undergraduates at Eton and Oxford respectively have been mentioned in passing. One wonders what the effect of the students would have been on the audience of townspeople in the rackets court theatres. Manager Henry Lee played in Abingdon during term time, possibly at the Lamb Inn theatre, to gain the support of the nearby Oxford students but soon realised that these denizens of the gallery merely came to ridicule:

> They began to be very annoying to the most respectable ladies
> and gentlemen in the boxes and other parts of the house:
> when silenced by the plaudits bestowed on the actors, by
> those who came to be entertained with the play, they...
> changed their manoeuvres into mock applause and deafening
> cries of 'Bravo! Bravo!'[12]

Their pelting of the orchestra with shilling pieces was more to the liking of the theatre staff. In addition to Abingdon, the Oxford students also trekked to Woodstock to see plays.[13]

Patronage

Thornton was in the happy position of enjoying the patronage of a number of aristocratic families, principally the Petre family of Thorndon Hall, West Horndon near Brentwood, Essex, whom he had assisted in staging plays at their private theatre, and the Margravine of Anspach residing at Benham, near Newbury. The Petres were regularly to be found at performances. For example, Robert Edward, the ninth baron, brought a party to the temporary theatre in the Ongar Assembly Rooms in 1790 and bespoke plays at the matinées during the race week of 1792 at Chelmsford.[14] After his father's death in 1801, the eldest son, also Robert Edward, continued the tradition of theatre visits and in 1804 the family was to be found requesting *The Heir at Law* and *Love Laughs at Locksmiths*.[15]

When Thornton built his Speenhamland theatre on the edge of Newbury in 1802 he had a box especially constructed at the rear of the auditorium for the Margravine of Anspach, the daughter of the Earl of Berkley and formerly Lady Elizabeth Craven, wife of the sixth Baron Craven.[16] Prior to this date, the Margravine braved the dark and inhospitable approach to the Northcroft Lane theatre occasionally. She desired

The Margravine of Anspach.
(Reading Local Studies Library)

on one occasion *Such Things Are* and *The Romp,* whilst on another night her choice fell on *Wives as they Were* and *Lock and Key,* light-hearted offerings which mirrored her own style of dramatic writing.[17] For an evening at the Speenhamland playhouse she chose *The School for Prejudice* and *St David's Day.*[18] Another comment on the forgetfulness of Thornton hinged on the Margravine's request for a performance of *Othello* in which the manager played the title role. On its completion Thornton, with lighted candelabra held high as at Windsor, escorted the Margravine into the theatre lobby where, unfortunately the flames blew out. She found her way to the carriage in the darkness and Thornton, discountenanced, went straight to bed, forgetting to remove his covering of lampblack and pomatum.[19] At times the Margravine would travel to Reading, where, for example, she desired *The Haunted Tower* and *The Jew and the Doctor.*[20] Her visits to the theatre ended in 1806 with the death of the Margrave, when she retired to Brandenburgh House in Hammersmith and then migrated to Naples to live in a replication of her Hammersmith House built on land given her by the king of the principality. She ended her days writing her memoirs and gardening, resembling, it was said, 'an Egyptian mummy'.[21] Although the Margravine attended the theatre, she did not seek Thornton's assistance with productions at her own private playhouses in Benham and London.

Another enthusiast for private theatricals, as indeed for many of the arts such as musical composition and collecting cameos and intaglios, was the 4th Duke of Marlborough whose family staged plays, again without Thornton's help, in the orangery of Blenheim Palace at Woodstock, near Oxford. Marlborough sporadically attended the Oxford Theatre, arriving in 1802 when he desired *Speed the Plough.*[22] The Duke's son, the Marquis of Blandford, who himself had played the part of Marlow in *She Stoops to Conquer* at the Blenheim theatricals, and who later resided at Whiteknights in Reading, was an inveterate theatre-goer requesting, as did his wife, *The Wheel of Fortune* and *The Prize* in 1800, *The Rivals* and *The Midnight Hour* in 1807 and *The School for Scandal* and *A Tale of Mystery* in 1811, to give but three examples.[23]

Of course, most of Thornton's patrons eschewed private theatricals of their own, gaining more satisfaction from making their choice of play but leaving its performance to the company. Sheer numbers allow one merely to list some of the manager's aristocratic patrons. The Marquis of Salisbury supported Mrs Thornton's benefit at Chelmsford, choosing *The Heir at Law,* in which she played Cicely Homespun and *The Wand'ring Jew,* an opportunity for Hatton to take the title role.[24] At Gosport Lady

Sarah Crespigny desired *The Clandestine Marriage* and *Bluebeard*; her mother had earlier supported Mrs Crouch at Reading, requesting she appear in *The West Indian* playing opposite Thomas Young's Belcour.[25] At the beginning of Barnett's period of management the seventh Earl of Craven became captivated by the actress Miss Brunton when she appeared at the Speenhamland Theatre.[26] A week after the Duke of Marlborough desired a play at the Oxford Theatre, Sir Digby Mackworth requested *The Busy Body* and *Of Age Tomorrow*.[27] Another enthusiast at the Reading Theatre was the Rt Hon Richard Neville, Lord Braybrooke, the Member of Parliament for the town. His taste was light; for one evening he chose *The Review*, during which a view of Windsor Castle was displayed, comic songs sung by David Pritchard's lad, *Sylvester Daggerwood* and *Obi*.[28] On reporting in the newspaper notable people in the audience, the manager would at times be at a loss: at the same theatre Thornton in 1800 mentioned that the audience was genteel, consisting of 'fashionable families in the neighbourhood'.[29] The families themselves who sponsored plays might also be coy in lending their names. There is an anonymity in the phrase 'the Ladies and Gentlemen of Great Baddow' who requested *Wild Oats* and *The Spoil'd Child* at the Chelmsford Theatre.[30]

Civic dignitaries also supported the theatres. The presence of the mayor of a town could be a useful draw. An instance is the Mayor of Newbury, Alderman Slocock, who supported the Barnetts on their benefit night, requesting as an after-piece *Not at Home*; a main piece was not advertised, possibly an indication of the limited dramatic knowledge of the mayor.[31] In Reading the Mayor was joined by the Corporation and they jointly requested *The Castle Spectre* and *St David's Day*.[32]

The stewards of the races often worked hand in glove with the theatre personnel: those at Chelmsford, for instance, at the first season of the permanent theatre desired *The School for Arrogance* and *The Lyar*. Two years later the stewards took on the patronage of the 'morning plays'.[33] Race meetings engendered excitement. The week before they began in Newbury in 1809 the newspaper announced that the 'the neighbouring mansions are already filled with the friends of the owners', that the 'ordinaries would abound with bustle' and that Lord Craven had presented the town with two fat bucks. Thornton added to the anticipation by announcing the engagement of Mrs Jane Powell from Drury Lane.[34] Once the meetings started the stewards could be helpful in ascertaining the likely times by which the sporting fixtures could finish: at Reading Thornton advertised vaguely that the curtain would rise 'immediately after the Races are over'.[35] The financial failure of the Reading Races in 1815 hit not only the

135

stewards but also the theatre and Thornton's note in his advertisement summarises the low morale: '...Although recent circumstances have so damped the spirit of this town that the races were suffered to fall without an effort to preserve that amusement, we hope, so far from being a detriment it will prove an additional stimulus to the public to support the rational entertainments they have so many years enjoyed from the exertions of Mr Thornton's company....'[36] At this juncture lay the interfacing of several financial interests.

People arrived in groups, by pre-arrangement supporting actors' benefits. The heads of educational establishments obviously chose with care the plays they wished to see. Mr Smith's Boarding School at Writtle, outside Chelmsford, requested the highly moral drama *Douglas* followed by *The Prize* in 1795.[37] The choices of Miss Jesse at Reading were adventurous: she selected for one visit of her school *Every One has his Fault* and *The Wandering Jew* and for another *The Battle of Hexham* and *Paul and Virginia*.[38] A differentiation seems to be made between 'the young gentlemen at the [Gosport] Academy' and the Principal Dr Burney: the former requested the comedy *Management* followed by the musical entertainment *The Padlock* whilst the principal, supporting Thornton's benefit, desired *The Jealous Wife* and *Catherine and Petruchio*.[39] The publicans and inn keepers of Chelmsford clubbed together to support the Fawcetts on their benefit night; the theatre put on *Blood for Blood* followed by a comic dance by Master Ivers.[40] Mention has been made of the Masons who supported the theatre thus adopting a totally different attitude to the nonconformists and some clergy of the Anglican church. The Free and Acceptable Masons of Cowes and Newport attended Thornton's new Ryde Theatre during its first season in 1813 when they desired *The Rivals*, *The Sleepwalker* and a dance by the late William Hatton's daughter.[41] At Reading three years later the Masons supported Barnett (himself a member) in *The Doubtful Son* and *Robin Hood*.[42]

By far the largest group to support the theatre were the service personnel who often attended on a regimental basis. Gosport provides an example of a town in which there was this homogeneity of audience. The vast numbers working in the yards of the Royal Navy took up much of the auditorium and most other seats were occupied by the tradespeople of the town.[43] George Parker, who in early life had been a midshipman, described in his memoirs the audience at a temporary Gosport theatre prior to Thornton's arrival:

> Our house in the place was chiefly supported by Jack-Tars, a
> whimsical race of mortals. These jolly Britons used to sing and

drink flip during the performance of the play, and hand occasionally on the stage bowls of punch to the Actors; no unwel-
come feast to the poor people who were starved by the rapacity
of the unfeeling manager.[44]

This manager whom Parker referred to as 'Mr C-.' was possibly
Thomas Collins, the leader of the Salisbury Comedians, who for a short
period managed a theatre in the vicinity of Rimes Alley, later known as
the King's Arms Passage. There is every likelihood that the same personnel later attended Thornton's Middle Street theatre. Ann Holbrook, who
joined the company for a year, playing at Gosport during the Napoleonic
Wars, took a more serious view than Parker of the audience:

Never shall I forget my sensations when, stepping on the stage,
so many brave defenders of the country met my view - not the
loss of legs or arms had power to check the hilarity that glowed
in their breasts.[45]

Between the pieces the actress recited a monody on the death of
Nelson; instantly there was a change in the atmosphere of the house as a
quiet attentiveness gripped the sailors. Another actress who spoke with
approbation of the Gosport audience was Dorothy Jordan. She arrived in
the town in November 1812 and then returned in December. 'I have met,'
she wrote to her son George FitzClarence, 'with great kindness and civili-
ties here from everybody both on and off the stage.'[46]

Other theatres had their measure of servicemen. At Chelmsford
plays were desired by Colonel Montagu and the Officers of the Wiltshire
Militia (*The Rivals* and *The Midnight Hour*); by the Officers of the Royal
Welsh Fusiliers and of the East Norfolk Regiment (*The School for
Scandal* and *The Agreeable Surprise* for the Dyers' benefit); by Captain
Tuffnell's Corps of Yeoman Cavalry (*The Road to Ruin* and *The Loyalist*)
and by the Officers of the Royal Bucks Militia (*The Mountaineers* and
The Sultan for the benefits of Mrs Skinner and Mr Fulton.[47] More often
a local regiment would desire a play; thus at Reading the Officers of the
Reading Loyal Volunteers desired *The Stranger* and *The Review* and the
regimental band played whilst at the nearby town of Newbury the
Officers and Men of the Newbury Troop of Cavalry desired on Smith's
benefit night *Hamlet* and *High Life Below Stairs*.[48] The business of bring-
ing a band to play increased in popularity in the early years of the nineteenth century. Thus in 1814 Colonel Sir John Elley brought from
Windsor to the Reading Theatre the distinguished band of the Royal
Horse Guards (the Oxford Blues) to play between presentations of *The
Heir at Law* and *Of Age Tomorrow*.[49]

Several societies also acted as patrons of performances. The Reading Association sponsored *The School for Scandal* and *The Poor Soldier* and the Association band in full uniform played before the show.[50] After the Congress of Vienna, at Chelmsford the Waterloo Society was patron of performances of *John Bull* and the 'loyal farce' of *The Rival Soldiers*. Appropriately, between pieces Starmer sang 'Darby Kelly or The Hero of Waterloo'. Strangely this was not some kind of civic or military benefit.[51]

Admission Charges

In many provincial theatres the prices of seats were 1/- in the gallery, 2/- in the pit and 3/- each seat in the boxes. At a given point in the evening the audience was admitted at half price. Changes in the charges occurred when the manager altered the disposition of parts of the house or engaged a visiting player whose name would command a high salary, the greater part of which had to be recouped from box office revenue.

Newbury posters demonstrate the normal seat prices for the theatre. At the playhouse in Northcroft Lane in April 1797 *The Way to Get Married* was presented followed by *The Agreeable Surprise*; the main piece gave the opportunity for Owens, the theatre painter, to create a new setting for Allspice's garden and hot-house and between the two pieces was a song given by Cross. The programme for the night was a routine one and the seat prices of 3/-, 2/- and 1/- reflected this.[52] What is surprising is that on turning to a bill for a benefit performance in January 1817 at Thornton's superior theatre in Speenhamland, Newbury, the prices are still the same and Kirby and Yarnold, the beneficiaries, have assembled a lively programme which included *The Castle Spectre*, a harlequinade, *Harlequin's Olio*, impersonations by Kirby of Grimaldi and a masquerade, first given at Covent Garden, terminated by a 'Grand Display of Fireworks'.[53] As late as 1830, during the recession following the Napoleonic Wars the price of seats would remain constant at some theatres. A bill for the Chelmsford Theatre for August 1798 advertising Mrs Thornton's benefit informs that *The Heir at Law* and *The Wand'ring Jew* were to be presented supported by such extras as Miss E Thornton singing 'Moss Roses' and Miss Binfield rendering 'The Negro's Festival'. Seat prices are given as the usual 3/-, 2/- and 1/-.[54] William Hall, who managed for a short time the Croydon Theatre and also took a lease on the Chelmsford, advertising himself as a pupil of Thornton's, staged a performance of *Black Eyed Susan* during the race week, drawing back the

By his Majesty's Servants,
(*From the Theatre Royal,* WINDSOR)

NEW THEATRE, NEWBURY,

On SATURDAY, APRIL, 22d. 1797, will be performed,

For the first Time,

A CELEBRATED COMEDY CALLED, THE

Way to get Married.

WITH ENTIRE NEW SCENERY.

As performed at the THEATRE ROYAL, *Covent Garden, upwards of* 100 *Nights*

Tangent,	Mr. HATTON——*Capt. Faulkner*	Mr. AICKIN
Allspice,	Mr. OWENS——*Caustic,*	Mr. CROSS
Dashall,	Mr. EVATT—*Mc. Queery,*	Mr. SWINDAL
Geoffry,	Mr. PARSONS——*Ned,*	Mr. BATEMAN
Postilion,	Mr. DUNN——*Undertaker,*	Mr. STANNARD
	Landlord, Mr. HARGRAVE	
Clementina,	Mrs. THORNTON——*Lady Sorrel*	Mrs. FARQUHAR
Julia,	Mrs. AICKIN——*Fanny,*	Mrs. PARSONS

In Act 2nd. *an* INSIDE VIEW *of*

ALLSPICES's SHOP.

IN ACT 5th.

Allspices's

GARDEN AND HOT-HOUSE.

Painted by Mr. Owens.

A FAVORITE SONG MR. CROSS.

To which will be added the Entertainment called, the

Agreeable Surprise.

Sir Felix,	Mr. OWENS——*Compton,*	Mr. SWINDAL
Eugene,	Mr. HARGRAVE—*John,*	Mr. BATEMAN
Thomas,	Mr. AICKIN——*Chicane,*	Mr. CROSS
Stump,	Mr. PARSONS——*Cadden,*	Mr. DUNN
	Lings, Mr. HATTON	
Cowslip,	Miss THORNTON—*Mrs. Cheshire,*	Mrs. FARQUHAR
Fringe,	Mrs AICKIN——*Laura,*	Mrs. SWINDAL

ON MONDAY——*Jane Shore* WITH *Lock and Key.*

BOXES, 3s.—PIT, 2s.—GALLERY, 1s.——TICKETS may be had at the *Theatre,* *Printing-Office, Inns,* and of Mr. *Simmons,* North-brook-street.

Playbill, Newbury Theatre, Speenhamland.
(From the collections of the West Berkshire Heritage Service)

former Miss Ivers to take the title role, and also provided a farce and a series of songs and dances at no increase in the admission charges.[55]

In the course of most evenings seats were offered at given times at half price. Thornton seems to have varied the arrangements for this concession. At Reading in August 1809 the seat prices included the stage boxes constructed in the 1801 renovation, for which a charge per seat of 4/- was made and other seats were at the usual rates. The doors opened at 6.00 pm and the entertainment started at 7.00 pm. After 8.00 pm the price of the box seats dropped to 2/- and after the start of the third act of the main piece, which varied each evening in selection and thereby timing, pit and gallery seats were an exact half price.[56] The earlier mentioned Chelmsford playbill of 1798 gives the starting time of the entertainment as 7.00 pm with a second price for the boxes at 8.15 pm and a half price for the pit and gallery at the end (rather than the beginning) of the third act. At Gosport in 1806, employing the usual starting time and admission charges, half price to the boxes was from 8.30 pm when seats were reduced to 2/-. No mention was made of a general half price, possibly because the visiting attraction was Palmer from the Haymarket.[57] Nearly ten years later in Gosport the reduced price, by then offered at 8.00 pm, was the same.[58] Seats in the stage boxes were sold for 5/- in Oxford at the rackets court theatre in Christ Church and a playbill of 1807 gives no indication of a half price concession.[59] Prices at Thornton's second Windsor Theatre were also higher than in most others: here in 1800 the stage boxes also sold for 5/- per seat and upper box slips at 2/6d.[60] By 1805 a price restructure had taken place, possibly due to the infrequent attendance of the royal family. James Winston gives the admissions as lower boxes 4/-, upper boxes 3/6d, slips 3/-, pit 2/- and gallery 1/-. When a half price was allowed the admissions were 2/6d, 1/6d, 1/- and 6d.[61] As with Palmer's visit, often Thornton would invite a celebrity to play and advertise that no half price would be allowed; but worthy causes, too, sometimes precluded a reduction, as, for example, the Voluntary Contributions for the Defence of the Country.[62]

Scant information is given in newspaper advertisements about the opening hours of the box office. The usual practice was for the box seats only to be booked in advance either at the theatre itself or at the box-keeper's house near the theatre. The box office at Guildford was open from 10.00 am until 2.00 pm in 1814.[63] Servants would normally make the booking on the day of the performance, later sitting on the seats to be taken by their employers as early as an hour and a half before the start of the performance.

The financial arrangements for the visits of the royal family to the Windsor Theatre are difficult to determine. The very presence of the court in the theatre drew a full house. In 1794 the king had given the company as a whole a sum of money for a benefit performance; unfortunately some of the actors had grumbled because Thornton had included as sharers a few actors who did not belong to the Windsor section but had arrived to augment the cast on the benefit night. The following year, in payment for another benefit, the king gave the playing company fifteen guineas to which the Duke and Duchess of York added a further five.[64] Whether payment was additionally given to Thornton remains uncertain.

Disorder and Law

Compared with the sheltered, well-behaved, secure theatre-goer of today, his Georgian counterpart suffered a number of risks. Even the journey to the theatre could be dangerous. Some members of the audience travelled a distance on horseback or by carriage. When Betty appeared at the theatre in Arundel families of 'rank and taste' travelled up to twenty miles to see the wonder.[65] The families travelling in from the villages to the centre of Oxford were terrorised by highwaymen at the end of the eighteenth century and the short journey was said to be made with ready loaded pistols.[66] Thornton usually listed any mitigation that would make the journey less hazardous such as moonlit nights. However, the weather could affect the size of the audience. Heavy rain at Chelmsford left the theatre 'indifferently attended' and 'foul weather' could raise the charges of the Gosport ferrymen.[67] Nevertheless, Bristow, on his benefit night at Gosport, expediently advertised that the show would be over by 11.00 pm and the 'waterman' would be attending.[68] The ferrymen were often a liability. Arrogant and demanding, some, such as George Brothers, sailed the wrong side of the law by helping, when bribed, prisoners to escape from the gaol at Forton. It was not until 1809 that an Act of Parliament was passed to curb the excessive charges of ferrymen after the journey had begun and to protect the passengers.[69]

Troubles could arise inside the theatres, often from the gallery. A German visitor to England in the 1780s remarked on the antithetical opinions of the box and gallery audiences:

> ...aristocrats and commoners are gathered [in the theatre auditorium], and the latter are bent on showing they consider themselves quite as good as the former... The upper gallery controls the whole house, even the actors being compelled to obey orders.[70]

From the heights of the gods the conditions were not conducive to a quiet enjoyment of the play. At an early theatre on Crown Hill in Croydon the way into the gallery was by an outside ladder.[71] At Oxford the town boys, too, were disruptive: in 1810 during Russell's season he threatened to publish their names and prevent future admission, a move applauded by the audience.[72]

Other sectors of the house than the gallery could hold troublesome elements. Pitt Lennox relates the occasion in 1814 when he saw *Hamlet* at Speenhamland with several of his friends. The small stage was hard pressed to contain an inner stage when 'The Murder of Gonzago' was acted and the squash was undignified. 'What stage effect,' Pitt Lennox cried from the vantage point of a box. The first Mrs Barnett came sweeping down to the footlamps and declared, 'Puppies are no judge of stage effect.' An authoritative actress could quell any nonsense that occurred too near the acting area.[73] At Gosport in 1806 army and navy officers, usually the takers of box seats, rioted over a number of evenings. The constables, called by Thornton, were in turn set upon. When the rowdy element was brought before the Revd Richard Bingham and Samuel Jellicoe at Portsmouth the men signed an apology and made a donation of £20 to the Patriotic Fund at Lloyds. The manager, realising that much of his livelihood depended on the armed services, waived criminal charges against the officers.[74] Other instances of unruly behaviour have already been mentioned: the audience pushing its way into a benefit before a box keeper was in attendance to take the money, the use of peace officers in the gallery or at the front of the stage when necessity arose and throwing victuals during a performance. In a demonstrative age, if there were no more than these infringements of behaviour, Thornton would appear to conduct his playhouses with firmness and propriety.

The sight of an audience could be touching to performers, as Ann Holbrook testified but so could its response to a favoured public figure. Let Fanny Burney witness to this. In 1798, along with the royal family, she went to the Windsor Theatre to see *The Heir at Law*:

> When the King entered, followed by the Queen and his lovely daughters, and the orchestra struck up 'God save the King', and the people all called for the singers, who filled the stage to sing it, the emotion I was suddenly filled with so powerfully possessed me, that I wished I could, for a minute or two, have flown from the box - to have sobbed; I was so gratefully delighted at the sight before me, and so enraptured at the continued enthusiasm of the no longer volatile people for their worthy, revered sovereign, that I really suffered from the restraint I felt of being forced to behave decorously.[75]

142

Audiences

Even when people queuing at the doors were unable to get into the playhouse for want of room, decorousness prevailed. *Pizarro* drew crowds to all of the theatres on the circuit and there were many times when numbers were turned away. The Oxford paper reported the amazing sight of seven hundred people quietly walking down Merton Street on a September evening in 1799, foiled in their attempt to see the last night of the play. Likewise for a performance of *The Rivals* in the same month, 'as many as could be received within the Court returned for want of room'.[76] The numbers turned away from *Pizarro* at Chelmsford were not so spectacular: £10 for lack of room on one evening but still a dignified acceptance of the situation.[77]

There was only one published mandate to which Thornton adhered: no one was allowed 'behind the scenes'. This prohibition continued to be made into the 1800s, in spite of the fact that the regulation was first enforced during David Garrick's management of Drury Lane. The dressing rooms, the green room and the space behind the wings were for the use of the actors only and Thornton's company was saved from the distraction of visitors.

1. John Man, *The Stranger in Reading* (Reading, 1810), p.75.
2. Britton and Brayley, *The Beauties of England and Wales*, 1. 95.
3. *Reading Mercury*, 10 September 1810.
4. Defector [Henry Gauntlett], *Letters to the Stranger in Reading* (Reading, 1810), p.10. Henry Gauntlett, *Sermons by the late Revd Henry Gauntlett, vicar of Olney, Bucks, with a Memoir of the Author* (1835), pp lx - lxvi.
5. Richard Graves, *The Spiritual Quixote* (1773), p.245.
6. Mavor, *Agriculture of Berkshire* , p.463.
7. Mary Russell Mitford, *Belford Regis* (1835), p.164
8. John Styles, *An Essay on the Character of the Stage* (Newport, IOW, 1806), pp 74-5.
9. *Southampton Guide* (Southampton, 1787) cited in the *Hampshire Antiquary and Naturalist* (1892), 2. 7.
10. Wilkinson, *Patentee*, 1. 105-115.
11. Rogers, 'Gosport's Lost Theatres', *Gosport Records*, 3 (1972), 14. Theatre Museum: Peter Davey Manuscript Notebooks, 7, Gosport. Local information from Mrs Jean Kirkwood of the Windsor Local History Research Group.
12. Lee, *Memoirs*, 2. 53.
13. James Townsend, ed, *News of a Country Town* (1914), p.14.
14. *Chelmsford Chronicle*, 17 September 1790 and 10 July 1792.
15. *Chelmsford Chronicle*, 27 July 1804. Thomas Wright, *The History and Topography of Essex* (1836), 1. 177.
16. Henry Godwin, *The Worthies and Celebrities connected with Newbury, Berkshire, and its Neighbourhood* (1859), 1. 175 and 2. 88.
The Margrave was the nephew of Frederick II of Prussia. At his death he was interred in Speen Church; a large memorial was set up in the grounds of Benham and later moved into the church. It remains at the time of writing.
17. *Reading Mercury*, 15 October and 5 November 1793.

18. *Reading Mercury*, 3 January 1803.
19. *Biography of the British Stage,* p.204.
20. *Reading Mercury*, 21 September 1801.
21. A M Boaden and Lewis Melville, *The Beautiful Lady Craven. Memoirs of Elizabeth Baroness Craven* (1913), 1. lxxxvi and cxxxiv.
22. *Jackson's Oxford Journal*, 7 August 1802. Marian Fowler, *Blenheim: Biography of a Palace* (1991), pp 116-7. James D Brown and S S Stratton, *British Musical Biography* (1897), p.51.
23. Sybil Rosenfeld, *Temples of Thespis* (1978), p.110. *Reading Mercury*, 8 September 1800, 2 September 1807 and 23 September 1811.
Whiteknights became the principal campus of the University of Reading.
24. Chelmsford Public Library: Playbill collection, Chelmsford, 24 August 1798.
25. *Portsmouth Gazette*, 1 April 1799.
26. Money, *A Popular History of Newbury*, p.102.
27. *Jackson's Oxford Journal*, 14 August 1802.
28. *Reading Mercury*, 21 September 1801. Richard Lord Braybrooke, *The History of Audley End* (1836), pp 54-5.
29. *Reading Mercury*, 8 September 1800.
30. *Chelmsford Chronicle*, 22 July 1796.
31. *Reading Mercury*, 8 January 1810.
32. *Reading Mercury*, 14 September 1801.
33. *Chelmsford Chronicle*, 27 July 1792 and 15 August 1794.
34. *Reading Mercury,* 14 August 1809.
Jane Powell received published appraisals from Leigh Hunt, F C Wemyss and Thomas Gilliland.
35. *Reading Mercury*, 27 August 1798.
36. *Reading Mercury*, 3 July and 21 August 1815.
37. *Chelmsford Chronicle*, 31 July 1795.
38. *Reading Mercury*, 17 September 1798 and 27 September 1802.
39. *Portsmouth Telegraph*, 24 March 1800. *Hampshire Telegraph*, 15 May 1809.
40. *Chelmsford Chronicle*, 28 July 1814.
41. *Hampshire Chronicle*, 29 June 1813.
42. *Reading Mercury*, 18 March 1816.
43. Thomas Pennant, *A Journey from London to the Isle of Wight* (1801) cited in Margaret J Hoad, *Portsmouth, as Others have seen it, 2, 1790-1900* (Portsmouth, 1973), p.6.
44. George Parker, *A View of Society and Manners in High and Low Life* (1781), 4. 53.
45. Holbrook, *The Dramatist*, p.24.
46. Aspinall, *Mrs Jordan*, pp 241 and 243.
47. *Chelmsford Chronicle*, 7 August 1795, 18 August 1797, 6 July 1798 and 9 August 1805.
48. *Reading Mercury*, 24 September 1804 and 15 January 1810.
49. *Gentleman's Magazine*, new series, 11 (1839), 430-1 and 12 (1839), 669. *Reading Mercury*, 19 September 1814.
50. *Reading Mercury*, 16 September 1799.
51. The Folger Shakespeare Library, Washington DC: Playbill collection, Chelmsford , 6 August 1817.
52. Newbury District Musuem: Playbill collection, 22 April 1797.
53. Newbury District Museum: Playbill collection, 21 January 1817.
54. Chelmsford Central Library: Playbill collection, 24 August 1798.
55. Chelmsford Central Library: Playbill collection, 21 July 1830.
56. *Reading Mercury*, 21 August 1809.
57. *Hampshire Telegraph*, 3 November 1806.
58. British Library: Playbill collection, 269, 31 July 1815.
59. Cheltenham Museum and Art Gallery: Playbill collection, 28 August 1807.
60. Theatre Royal, Windsor: Playbill collection, 28 June 1800.
61. Winston, *Tourist*, p.54.
62. *Chelmsford Chronicle*, 18 June 1798.

63. Guildford Muniment Room: Playbill collection, 17 June 1814.

64. Everard, *Memoirs*, p.152.

65. *Hampshire Telegraph*, 12 December 1807.

66. G V Cox, *Recollections of Oxford* (1870), p.5.

67. *Chelmsford Chronicle*, 4 August 1809. *Hampshire Telegraph*, 3 May 1802 and 28 August 1809.

68. *Portsmouth Telegraph*, 19 May 1800.

69. L F W White, *The Story of Gosport* (Southsea, nd), pp 96-102.

70. A Wendeborn, *Der Zustand des Staats* (Berlin, 1784) cited in J A Kelly, *German Visitors to English Theatres* (Princeton, 1936), p.121.

71. Croydon Central Library: Notes and cuttings of J C Anderson referring to the Croydon theatres.

72. *Jackson's Oxford Journal*, 18 August 1810.

73. William Pitt Lennox, *Fifty Years of Biographical Reminiscences* (1863), pp 126-8.

74. *Hampshire Telegraph*, 13 January 1806.

75. Frances Burney, *The Diary and Letters of Madame D'Arblay,* ed C F Barrett (1846), 6.174.

76. *Reading Mercury*, 30 September 1799. *Jackson's Oxford Journal*, 14 September 1799.

77. *Chelmsford Chronicle*, 30 August 1799.

Under Two Managers

CHAPTER 10
HENRY THORNTON AND THE PRIVATE THEATRES

The Margravine of Anspach at Benham

Even before Henry Thornton moved from his makeshift premises in Northcroft Lane, Newbury, to the superior theatre at Speenhamland the Margravine of Anspach was supporting the company and the manager would have become aware of 'Her Serene Highness's' interest in the theatre.[1] The townspeople were introduced in 1778 to the then Lady Elizabeth Craven when she presented and performed in her English version of *La Sonambule (The Sleep Walker)* at the Assembly Rooms which then stood to the north-west of the Market Place.[2] Further plays followed and an open air theatre was made in a bosky grove at Benham Valence, her home both as a Craven and as Margravine, in 1782.[3] There is no record of the Margravine employing Thornton to help with any of her theatricals, whether in the transformed riding school at Benham or at her house in Hammersmith.[4] Why was this? Possibly Thornton fought shy of the Margravine on artistic grounds: her plays were written in verbose blank verse and tended to praise 'Spousy', the Margrave, and 'her dear sweet self' added to which her acting powers fell short of the tolerable.[5] Socially, the Margravine was an outcast: her marriage to the Margrave immediately after the death of Lord William Craven had offended many susceptibilites and this would have made Thornton's relations with the members of the royal family difficult. It was unusual, nevertheless, for Thornton not to have pressed his company's services on to an illustrious aristocrat.

147

Lord Barrymore at Wargrave

January 1789 saw an interesting and novel development of Thornton's spheres of activity. He was invited by Richard Lord Barrymore to bring the women of the Reading theatre to Wargrave, a small town situated a couple of miles south of Henley, to assist at the Earl's recently opened private playhouse. Then twenty years old and a member of the Berkshire militia, Barrymore hit on the idea of getting his army friends to fill the male roles for the theatricals, augmented by the local professionals.

The earl first gained his interest in the theatre through his love of horses, investing money in the livestock of the Royal Circus.[6] His own theatricals had begun in 1786 in a barn, as had some of Thornton's, attended by an audience of rustics; by 1788 he had employed Gabriel Cox, the carpenter to Covent Garden, to build him a theatre on the opposite side of the Henley Road from his cottage residence. Tobias Young, whom we have already met, Emmanuel and possibly Scot were employed as scene painters. Within the next three years a sum of £60,000 was to be spent on improvements and additions at a time when a decent theatre could be erected in a town for £1,000, as at Winchester by Thomas Collins in 1785. Such reckless spending drove the earl to a state of bankruptcy.[7]

Lord Barrymore's Theatre at Wargrave from The General Magazine and Impartial Review *(1792).* (Reading Local Studies Library)

148

Henry Thornton and The Private Theatres

The first performance under this new arrangement on 31 January 1789 was attended by Mrs Lybbe Powys, a local resident from Harwick House, who delighted to engage in the milieu of aristocratic sociability. Her interest lay in the plays, performers and refreshments: *The Confederacy* and *The Midnight Hour* were given. Lord Barrymore played Brass in the main piece; his friend Henry Angelo - famous for his fencing skill and passion for dramatics - Dick; John Edwin, an actor - 'incomparable' remarked Powys - played in the afterpiece the transvestite role of Mrs Amlet paired with the only other male professional, Ryder, who took the part of Mrs Cloggit. Mrs Thornton played Clarissa and the other actresses appearing were Mrs Jackson, Mrs Benson and Miss Briderson. Costumes and scenery in the afterpiece gained enthusiastic commendation locally but an unidentified London newspaper was more stringent: 'On the first night some irregularities occurred, but on the second everything went off with improved effect'.[8] Between the acts cake, negus and a variety of wines were provided.

Members of Thornton's company were treated with respect and deference by Barrymore. In spite of the shortage of space in Barrymore's cottage, they took their meals with the guests in the dining room, simply sitting at a separate table. Unused to the champagne, claret and servants, their requests became imperious, which upset Dennis the Irish footman who referred to the actresses as 'the precious swappings of hell'.[9] Sleeping arrangements were primitive. Eight beds were placed in one room for the men; Angelo reported that others unaccommodated were left to scramble in the cottage for what they could get, possibly the fate of Thornton's actresses.[10]

Come August 1789 the theatre was again put to use and on this occasion an invitation was sent to the Prince of Wales. Twenty-five inmates were squeezed into the cottage, the only place for them as there was no inn at Wargrave. Revelry was kept late into the night: Dennis claimed it was the rising sun brought daily peace. In this atmosphere Barrymore decided that the Prince would best be accommodated with a friend, Hill, who owned a spacious house on the edge of Wargrave. Before the visit *The Beaux' Stratagem*, with Barrymore playing Scrub - 'amazingly well' according to Mrs Lybbe Powys - and *The Romp*, in which Barrymore chose the part of Young Cockney, were performed. As before some of Thornton's actresses played the women's roles.[11] On 21 August the Prince of Wales arrived from Brighton and after dinner, with the distinguished visitor sitting in the box which had been especially constructed, the curtain rang up at 9.00 pm. Because of the lateness *The Romp* was omitted. At the end of the performance, possibly tongue in cheek, Mrs Thornton spoke the epilogue:

149

What tho' untaught in the theatric air,
We want the measur'd step, the practis'd stare,
Fearful t'offend, solicitous to please,
We fail t'attain an unembarrassed ease.[12]

A milliner's notice in the Reading paper heralded the approach of the Christmas season of theatricals at Wargrave for which *The Constant Couple* and *The Citizen* were in preparation.[13] Barrymore took on the roles of Beau Clincher and Young Philpot. Edward Cape Everard together with a small selection of Thornton's actresses represented the professional company.[14] Through Angelo's good offices Charlotte Goodall of Drury Lane was persuaded to join the thespians in the breeches role of Sir Harry Wildair, as none of Thornton's actresses was judged to be suitable.[15] Other offerings for the season were *The Citizen*, in which her husband Thomas Goodall, never before seen on the stage, was requested by Barrymore to play Dapper, which he did, and Carlo Delpini's production of the pantomime *Don Juan*. To gain a long vista of the 'infernal regions' in this last presentation the stage of the theatre was extended almost a further twenty feet to the rear of the building.[16] As manager of pantomimes Delpini was to become an important presence at Wargrave. He was not only a successful clown, playing Robinson Crusoe to Grimaldi's Man Friday, for example, but also an expert with stage machines and illusions.[17] After *Don Juan*, *A Trip to the Jubilee* was given.

There was a contrast between the audience at the dress rehearsal and at the performances. Ploughboys, shepherds and maids, 'cabbages arranged in Covent Garden Market', came to the former but the following nights gentry arrived from many miles around, including the Duchess of Bolton, Lord Inchiquin, General Conway, Lady Ailesbury and a rare visit together of Lord and Lady Craven.[18] The festivities reached their apogee in the visit, again, of the Prince of Wales, this time accompanied by his brothers and the Duke of Orleans.[19] As a representative of Thornton's company Everard came to the end of his stay and marvelled at the splendid production of *Don Juan*, the richness of the hospitality and the liberal reward of £10 each which he and his Reading theatre colleagues had received.[20] Unfortunately this was the company's point of severance with the Wargrave theatricals.

As soon as the new year entertainments of 1790 had drawn to a conclusion the theatre was dismantled in preparation for a sumptuous rebuilding. Whilst this was taking place Barrymore ventured to appear during August at the Richmond (Surrey) theatre to support Edwin at his benefit.[21] It is possibly for this reason that when the rebuilt Wargrave pri-

Lord Barrymore as Scrub in The Beaux' Stratagem.
(The Royal Collection ©2000, Her Majesty Queen Elizabeth II)

151

vate theatre opened in September as part of the earl's coming of age celebrations performers from the Richmond, rather than the Reading, theatre took part in the plays; whether the company was as good is doubtful for 'though there were the means of comparison between the gentlemen who performed for their amusement, and the ladies who made acting their profession, the former did not suffer even by the severity of the test'.[22] As we have seen, Barrymore later bespoke a benefit for the scene painter Young, at the Reading theatre.[23]

Unfortunately a series of calamities struck Barrymore. Gabriel Cox sued the earl for £449, a proportion of the outstanding debt on the theatre and after a hearing at the King's Bench before Lord Kenyon, the Sheriff of Berkshire seized the theatre, greenroom, furnishings, costumes and properties.[24] These were sold at Christie's. The following year, whilst escorting French prisoners of war from Rye to Dover, Barrymore's gun accidentally fired on Folkestone Hill, killing him. He was twenty-four years old.

The Petre Family at Thorndon Hall, West Horndon

In addition to the Earl of Barrymore Thornton also assisted the Petre family of Thorndon Hall, West Horndon, two miles south-east from Brentford, but whereas the activities at Wargrave are fully documented there is remarkably little written of the Thorndon theatricals. The hall, a splendid white-brick Palladian mansion built on an eminence in rolling parkland, was designed by James Paine and erected by the ninth earl, Lord Robert Edward Petre, from 1764 to 1770. Petre was a Roman Catholic aristocrat, the first to be visited by an English monarch, and strangely, as membership had been forbidden by the papacy, also a Freemason.[25]

A notice of the Thorndon plays appeared in the Chelmsford newspaper in 1792. This may be a case of one door closing at Wargrave in 1790 and another opening in Essex or of Thornton searching for an opportunity to use his company in private productions at an estate reasonably near one of his theatres. A satisfied visit of the family to the theatre may have been the means of the manager's entry. A matter of weeks after the permanent theatre at Chelmsford opened at least three days of dramatic entertainments were held at Thorndon. The saloon made an elegant theatre and both this transformation and the performances were under the direction

Thorndon Hall, West Horndon, Essex.
(Essex Record Office, Chelmsford)

of Thornton. The plays given were *The Busy Body* and *Rosina; The Rivals* and *No Song No Supper;* and *The Road to Ruin* and *The Farmer.* Thornton wrote a poetic address ostensibly on the theatricals but in reality it was an epithalamium on the continuing conjugal happiness of Lord and Lady Petre. He does make one reference to the theatre: an elaborate frontispiece formed the proscenium arch above which was inscribed a motto suitable for the transitory nature of the drama, 'The Follies of the Day', and this Thornton contradicted:

> No folly sure these festive Scenes display;
> They show the goodness of a Noble Pair...[26]

It is interesting that in this instance the organisation of the theatricals is ascribed to *Lady* Petre.

On the death of his father in July 1801, the tenth baron, also Robert Edward, succeeded. The new Lord and Lady Petre contented themselves with occasional visits to the Chelmsford Theatre.[27]

1. *Reading Mercury*, 15 October 1793.
2. *Reading Mercury*, 18 May 1778.
3. *Reading Mercury*, 5 August 1782.
4. Henry Angelo, *The Reminiscences of Henry Angelo* (1825), 2. 32. *Thespian Dictionary*.
5. *Morning Herald*, 26 April 1793. A remark of Charles Sharpe on the Margravine's acting cited by Boadley and Melville, *Lady Craven*, p xcv.
6. E Beresford Chancellor, *Old Q and Barrymore* (1925), pp 141 and 156. John Williams, *The Life of the Late Earl of Barrymore* (1793), pp 159 and 163.
7. Angelo, *Reminiscences*, 1. 209. Williams, *Barrymore*, pp 14-18. Winston, *Theatric Tourist*, p.71. Herbert J Reid, *The History of Wargrave* (1865), p.123.
8. British Library: 'Burney Collection of Private Theatre Playbills, 1750 - 1808', newspaper cutting dated 29 January 1789, 937 g 96. Mrs Philip Lybbe Powys, *Passages from the Diaries of Mrs Philip Lybbe Powys, 1756-1808*, ed E J Climenson (1899), pp 238-9.
9. Angelo, *Reminiscences*, 1. 313. Williams, *Barrymore*, p.111.
10. Henry Angelo, *Pic Nic* (1905), p.211. The building, which no longer exists, was referred to as a 'cottage' by a number of contemporary writers; it is likely to have been a 'cottage orné', a country house in rustic style offering slightly more room than the word at first suggests. Nevertheless, friends of Barrymore point out that the quarters were cramped.
11. *Reading Mercury*, 24 August 1789. British Library: 'Burney Collection of Private Theatre Playbills', 21 August 1789. *Public Advertiser*, 25 August 1789. Chancellor, *Old Q and Barrymore*, p165. *European Magazine*, 16 (1789), 136-7. Bell's edition (1791) of *The Beaux' Stratagem* contains an engraving, based on Samuel De Wilde's painting, showing Barrymore and Wathen in the roles of Scrub and Archer.
12. *Public Advertiser*, 3 February 1789.
13. *Reading Mercury*, 12 December 1789.
14. *Reading Mercury*, 5 January 1790.
15. Angelo, *Reminiscences*, 1. 246, 231, 2. 310. A portrait by Samuel De Wilde of Charlotte Goodall in the role of Wildair is in the Garrick Club.
16. Unidentified newspaper cutting in the British Library, Burney Collection, cited by Rosenfeld, *Temples of Thespis*, p.21.
17. Stephen and Lee, ed, *DNB*, 5.778.
18. Williams, *Life of the Late Earl of Barrymore*, p.20.
19. *Reading Mercury*, 18 January 1790.
20. Everard, *Memoirs*, p.139.
21. *Public Advertiser*, 13 August 1790.
22. *Gentleman's Magazine*, 60 (1790), 852.
23. *Reading Mercury*, 13 June 1791.
24. *Gazetteer*, 25 June 1792.
25. Alfred Franks, 'Historic Essex Mansion to Disappear', *Essex Countryside*, 13 (1965), 354. Thomas Wright, *The History and Topography of the County of Essex comprising its Ancient and Modern History* (1842), 2. 553.
26. *Chelmsford Chronicle*, 28 September 1792.
27. An instance is given in the *Chelmsford Chronicle*, 27 July 1804.

CHAPTER 11
CHANGES OF MANAGEMENT

The Retirement and Death
of Henry Thornton

The last two years of Henry Thornton's life were marked by personal loss and managerial difficulties as well as by increasingly poor health. At the beginning of 1816 Elizabeth Thornton became unwell for a short period and then died on 14 March. It was the day on which the company at Reading was performing *Where to Find a Friend* and this his wife had certainly been to Thornton. It must have required considerable tact and expertise to weld the various members of her family into a company in which there was the freedom to leave or arrive as the London seasons permitted. Thornton's gout and the sudden sacking at Oxford of a third of the total company suggest that in old age he had grown irascible and his wife was possibly the appeaser. However, the *Reading Mercury* summed up her theatrical life in the single sentence: 'In her professional pursuits and all the relations of life she was deservedly esteemed'.[1] The manager's benefit was due to be taken in the week after his wife's death and it is an indication of the need to maintain a public life that this was duly advertised in the *Mercury*, although the title of the play was not given, a rare omission on Thornton's nights. Friends and family lent their help. *The Belle's Stratagem* was eventually selected, Sally Booth arrived from Covent Garden and Edward Barnett appeared as Flutter.[2]

By August 1817, after the fiasco of Dawson's decampment with the company's takings at Chelmsford, the manager was making his farewell tour to some of the theatres of the circuit, appearing as Sir Christopher Curry in *Inkle and Yarico*.[3] Between appearances he returned to Chelmsford and settled with his son-in-law, Robert Kelham, ready to allay any fears of the townspeople which lingered after the financial debacle.[4] Various towns had provided a home to the manager during his peripatetic career: a house for the manager was built beside the theatre at Windsor

Inkle, son of Sir Christopher Curry, discovers the savage maiden Yarico in Inkle and Yarico *by George Colman.* (Author's collection)

and after disposing of this property he discovered a winter home in Gosport. His last was with one of his daughters and her husband in Essex, nostalgically as near as he could reach to his birthplace at Clare. At Chelmsford, though, he lived for less than a year before he died at the house in the High Street. He was buried during a service conducted by the Revd James Hutchinson in the churchyard of St Mary's, a building later to become the Cathedral, in a grave now lost.[5] A visitor to the pleasant garden, the transformed churchyard, knows only that somewhere in this quiet oasis the remains of a Georgian theatre manager are interred. Perhaps this is as it should be, a metaphor of the fleeting nature of the actor's art whose roles disappear at his death.

156

The parish church of Chelmsford, now the cathedral.
(The Provost and Chapter of Chelmsford Cathedral)

The Circuit changes Hands:
Bronsdorph and Jones

Although a number of the theatres which Thornton had leased or bought had been disposed of, enough remained to constitute a circuit composed of Newbury (Speenhamland), Reading, Guildford, Gosport, Chelmsford, Oxford, and Ryde. These theatres, with the exception of Oxford, Ryde and possibly Gosport, passed after Thornton's retirement into the hands of Bronsdorph and Jones. The Barnetts, busy at the Haymarket as well as provincial theatres on other circuits, either forfeited the opportunity to take over the management or were contentedly otherwise occupied at the time. A note in the *Reading Mercury* is a typical announcement of the new regime:

> Messers Bronsdorph and Jones, having taken the whole of Mr
> Thornton's Theatres [an inaccurate claim] for a term of years,
> they will have the honour of commencing their management in
> this town [Reading]; when assiduous attention to the comfort
> and convenience and entertainment of their auditors, it is
> humbly anticipated, will secure for them that patronage it will
> ever be their study to deserve....

157

The couple nailed their colours to the mast of propriety, promising to cut from the plays anything 'immoral or indecent'.[6]

Bronsdorph had been a player in Thornton's company (he advertised himself as a 'veteran Actor of acknowledged celebrity') but on entering management he relinquished this for the post of box-keeper at the Reading Theatre; Jones was an actor and Mrs Jones served as money taker.[7]

Members of Thornton's family seemed to get on well with the new administrators; the Barnetts, for example, continued to act with the company. Edward Barnett was appointed 'supervisor' at Newbury; at Guildford, although Bronsdorph was advertised as manager, Barnett was 'in sole control' and at Chelmsford he was appointed by Bronsdorph to be 'stage director and acting manager'.[8]

Possibly hoping to dispel any shabbiness of image that lingered from Thornton's day, Bronsdorph and Jones may have decided to decorate all of the theatres on the circuit, and a beginning was made with that at Reading. Franklin, who as well as being the scene painter and mechanist at Reading was also an artist at the English Opera House in the Haymarket, undertook the work.[9] Few people of any theatrical standing came to play in the theatres: the appearance of a fourteen year old youth, Duff, as Octavian in *The Mountaineers* at Guildford was a typically uninspired engagement.[10]

Chelmsford: Amhurst

Thornton's son-in-law Henry Robert Kelham held a financial interest in the Chelmsford theatre, regularly selling places for the boxes at his circulating library.[11] He invited J Amhurst to become joint-manager with himself, thus making Barnett, whom Amhurst claimed did not get on with Kelham, redundant. Amhurst was formerly manager of the Woolwich theatre and joint-manager of the Margate ; he had appeared unsuccessfully at Covent Garden but with approbation at the Haymarket as, amongst other roles, Shylock. Latterly he was a performer in the theatres at Bath and Bristol.[12] The season began in a 'spirited manner' with Amhurst taking leads in *Richard III*, *The Stranger*, *The Dog of Montargis*, *Rob Roy* and *The Blind Boy* but in spite of these performances and the redecoration of the interior of the playhouse, audiences were small. Some potential patrons were deflected to the temporary theatre hastily set up on Galleywood Common at the races by one Dobrée.[13] The following year difficulties were exacerbated by a quarrel between the Amhursts - Mrs

Amhurst was an actress in the company - and Kelham. Amhurst accused Kelham of denigrating the company before people in Chelmsford. Soon a backstage row errupted. Amhurst's account of this is graphic:

> A few evenings after [receiving a threatening letter from
> Kelham], I performed at the theatre. Mr Kelham took the
> opportunity, when he found me on the stage, of intruding him-
> self behind the scenes, and grossly insulted Mrs Amhurst.
> Feeling the insult she naturally (and all will commend her)
> detained him forcibly, until I was disengaged from the scene.
> Passion for such an insult, got the better of reason, and had I
> not, by actual force, been overpowered by my friends, I cannot
> answer but the consequences might have been fatal to this ruffi-
> an.[14]

The contending parties issued several broadsheets from one of which the above is taken. Amhurst feared for his licence. Imagining that stage spectacle might save the day, the manager announced on the bill for his wife's benefit that in two months he had spent over £600 on the enter-tainments, a sum impossible to recoup 'in the present state of Theatrical Performances'.[15] But Amhurst's hold on the theatre was short-lived. By 1821 he had disappeared from the Chelmsford scene.

Edward Barnett

Soon Bronsdorph and Jones, too, fade from the theatres and it becomes obvious that Barnett replaced them as manager and sometimes proprietor at most of the theatres. This was a sad time for Barnett for his wife, Thornton's daughter, died in the early 1820s. However, whereas a simi-lar event prompted Thornton to retire, Barnett continued quietly with his work, marshalling the company and giving its members a new lease of life. In tracing their progress around the theatres it is clearest to consid-er each in turn. There were few innovations in the productions and little by way of building took place; the great strength of Barnett and his sec-ond wife was their ability to keep the playhouses going through a period of economic depression and reaction against the theatre. A new spirit of religious fervour and earnest learning was on the increase with the set-ting up of various scientific, literary and philosophical institutes. Activities at home, such as singing and instrumental music, became more popular and, together with the reading of three-volume novels, they all contributed towards the neglect of the playhouse.

159

1. *Reading Mercury*, 18 March 1816.
2. British Library: Playbill collection, 299, 28 March 1816.
3. *Chelmsford Chronicle*, 29 August 1817.
4. *Chelmsford Chronicle*, 27 June 1817.
5. St Mary's Cathedral Church, Chelmsford: Burial Register, 16.67.
6. *Reading Mercury*, 24 November 1817.
7. *Reading Mercury*, 2 February 1818 and 3 November 1817. British Library: Playbill collection, 299, Reading, 24 November 1817.
8. *Chelmsford Chronicle*, 26 June 1818. *Reading Mercury*, 1 February 1819. Godfrey Harding, *The Opening of the Yvonne Arnaud Theatre, Guildford; Supplement to the Surrey Advertiser* (Guildford, 1965).
9. *Reading Mercury*, 8 November 1817 and 26 January 1818.
10. *The Theatre*, 2 (1819), 13.
11. Chelmsford Central Library: Playbill collection, 28 July 1819. Folger Shakespeare Library, Washington, DC: Playbill collection, Chelmsford, 5 August 1817.
12. *Chelmsford Chronicle*, 16 July 1819.
13. *Chelmsford Chronicle*, 23 and 30 July 1819. The *Theatre*, 2 (1819), 47. John Kennedy Melling, 'The Theatre at Chelmsford' in the *Essex Chronicle*, 19 December 1958.
14. Chelmsford Central Library: Broadsheet, *The Actor's Defence* (1820).
15. Chelmsford Central Library: Broadsheet, *The Accuser's Reply* (1820). Playbill collection, 8 October 1820.

CHAPTER 12
EDWARD BARNETT:
MAINTAINING THE CIRCUIT

The following theatres, originally set up by Henry Thornton, were taken over by Bronsdorph and Jones and then by Barnett, following the retirement of Henry Thornton.

Reading Theatre

The Reading Theatre season opened in September 1821 with Edward Barnett as manager; there were four playing nights in each week, Monday, Wednesday, Thursday and Saturday. Looking at the plays in the repertoire one recognises many old favourites, once staged under Barnett's father-in-law's direction. In the second week *The Honey Moon* was presented followed closely by the arrival of William Dowton in such tried pieces as *The School for Scandal* (Sir Peter Teazle), *Henry IV* (Falstaff) and *The Soldier's Daughter* (Governor Heartall). Before Christmas came Barnett's benefit, an evening of nostalgia with *The Way to Get Married* followed by his comic and serious songs.[1] The following years the plays and visitors were even more conservative: a 'wonderful' bear and 'sagacious' dog were the first to arrive, presented by Hector Simpson; the two animals gave a dance based on the plot of the popular pantomime *Valentine and Orson*, as well as taking part in a melodrama, *The Treacherous Indian*, in which the advertisement for the Newbury presentation of the show promised that the dog, Carlos, would 'evince a sagacity which, unless witnessed, could scarcely be believed'.[2] The two animals were followed by John Pritt Harley, comedian and singer at Drury Lane, playing Marplot in *The Busy Body*. Relying on his links with the Haymarket Theatre, Barnett sent for a copy of the operetta *Sweethearts and Wives* by James Kenny which had been performed there the previous season.[3] Then in 1824 came more old favourites: a visit from Mrs

Fitzwilliam of the Surrey Theatre and Drury Lane in *The Country Girl* and the theatre artist, Maxwell at this time, produced new scenes for his benefit performance of *Tekeli* in which 'a gentleman of Reading' took the role of Isidore. The theatre opened as early as February in 1825 with Dr Valpy's version of *The Merchant of Venice* (Shylock's departure at the end of Act 4 marked the finish of the play), the melodrama *The Castle Spectre* and *Pizarro* given during the early part of the season.[4] Later in the decade the standby of the juvenile phenomena re-appeared: a three year old Master Burton recited Cato's 'Soliloquy on Immortality' and Master Herbert, six years old, played in *John Bull*.[5]

In August 1825 Frances Wolfe, then twenty-six, married the fifty-five year old Edward Barnett at Newport on the Isle of Wight.[6] The pair had been born on the island and Barnett was eventually buried there. Frances was an actress with a wide repertoire at her command and a fund of prattle about the theatres in London, Chichester, Winchester, Gosport, Portsmouth and Ryde where she had performed.[7] It was his good fortune that Barnett had found another partner who was popular with the audiences and could help manage the company as well as join him on the stage. When the new Mrs Barnett appeared in the winter of 1826 she was greeted with applause and performed with her 'usual intelligence'.[8] She was petite and able to play, for example, one of the two wandering boys in the play of that title or take the lead in *The Little Jockey*.[9] There was, too, a youthfulness in her stage presence which for over a decade allowed her to play Cora, Alonzo's young bride whom she made 'interesting', in *Pizarro*.[10] Taste was changing, however, and the play which had drawn such crowds to the building was deemed to be faulty and Rolla's patriotic oration was dubbed by the local critic 'the claptrap speech'.[11]

But what of her husband's capabilities in comparison? Certainly he was a character, although in different ways to Thornton. Whatever the time of day, he wore evening dress, complete with white choker, pumps and black silk stockings. If he were about to perform, he substituted a doublet for his coat and the remainder of his clothes were as before.[12] A brief portrait of Barnett's acting style at this age shows him as Tony Allspice in *The Way to Get Married*:

> [He] reminds the spectator at once of Munden, Mathews and
> Oxberry, yet the resemblance seems to proceed from nature and
> not from imitation. At the reading of the will, he portrayed the
> feelings of hope and disappointment with great comic breadth
> and effect; and his parting with the five thousand pounds was
> rich, though rather overcharged.[13]

162

The latter was a common failing as when performing Sir Abel Hardy in *Speed the Plough.* Naturally he often assumed older roles such as Squire Hardcastle in *She Stoops to Conquer,* Crabtree in *The School for Scandal* and Polonius in *Hamlet.*[14]

One learns of the personnel of the company surrounding the Barnetts from a playbill dated 1829: the men include Barnett, Cathcart, Ennis, Hamilton and his young son, Hastings, Lockwood, Morris (also the scenic artist), Paice and Wyatt; the women include Mrs Barnett, Miss Dunbar, Mrs Ennis, Mrs Hamilton, Mrs Lockwood and Miss Walton.

References on bills and in the papers hint at the everyday theatre life under Barnett. The seats were still 3/-, 2/- and 1/- with half price admissions from 8.00 pm to the boxes at 2/- and the remainder of the house from 8.30 pm at 1/- and 6d. At the opening night of the 1829 season the box office takings of £35 were commended and this sum in spite of inclement weather.[15] Barnett, the source of places for the boxes, regularly lodged at Mr Sweetman's in the Butts.[16]

Little seems to have been done to the theatre fabric. Barnett advertised a 'considerable improvement' but the evidence was scant and the following year the building enjoyed a 'complete repair' affording 'additional comfort'.[17] Few serious structural repairs or additions appear to have taken place and as late as 1841 a town guide mentioned improvements.[18] From time to time a painter, Henry, touched up the interior.[19]

As the 1820s drew to a close, two people did much to attract interest in the Reading Theatre. The first was a local resident, Mary Russell Mitford and the second an actor in the company, James Cathcart. Mary Mitford lived outside Reading at Three Mile Cross. Although descriptive prose was her principal genre, she became interested in the drama at the age of four when she was taken to a barn theatre at Alresford and subsequently, as an adult, wrote a number of plays, two of which were staged at Reading during May 1829, *Foscari* and *Rienzi .*[20] *Foscari* was a domestic tragedy centred on the doge of Venice. Three years earlier the piece had been presented at Covent Garden, after much re-shaping.[21] 'All the actors were good,' wrote Mitford of the London production to her mother; they were headed by Charles Mayne Young in the title role and Stephen Kemble playing Francesco, the son of the doge.[22] Added to this the Venetian settings, a favourite for his easel paintings and dioramas, were designed by Clarkson Stanfield.[23] Audiences, too, were good: 'It was so immense a house that you might have walked over the heads in the pit; and great numbers were turned away in spite of the weather'.[24] Conditions were different in Reading. The playbills gave no indication of specially prepared scenery;

possibly it was the unattributed work of Morris, the scene-painter. The role of Foscari was played by James Cathcart and Frances Barnett took that of Camilla. Apart from admitting that the play was 'Miss Mitford's celebrated and highly-admired Tragedy' the advertising was for a run of the mill drama with the result that the house was only half full.[25]

Louder trumpets proclaimed the 'splendid production' of *Rienzi* later in the month. For this Morris painted new scenes. Cathcart took the title role of Cola di Rienzi, Barnett played the Captain of the Guard, Alberti, and Mrs Barnett Claudia, Rienzi's daughter, a comment on the years separating the pair. As well as undertaking the painting, Morris took on Savelli, a Lord of the Collona faction. The first run of the play had been at Drury Lane in October 1828. The plot was based on an incident related by Edward Gibbon concerning Rienzi, the Tribune of the People and a friend of Petrarch. William Charles Macready, then manager of Drury Lane, had insisted from the start - 'I think it extremely clever; some scenes are very powerful, and capable of being wrought into a most effective play' - that considerable changes, including the running together of Acts 2 and 3, should be made.[26] On completion, he was reported to have remarked patronisingly that the drama was 'a wonderful tragedy for a woman to have written'.[27]

A further drama of Mitford's, *Charles I*, was also staged in Reading. Initially (1834) it was presented in Lambeth at the Royal Victoria (later the Old Vic) Theatre, with Abbott, the manager, taking the title role and Cathcart the part of Cromwell. Macready saw the production which he disliked:

> The play is wretchedly constructed, with some powerful scenes, many passages of power and considerable effect in the sketch of Cromwell's character, which, deserving first-rate support, was consigned to the murderous hands of Mr Cathcart - a very poor pretender indeed. There was so little plot in it that I could not remember the order of the scenes.[28]

However, Mitford, who for several years reviewed for the *Reading Mercury*, enthused over the skill of Cathcart to such an extent that her counterpart on the *Berkshire Chronicle* remarked on one occasion that whilst he thought Cathcart was competent, he did not approve of Mitford's 'sickening eulogy'.[29] Cathcart had served in Burton's company - and, incidentally, performed in the Arundel Theatre - and then joined that at Bath. This he left in 1829 for the Barnett company.[30] He was married, with several children and, it was rumoured, kept a mistress.[31] An attractive man, he was slight, fair-haired, spoke fluently, though some-

MISS MITFORD's
SPLENDID PRODUCTION OF

R I E N Z I

Will be presented on FRIDAY, for the LAST time.

THEATRE, READING.

On FRIDAY EVENING, MAY 22, 1829,

Will be performed Miss MITFORD's last new popular Tragedy of

As performed at the Theatre-Royal Drury-lane, nearly FORTY Nights, with unceasing attraction and universal approbation.

The New Scenery painted by Mr. MORRIS.

Cola di Rienzi, (afterwards Tribune of the People,) Mr. CATHCART.
Stephen Colonna, (a great Nobleman of Rome,) Mr. HAMILTON.
Angelo Colonna, (his Son,) Mr. HASTINGS.
Ursini, (a great Nobleman, rival to Colonna,) Mr. LOCKWOOD.
Savelli, (a Lord of the Colonna Faction,) Mr. MORRIS.
Frangipani (a Lord of the Ursini Party,) Mr. PAICE.   Alberti, Captain of the Guard, Mr. BARNETT.
Paolo, a Citizen, Mr. WYATT.   Camillo, Rienzi's Servant, Mr. ENNIS.
Berta, Miss DUNBAR.   Tensa, Mrs. ENNIS.   Rosa, Miss WALTON.
Attendant, Mrs. HAMILTON.   Lady Colonna, (Stephen Colonna's Wife,) Mrs. LOCKWOOD.
Claudia, (Rienzi's Daughter,) Mrs. BARNETT.
Citizens, Guards, Attendants, &c. &c.

INCIDENTAL TO THE PLAY,

A Duet, by Miss Dunbar and Mrs. Ennis.

END OF THE PLAY,
" Barney Brallaghan's Courtship," by Mr. WYATT.
" THE KING, GOD BLESS HIM !" by Mr. LOCKWOOD.
A Song, by Miss DUNBAR.
A HORNPIPE, by a YOUNG GENTLEMAN of Reading.

After which the highly popular Comic Entertainment, called

RAISING the WIND.

Old Plainway, Mr. ENNIS.   Fainwou'd, Mr. LOCKWOOD.   Richard, Mr. HASTINGS.
Sam, Mr. WYATT.   Waiter, Mr. PAICE.   Servant, Mr. COX.
Jeremy Diddler, Mr. CATHCART.
Miss Laurelia Durable, Mrs. ENNIS.   Peggy, Miss WALTON.

Doors to be opened at Six, and to begin at Seven o'Clock.—Boxes 3s Pit 2s. Gallery 1s.
Admission to the Boxes at Eight o'Clock, 2s.—Half-price generally to the House at half-past Eight.
TICKETS to be had, and Places for the Boxes taken, of Mr. BARNETT, at Mr. Sweetman's, in the Butts,
R. Snare, Printer, Reading.

Playbill, Reading Theatre.
(Reading Local Studies Library)

times 'mincingly', and in conversation had a light, and at times, common, tone. However, in dealing with poetry or under the influence of passion, he gained strength and rose to dramatic heights.[32]

In 1830 Mitford daringly compared Cathcart's performance as William Tell with that of Macready:

> Mr Cathcart's William Tell is a most splendid performance, resembling Mr Macready's in intensity and power and differing from that great actor, in the absence of the colloquial familiarities which form the distinctive peculiarity of his style, and in the higher tones of personal dignity thrown over the individual character... Dignity and deep feeling were the principal characteristics of Mr Cathcart's representation of the part.[33]

The lack of men actors dictated that their roles should be played by some of the women of the company. Mitford felt it was as a Shakespearean actor that the admired reached his zenith. In 1831 *Hamlet* was staged in Reading with Cathcart as the prince. Mitford wrote:

Mary Russell Mitford.
(Reading Local Studies Library)

Edward Barnett: Maintaining the Circuit

> The mellow beauty of Hamlet's soliloquies; the gracefulness and
> variety with which he delivered the infinitely varied dialogues;
> the perpetual undulation of feeling which he threw into the
> part, and above all his time and fervid passion in the play and
> closet scene, and the terrible reality of his death, can hardly be
> too much praised.[34]

That year *As You Like It* had opened the season with Cathcart's Orlando
playing opposite Frances Barnett's Rosalind. Mitford concentrated on the
actor's vocal prowess: '[Cathcart] delivered the fine poetry of the part
with a nice perception of the sense, and a delicious embodying of the
music of the verse, rarely equalled on any stage'.[35] Of Frances she commented primly that the actress had 'preserved the tenderness and delica-
cy of the woman, under the doublet and hose'.[36] In the same season
Cathcart also gave Reading *Macbeth* - this time Mitford's over-zestful
comparison of her hero was with John Philip Kemble - and Shylock. 1832
brought the opportunity to perform with Miss Phillips of Drury Lane in
Romeo and Juliet. Cathcart's 'intonation in some of the earlier dialogues
with Juliet (Phillips) came over the ear like strains of sweet music, whilst
his energy and pathos in the last act bore along the feelings of the audience with an irresistable sway'.[37] It was reported that Miss Phillips was
delighted with her co-star.

Cathcart appears to have had an arrangement with Barnett that he
would be released each year from the end of May to play for a short season at Covent Garden. Here was an opportunity for him to stretch his
wings and to discover a less partial critique of his work than that supplied
by Mitford.[38]

At the time of the theatre's construction Friar Street appeared to be full
of new buildings but by 1841 it had succumbed to time's ravages. The
area between the playhouse and Broad Street had become a maze of narrow courts in which the poor resided. Drainage was defective; several
households shared a single tap as well as a privy; the reek from a slaugh-
ter-house was overpowering; the noise from the pig market at the rear of
the theatre was disturbing and cases of cholera were common.[39] Although
in this year Barnett prepared for the season by 'improving' the theatre,
the next few years saw, as might be expected in an unsalubrious district,
indifferent audiences.[40] The redecorations seemed to be merely cosmetic
and by 1847 Henry, another painter, was working on the auditorium, in
addition to creating the scenes and acting.[41] A bill for Barnett's benefit at
the end of the 1841 season reveals that Mrs Barnett appeared in lieu of
the veteran, hot foot from the farewell performances to Alfred Bunn at
Drury Lane. She repeated the role of Meg Merrilies in *Guy Mannering*.[42]

By 1853, in his eighty-fourth year, Barnett had decided to retire from management at Reading. A report made in that year suggests it was a good time to go: the playhouse was 'such a mass of ruins that playgoing folk did not feel certain that they would come out again safe and sound and if this was escaped, more assuredly cold and rheumatism would not pass them scatheless'.[43] The benefits that year brought in larger numbers than other performances had. On the final night of the season Mrs Barnett held hers, playing in *The Honey Moon*, supported by the London actress Miss Beaumont. The manager was too elderly to appear and earlier the 'gentlemen amateurs' of the town had presented to him their tribute prologue. A subscription was opened to make a financial testmonial to him; the advertisement for this claimed that he had been manager for over fifty years at Reading. The miscalculation may have arisen by counting from one of the times when Thornton left his son-in-law in charge of the theatre and company during periods of sectionalisation.[44]

Newbury

As a young officer Lord William Pitt Lennox was stationed in 1817, the year of Barnett taking on the management of the theatre under Bronsdorph and Jones, at Donnington, a village a mile outside Newbury.[45] Thirty years later Lennox incorporated his visits to the Speenhamland playhouse into the plot of his novel *Percy Hamilton*. Some sentences give a first-hand impression of a performance under the Barnetts. The three principal characters, a couple of young bloods and Hamilton's tutor, were lodging at the Pelican, one of the most expensive inns in the vicinity.[46] They set out one morning to lionize the town and began with the theatre where they hid in the gallery:

> 'Strangers in the house,' shouted the young, black-eyed syren, who was *en dishabille* in a morning wrapper, a coat ornamented with cat-felt fur, hair dressed en papilotte, a faded black velvet bonnet, with a tarnished red feather dangling from it... 'Mr Budd,' continued the enraged prima donna, addressing the prompter, 'if people are allowed to come into the theatre during the rehearsals, I'll throw up my engagement.' 'Clear the gallery,' shouted the manager in a voice that would have scared even the privileged few that are admitted into St Steven's; 'if such an occurrence happens again, I'll dismiss the door-keeper.'[47]

Edward Barnett: Maintaining the Circuit

That evening Hamilton together with Heythrop, Beaufort and Hook took seats in a stage box for the benefit night of Miss Levison with whom Hook had fallen in love. The mainpiece, *The Merchant of Venice* had ended, and the entre-acte entertainments had begun:

> ...after a pause, the curtain drew up for the characteristic dance, and discovered a gentleman in 'fleshlings', pink tunic, light flowing locks, and a young lady dressed, if such a word can justly be applied to one whose only garments consisted of a low blue satin bodice, ornamented with ribands, and a thin scant white guaze dress.

> The side wing prevented my getting a full view of the dancers; all I could see was the lover upon his knee, and the lady standing upon the light fantastic toe, her other limb extended in the air, her body thrown back, and supported by a wreath of artificial roses.... After remaining in this attitude for a few seconds, amidst the plaudits of the house, mingled with the 'Oh, dears!' of a few straight-laced antiquated spinsters, who were hiding their wrinkled visages in their fans, and who were evidently shocked by the Terpsichorean display, both dancers recovered their equilibrium, and, encircled by each other's arms, tripped towards the footlights. Another burst of applause welcomed this movement, when, judge of my horror and dismay at finding the gauze-apparelled dancer to be the object of my daily thoughts - my own long-lost Celine! My brain was on fire; my pulse beat high; I felt as if I could have sunk upon the spot.

Hamilton staggered from the box, through the lobby and into the square. Lennox's thumbnail sketch of Gilder's Square, not flattering, is worth quoting, for it reflects the response of many Newbury theatre-goers attending the winter seasons in the nineteenth century:

> The keen and biting wind whistled through the small, dreary space that led to the theatre; the snow that had fallen for the last hour had given a bleak, desolate look to the scene....

Though Barnett tended to invite few visiting actors to the stage of the Newbury playhouse, several performers may be mentioned. In March 1823, recently returned from a tour of America, Edmund Kean brought with him the Shakespeare parts he had performed there, the title roles in *Richard III*, *Othello*, Shylock (*The Merchant of Venice*) and *King Lear* ; additionally he presented Sir Giles Overreach (*A New Way to Pay Old Debts*). In London Lord Byron had been reduced to a state of hysteria by the final moments of the last play. A similar effect in Newbury is not

169

reported.[48] After Kean's visit Simpson brought his dog and bear and finding that there was a calling for these animals, Barnett followed up their visit in 1825 with the spectacular Bohemian horse drama *Der Freischutz*. The mayor attended and it was agreed that here was an opulent production mounted to great effect.[49] Unmoved by the troubles Thornton had experienced when employing horse troupes, Barnett went on to engage that of Woolford and West. Short of accommodation, the horses were stabled in a slatted gallery above the passage from the actresses' dressing room. A performer, Robert Dyer, told of a mishap:

> Mrs Kendal, a most lady-like woman, arrayed in all the finery of
> a Slave, was waiting her call, when a fall of water deluged her
> splendid attire, and made her appearance, in time for that
> evening, an impossibility. She sent the dresser to Barnett, stating
> her pitiable condition; he replied: 'My compliments to Mrs
> Kendal, I excuse her attendance, as I feel satisfied it is impossible
> to appear under the auspices of Messers Woolford and West'.[50]

Other visitors were less hazardous. Master William Robert Grossmith, an infant phenomenon, travelled from the Reading Theatre to appear in Newbury in 1826 and then proceeded to Hungerford, Ramsbury (a small village on the Berkshire/Wiltshire border where the theatre was a temporary fit-up) and on to Salisbury.[51] The Grossmith family - William Robert, brother Benjamin and their father - arrived later in 1840 but by that time the playhouse was intermittently shut for long periods so that they played in the Mansion House.[52] Three visiting pugilists were a novelty: Crawley, Richmond and Randall gave a demonstration of 'The Art of Self-Defence' which was followed by *The Beaux' Stratagem* in which a gang of rogues attack and enter Lady Bountiful's house - a possible further employment for the boxers.[53]

Gilder, as proprietor of the theatre, was responsible for the good order of the fabric which in 1829 was fitted with a new interior. Gas lighting had been installed in 1825 and the time had come to rectify the wear and tear caused by audiences.[54] Although little indisciplined behaviour is reported, on one occasion a couple of years before the renovation, three local boys threw crackers from the gallery into the boxes which caused consternation.[55] The boxes and gallery were constructed of wood - hence the danger of the misdemeanour - and when renewed were painted by Morris. Gilder took the opportunity to construct a set of upper boxes which may indicate that the audience, unlike the diminishing numbers at Reading, was composed of a wide social structure.[56] Appropriately at this time Barnett decided that the company as well as the building could be

170

overhauled and on their return to Newbury from Andover - an untypical visit on a temporary lease - this was put into operation. After the races the company opened at Reading.[57]

Barnett jogged along quietly until 1833 when he paid his final visit to the theatre at Speenhamland. Whether the finality was premeditated or not is difficult to say. Then the manager journeyed to Guildford.

Guildford

Having been appointed in 1819 by Bronsdorph and Jones, Barnett had taken the lease on the Guildford Theatre by 1821.[58] Untypically, from the start of his management Barnett invited a long line of visitors. Here, as at Reading, came Harley singing in his counter-tenor voice, followed the next year, 1823, by Paulo the clown and Heath, the 'inimitable Harlequin'. There was, of course a harlequinade after which Paulo gave a show of strength: a 600 lb weight was placed on his body and three Guildford smiths struck it sixty times with sledge hammers. Supporting this entertainment was *John Buzzby* with Barnett playing the title role.[59] That same year, as part of the tour of his theatres, Barnett brought Edmund Kean to Guildford where he again surprised people with the ferocity of his Richard III and Sir Giles Overreach.[60] In 1826 a former member of the company who had gone on to play at the Haymarket, the Lyceum and Covent Garden, Mrs Orger, arrived and was seen in *A Day after the Wedding* and for her benefit *Midas*.[61] Maria Foote of Drury Lane and Covent Garden performed in the extremely cold winter of 1827 the role for which she was famed and reckoned to be more skilful than Madame Vestris, Maria Darlington in *A Roland for an Oliver*. Renowned for her transvestite roles, Foote played Rosalind (*As You Like It*) with aplomb and also took the roles of Lady Teazle (*The School for Scandal*) and Letitia Hardy (*The Belle's Stratagem*). Here was an opportunity for Barnett to raise the box seats to 4/- and those in the pit to 2/6d.[62] Clara Fisher from Drury Lane followed immediately with her battery of comic songs as well as the serious male role of Young Norval in *Douglas*.[63] Mrs Barnett must have been thrilled to play Catherine (*The Taming of the Shrew*) opposite the Petruchio of Henry Johnston of Covent Garden. A swash-buckler, he also gave the title role of *Rugantino*, written especially for him by Matthew Gregory Lewis.[64] *Black Ey'd Susan* enjoyed an enormous popularity and it was an added incentive to visit the theatre in 1832 to see the initiator of the role of William the sailor, T P Cooke. He also played Long

Tom Coffin in *The Pilot*.[65] David Fisher III who had led an East Anglian touring company with, amongst others, a theatre at Sudbury near to Thornton's birthplace, maintained the link by joining Barnett's company at Guildford for the 1838 season and was useful in his two capacities as actor and violinist.[66]

There was a regularity about the patronage at the Guildford Theatre. Two of the dancers, Miss Lidia and Miss Thomassin were sponsored on each of their benefit nights by the 'Batchelors of Guildford'. In 1836 the two women played no part in the dramas staged on their benefit nights but between pieces they performed a variety of dances including a Highland Fling, a Bolero and the two paired for a Garland Dance. In his end-of-the-century guide to the town, John Mason declared that these two performers were, together with Wyatt the comedian, the 'stars of the company'. The following year Miss Lidia, under the same patronage, took the role of Julietta in *The Dumb Girl of Genoa*.[67] Miss Gordon had belonged to the Barnett company before she progressed to Drury Lane, playing such roles as Gertrude in *Hamlet* and Emilia in *Othello*. From 1834-8 the Town Clerk, Joseph Hockley, sponsored five of the annual benefits the tragic actress earned on her return visits to Guildford. Hockley's death in the last benefit year at the early age of 52 put an end to Miss Gordon's appearances here.[68] Officials of this town were more inclined to bespeak performances than those in other places. The Mayor desired *Speed the Plough* when Wilkinson arrived from the Haymarket Theatre; the Bailiffs supported Mrs Barnett's 1827 benefit when she played in *The Clandestine Marriage*; and the Aldermen of the Borough sponsored W Keene's benefit performance of *The Cure for the Heart Ache*.[69] Lord and Lady Grantley regularly offered their financial support at benefits and other times.

Barnett appears to have pursued a policy of gradually redecorating each of his theatres during the mid-1820s and he had obviously hoped to do this at Guildford by 1825. However, patrons had to wait until the following year to see any improvement in the interior; possibly the artist had been too busy with his scenes for *Der Freischutz*, Channing, also an acting member of the company, was responsible for redecorating the auditorium here. Stressing the difference in the appearance, Barnett misleadingly referred to the building as the 'New Theatre'. The major improvements were on stage where there was a recently painted front curtain, an act drop and various new scenes.[70] At the beginning of the 1840 season Barnett announced again that a new act drop and 'a variety of new scenery' had been created by Channing.[71] Presumably this consisted of stock subjects as there is no indication in advertising *The Rivals* that new scenes were to be used. In the early 1840s structural alterations were made to the auditorium with the addition of an extra tier of boxes. Barnett readjusted the admission prices by lowering them - a most unusual ploy at this time - to 6d (gallery), 1/- (pit), 2/- (upper boxes) and 2/6d (lower boxes).[72] The only other change to the house was the introduction of gas lighting as late as 1847.[73]

Some indiscipline occurred in 1839 in the gallery. An episodic version of the newly published serial, *Nicholas Nickleby*, was presented by two visiting players, Mr and Mrs Charles Hill. The bill of the day gave details of the lengthy series of scenes and at the end of each the orchestra struck up with the first eight bars of 'The Light of Other Days'. These repetitions were more than the gallery was prepared to tolerate; volleys of orange peel hit the deck amidst much whistling with the result that Barnett was forced to employ a Peace Officer (three of these and a sergeant were available in the town) to eject any of the unruly. However, this breach of decorum seems to have been exceptional. That places for the boxes at this time could be obtained from the circulating library, indicates the general respectability of the Guildford theatre.[74]

The theatres at Oxford, Gosport and Ryde seem not to have been a part of Bronsdorph's and Jones's short-lived circuit but to have been managed by Barnett from the date of Thornton's retirement, 1817.

Oxford

Thornton's last visit to Oxford had been made in 1815 and it was not until 1827 that Barnett was advertising that the rackets court in Blue Boar Lane would be fitted as a theatre ('our little elegant theatre' it was soon termed) in preparation for an eight week season.[75] There was a small rise in admission prices to 3/6d for a box seat with the pit and gallery remaining at 2/- and 1/- respectively. A season ticket cost three and a half guineas. Box places could be reserved at Randall's the boot maker and hatter in the High Street. The gallery doors opened at 6.15 pm and other parts of the house could be entered at 6.30 pm ready for a 7.00 pm start. There was the usual stipulation that backstage admittance was not allowed. Performances were given on six nights of the week, a burden first imposed in Thornton's day.[76]

The repertoire of the first week showed an extreme conservatism but Oxford approved and there were shouts of applause at the close of each play: the opening entertainment was *The School for Scandal* and other

Blue Boar Lane: the theatre in Christ Church lay to the left of the lane.
(University of Oxford, ms Top Oxon. a. 48, no 41)

familiar titles such as *Macbeth, The Merchant of Venice, The Steward, The Way to get Married* and *Speed the Plough* followed.[77] During the season the diet was one of Shakespeare, Sheridan (the comedies and *Pizarro*), Lewis (inevitably *The Castle Spectre, Raymond and Agnes* and a spectacular revival of *The Wood Daemon*), Goldsmith, Mitford (*Foscari*) and Pocock (*The Miller and his Men* desired by the students of Mr Allen's Seminary at Kidlington). Various amateurs appeared on the stage and one wonders whether they filled a role in an emergency or were ready to pay for stage experience. One, 'well-known in the fash-

ionable world' took the role of Moses in *The School for Scandal*, requested by Lady Churchill; another, who unfortunately did not know his
lines, played Caleb Quotem in *The Wags of Windsor*; Dr Pangloss in *The
Heir at Law* was also played by a non-professional. Miss Taylor received
a double-edged compliment for her performance of the title role in Jane
Shore: 'her deportment throughout was ladylike and good; and in the
fifth Act in excellent keeping with the character; if, as has been inti-
mated, it was the first time of her undertaking it, there can be little
doubt but she will, on the second representation, do it infinitely better'.
No repetition was given in Oxford. A catastrophe occurred during
Romeo and Juliet. Hooper of Drury Lane, playing Mercutio, was badly
cut by Tybalt, using a sharp pointed officer's sword. Mr Cleobury, a
surgeon, was in the house and dressed the wound. At the end of the
season the newspaper editor looked forward to Barnett receiving permission to perform the following year; in his final curtain speech the
manager reinforced this expectation, stressing that no immorality lay in
stage representations.[78]

In 1828 Barnett failed to materialise. There are various possible reasons: permission may have been refused by the Mayor and Vice-
Chancellor; there may have been a difficulty in leasing a suitable hall; or
limited finances may have prompted Barnett to work on a reduced scale.
The following year the company was again performing in the Christ
Church rackets court. Plays of the 1827 season were repeated with only
two new works: *Invincibles*, a musical comedy long in preparation, was
presented for a week as the after-piece and Mitford's *Rienzi* was given a
showing. That Oxford was looking for family entertainment is evident
from the 'juvenile night' when children were admitted to the boxes at
half-price to see *The Midnight Hour* and, unsuitably, *Blue Beard*. By the
last night of the season, when *The Way to Get Married* was shown, the
company had become so popular that the orchestra was forced to move
behind the scenes in order to release the space for spectators.[79]

The inexperienced again took major roles: Miss Hamilton played
Rosalind in *As You Like It* and a pupil of George Bartley of Covent Garden
arrived from London to play Juliet. Notes on the company players in the
former piece were given in the Oxford paper. Mrs Barnett was praised for
the entertainment value of her roles, the singing of Miss Gaunt and
Yarnold was commended, Miss Gordon (a good Celia) was thought to be
inexperienced 'but should prove capable' - a forecast which, with her
translation to the patent house, came true - Miss Dunbar (Phoebe) tended to be dismissed as a player of small parts, Gattie (Touchstone) con-

fronted his audience with 'truth', Hooper (Orlando) was a 'decided favourite', Mr and Mrs Renaud were correctly respectable and Wyatt was noted for his comic songs.[80]

In passing it may be noted that Jackman, the manager of the Banbury, Woodstock and Aylesbury theatres, was performing at Bicester during Barnett's Oxford season. *Pizarro* was one of the dramas given with Alonzo played by a loudly applauded local amateur; Rolla was also due to be taken by an amateur but the manager received a note an hour before the performance that he would 'not be allowed to perform'. Was this an Oxford student aspiring to the stage who thought of venturing to Bicester only to be barred by university officialdom? Somehow the gap was plugged.[81]

When the company returned in 1831 the long prologue to *Hamlet*, written by Mary Mitford, was spoken by Cathcart:

> Romantic Oxford! mid thy cloister'd bowers,
> The tapering spires, bright domes and fretted towers,
> Thy world of antique beauty, throned high,
> Sits the proud muse of Grecian Tragedy.

The progress of the muse was traced from Thebes through to Stratford and the writings of Shakespeare:

> Hamlet the Dane! oh! but to follow well
> The lessons which he gives were to excel
> In our great art - the very rules we tell
> Might we but practice, little were our need
> For your indulgence even now we plead:
> Yet plead we must, yet hopefully, for here
> In this fair circle, small our cause of fear;
> Kind were ye ever! and our greeting blends
> Warm thanks to pass with hope of future friends.[82]

Mitford's work was seen several times during the season. In September her play *Julian* was staged and the author journeyed from Reading to Oxford to see Cathcart in the lead and then returned the following week for *Foscari*. Other than this new writing there was little of note in the repertoire.

The spirit of discipline at the Oxford Theatre, commended the previous season, was smirched when during *The Rivals* Miss Gordon (playing Julia) was hit by an object flung from the gallery; she was escorted off the stage by Cathcart.[83] Other performers fared better: an 'interesting little prodigy', Fanny Marshall, took part in the dancing; Barnett as Marmaduke Magog in *Wreck Ashore*, was described as an authority-conscious parish beadle and his characterisation of Mr Timid in *Dead Shot* was reported to be a 'gentleman of forty with very weak nerves [who] exerted himself to the utmost and kept the house in a constant roar of laughter'. Mrs Barnett's Rosalind (*As You Like It*) was praised for 'vivacity and good taste'.[84]

A cholera epidemic broke out in the city in 1832 which may explain why there was no theatre season; however, not only did Barnett return in 1833 but also to a new location.[85] Possibly Christ Church was unable to provide the rackets court; instead that in St Mary Hall (now subsumed within Oriel College) was 'handsomely and commodiously fitted up'.

The exterior of the St Mary Hall (now subsumed within Oriel College) real tennis court.
(Oxford City Council)

The court is tucked behind the houses on the west side of Oriel Street and that its walls were made only of rubble would have mattered little to Barnett.[86] The company welcomed some new performers: Brooks, Brougham, Hutchings, Langley and Stuart were accompanied by Miss Andrews, Miss George and Miss Scruton. Some former members - and comparisons may be made with the company of four years previous, recorded above in the Reading section - were Gattie, Morris, Renaud, White and Wyatt; Mrs Barnett, Mrs Brooks, Miss Gordon and Mrs Renaud. As before the orchestra was under the direction of Richard Barnett, the manager's son. The season began with *Rob Roy* with an opening address, written by an Oxford citizen and delivered by Hannington. In it he presents, for us, a conundrum:

> ...for though forced to roam
> From yonder spot that was our former home....

Why the company had roamed - and were they forced? - still needs to be solved.[87]

The players, of course, continued to be banned during term and in the vacations students were not allowed to attend the theatre. With these strictures in mind verses, 'Oxford in Vacation', were published in the local newspaper. Out of term the town was accused of being dull but the theatre offered some light entertainment:

> There's a theatre, too, to amuse
> Conducted by one, Mr Barnett
> And (however Bullees may abuse,
> And call him a devil incarnate,
> Or the swells with comparisons odious
> May sigh for the joys of Old Drury):
> He has actresses fair and melodious,
> And actors all right, I assure ye.
>
> Miss Crawford's black hair and bright eye
> Are indeed most remarkably pretty,
> I've a sympathy quite with her sigh -
> Or smile - when her mood's to be witty:
> It does one quite good in the dance
> Miss Lidia's dear person to ogle;
> And Miss Western's [ie Weston's] sweet sparklers enhance
> Her archness when acting some low girl.
>
> Mr Balls is excessively funny,
> Nor less so are Gattie and Wyatt;
> They've an Irishman worth any money,
> And Stuart, one may actually sigh at...[88]

St Mary Hall proved to be impracticable and Barnett decided that when he visited the city in 1836 his location would be a purpose-built theatre. He obtained a site in Red Lion Yard and kept a careful eye on the builders, although his description of the new structure is imprecise:

'The boxes are on nearly the same scale as on former occasions; the pit much more capacious and the gallery smaller than before'.[89] This may be a reference to the St Mary Hall theatre which was noticeably narrower than the court at Christ Church.[90] A sketch published by Shrimpton and Son shows the front stage right, orchestra and side boxes. The whole internal structure is made of wood; a proscenium stage is flanked by proscenium doors and a row of Argand lamps stands across the front of the acting area; the orchestra pit allows only for a single row of musicians; behind them people are arranged on backless benches; two tiers of boxes may be seen each crowded with an influx of half a dozen spectators, some of whom sit on the front ledges. When undergraduates attended Barnett's Victoria Theatre - as they might for variety shows and musical events but not the drama - they found the place 'a glorified barn which afforded a fine field for low-class representations of every kind...'.[91]

A row of shops in Magdalen Street ran in front of the theatre; next to that of Richard Stevens, a fruit-seller at number 9, was a doorway through which the box seats were approached and places for these could be booked at the shop at 3/6d each. Pittites entered from George Lane (now Street) at an admission of 2/- and the gallery at 1/- was entered through Red Lion Square. Season tickets could be purchased for £4.4/- (boxes) and £2.10/- (pit). Barnett claimed that his theatre was 'compact and convenient' and that the whole audience sat near the stage. It was also well-lighted and ventilated.[92] This building served Barnett for the remainder of his professional life until his retirement.

Gosport

Barnett's visits to Gosport were by no means as regular as Thornton's and the seasons were much shorter. The company, after a 'long absence' appeared in October 1823, opening with the tried favourites of *Rob Roy* and *Past Ten O'Clock*. A completely repaired and newly painted theatre was commended to Barnett's patrons in advertisements. Four performance nights a week, Monday, Tuesday, Thursday and Saturday, were advertised. Major Despard of the Seventeenth Regiment desired *Exchange No Robbery* and *Simpson and Co*, allowing the band to play on this night. In November Dr Burney of the naval college desired *Town and Country*; an 'Ode to Freemasonry', especially written by Fortescue and spoken in the 'proper costume', hints at Burney's affiliation.[93]

Under Two Managers

At the end of the 1825 season a couple of days before Christmas, having played Paul Pry in John Poole's play of that name, Barnett gave a curtain speech in the manner of John Liston, a London actor who specialised in the role. Barnett and Liston would have known each other from Barnett's visits to play at the Haymarket Theatre where Liston was employed on a permanent basis. Looking at a couple of sentences one wonders whether Barnett was aware that he would be without the theatre building when he returned to Gosport the following year:

> I hope I do not intrude [words of Paul Pry which became the tag
> of Liston], but if it is not an impertinent question, may I ask
> have our exertions during the season met with your approval,
> eh?... I wish you'd ask me to dine. I should like to breakfast,
> dine and sup with you for three months to come, at any rate I
> shall leave my umbrella; and so will some of the performers
> you've supported and just drop in for us next session, when I
> hope to see the same merry faces I saw.[94]

When he returned ten months later he discovered the doors of the playhouse shut against him:

> Mr Barnett feels that in announcing the commencement of a
> Season, the Public will naturally expect some explanation that
> they should be invited to a Temporary Theatre, when for so
> many years they have by their liberality supported a regular
> one: at a moment when the whole proceedings of this extraordi-
> nary ejectment are undergoing a legal enquiry, it might appear
> invidious and unjust to prejudice the public mind by an
> 'exparte' statement of the circumstances.

Removed from the theatre in Middle Street - negotiations were in hand between the proprietor and an Independent congregation to buy the building and adapt it as a chapel under the ministry of the Revd Mr Macconnell - Barnett set about looking for a base, which he discovered in the Market House and created a fit-up there. Performances were projected for Mondays, Tuesdays, Thursdays and Fridays. Again, the plays selected were those frequently presented, *The Rivals*, *A Roland for an Oliver*, *Speed the Plough* and, for the opening night, along with a choral rendition of the National Anthem, *The School for Scandal*.[95] Subsequent visits seem to have been few. A poster exists for a performance of *The West Indian* for Stanley's benefit under the patronage of the 'Gentlemen Subscribers to Messers Martin and Cox's Reading Room' and is dated possibly 1833 (the print has faded). By this time performances were given in the Town Hall although Barnett refers to the building simply as

'Gosport Theatre'.[96] This may have been the company's last appearance in the town. In spite of Gosport's position on the south coast, the company does not appear to have combined a visit to Gosport with the journeys to Ryde.

Ryde

The administration of the Ryde Theatre was taken over by Barnett in 1818 and he continued until 1853.[97] John Coleman, who acted in this theatre, has left a list of the company members at the time when Barnett became manager: Harry Craven, Tom Fry, William Shalders, Francis Waldron (who died in 1818) and his son; the women, who outnumbered the men, were Mrs Addison, Miss Clare (Mrs Barnett's niece), Miss Eardley, Miss Fanny Hughes (later Mrs Gaston Murray), Miss Agnes Kemble (later Mrs Clifford Cooper) and Miss Love (later the first Mrs Herman Vezin). This company differs in personnel from that on the mainland. Performances were given on only three nights of the week to 'pretty good' houses. Coleman writes of the time he worked with Barnett, playing the part of Francis the servant, in *The Stranger*. Giving the command to bring his two children from the nearby town, Coleman's order was followed by a long howl from a small child in the gallery. 'Beg pardon, sir,' interpolated Barnett, 'but isn't that one of 'em up yonder?'[98]

For his benefit Coleman chose *Hamlet*. The gender imbalance dictated that many of the younger and more flamboyant men had to be impersonated by women. The prince was surprised to be presented with a Hamlet costume by these members of the cast and equally amazed to find that Charles Kean and his wife had arrived at curtain-up to join the audience in the boxes. 'You've knocked 'em,' was Barnett's cheery commendation after the play.

By the 1820s, as the following newspaper report shows, Ryde had been established as a seaside resort:

> Our season may now be said to be at its height and never at any former period has it been so crowded with fashionable and most respectable company. The marine Promenade, the Pier which affords an ever varying scene is thronged to excess every evening until dusk when the public rooms at the Library become the scene of attraction... Our Theatre, which has been newly decorated, opened on Monday last to a very good house, and we hope the exertions of Mr Barnett, the manager, will meet with every success.[99]

Under Two Managers

A ball at the Library and the Regatta offered opportunities of patronage and in this Earl Spencer took the lead. One of the most popular visitors of this season was Mrs Orger.[100]

By the 1840s something of this pizzazz had evaporated leaving a workmanlike group, efficient but not inspired. The Barnetts' daughter was appearing in the plays – conservative to a degree with revivals of *Lodoiska*, *The Poor Gentleman* and *Lovers' Quarrels* – under the patronage of Sir James Caldwell.[101] It has to be admitted that not many visiting performers of renown traversed the Solent to Ryde, although mention may be made of T P Cooke, Charles Mathews, Benjamin Webster, Madame Celeste and Kate Terry (the sister of Ellen).[102]

1. *Reading Mercury*, 24 September, 1, 22 October, 3 December 1821.
2. *Reading Mercury*, 10 March 1823.
3. *Reading Mercury*, 7 October 1822, 22 December 1823.
4. *Reading Mercury*, 19 January, 16 February 1824, 7, 14 and 21 February 1825, 4 July 1831. Dr Richard Valpey, headmaster of Reading School, was in the habit of adapting Shakespeare's plays for the pupils to perform; earlier his version of *King John* was given at Covent Garden and described in the *Monthly Mirror*, 15 (1803), 347.
5. *Berkshire Chronicle*, 4 April 1829. *Reading Mercury*, 12 May 1828.
6. *Hampshire Telegraph*, 8 August 1825.
7. *Berkshire Chronicle*, 26 February 1870.
8. *Berkshire Chronicle*, 4 March 1826.
9. *Reading Mercury*, 31 May 1830.
10. Reading Central Library: Playbill collection, 11 and 25 April 1829.
11. *Reading Mercury*, 6 June 1831.
12. Coleman, *Fifty Years of an Actor's Life*, p.493.
13. *Berkshire Chronicle*, 12 February 1825.
14. *Berkshire Chronicle*, 4 March 1826. Reading Central Library: Playbill collection, 4 and 18 May and 8 June 1829.
15. Reading Central Library: Playbill collection, 7 April 1829. *Berkshire Chronicle*, 11 April 1829. *Reading Mercury*, 13 April 1829.
16. *Reading Mercury*, 24 September 1821.
17. *Reading Mercury*, 7 October 1822 and 24 November 1823.
18. William White, *A Description of the Town of Reading including its Origin and History* (Reading, 1841), p.55.
19. *Theatrical Times*, 2 (1847), 367.
20. Mitford, *Dramatic Works*, p.viii.
21. W J Roberts, *The Tragedy of a Blue Stocking* (1913), p.218. W A Coles, 'Mary Russell Mitford,the inauguration of a Literary Career', *Bulletin of the John Rylands Library*, 40 (1957), 33-46.
22. Mitford, *Dramatic Works*, p.83. Phyllis Hartnoll and Peter Found, *The Concise Oxford Companion to the Theatre* (1992), p.559.
23. Roberts, *Blue Stocking*, p.277.
24. Constance Hill, *Mary Russell Mitford and her Surroundings* (1920), p.224.
25. Reading Central Library: Playbill collection, 8 May 1829. *Reading Mercury*, 11 May 1829.
26. Philo-Dramaticus, 'A Letter to Charles Kemble. Esq., and R W Elliston, Esq., on the Present State of the Stage', *Blackwood's Edinburgh Magazine*, 17 (1825), 727-731. Mary Russell Mitford,

Edward Barnett: Maintaining the Circuit

The Friendship of Mary Russell Mitford as recorded in letters from her Literary Correspondents, ed A C L'Estrange (1882), 1. 151.

27. S C Hall, *A Book of Memories of Great Men and Women of the Age* (1871), p.438.

28. William Charles Macready, *The Diaries of William Charles Macready*, ed William Toynbee (1912), 1.164.

29. *Berkshire Chronicle*, 21 May 1830.

30. *Reading Mercury*, 13 April 1829. Odell, *More about the Old Theatre, Worthing*, p.68.

31. Vera Watson, *Mary Russell Mitford* (nd), p.186.

32. *Reading Mercury*, 31 May 1830.

33. *Reading Mercury*, 24 May 1830.

34. *Reading Mercury* 16 May 1831.

35. *Reading Mercury*, 9 May 1831.

36. *Reading Mercury*, 9 May 1831.

37. *Reading Mercury*, 1 June 1832.

38. *Berkshire Chronicle*, 28 May 1829.

39. H Lee, *Report to the General Board of Health on a Preliminary Enquiry into the Sewage, Drainage and Supply of Water* (1850), pp 22, 32 and 34. Reading Central Library: John Snare, map of Reading (1842).

40. White, *Reading*, p.55.

41. *Theatrical Times*, 1 (1846), 207; 2 (1847), 367.

42. Reading Central Library: Playbill collection, 20 December 1847.

43. Daphne Phillips, 'Troubled Theatre of Reading' in *Heritage*, no date; cutting in the provincial files in the study collection of the Theatre Museum. The citation is unattributed.

44. *Reading Mercury*, 12 March 1853. *Berkshire Chronicle*, 19 March 1853. *Jackson's Oxford Journal*, 19 March 1853.

45. Lennox, *Recollections*, p.644.

46.   The famous inn at Speenhamland
          That stands below the hill
          May well be called the Pelican
          From its enormous bill.

Cited by Roberts, *And so to Bath*, p.287.

47. William Pitt Lennox, *Percy Hamilton* (1851), 2. 181.

48. J Fitzgerald Molloy, *The Life and Adventures of Edmund Kean* (1888), 1. 248.

49. *Reading Mercury*, 16 and 30 May 1825.

50. Dyer, *Nine Years of an Actor's Life* , p.225.

51. *Reading Mercury*, 7 and 14 August 1826.

52. *Reading Mercury*, 25 April 1840. Derek Forbes, 'The Earliest Grossmiths and their Pictorial Playbills' in *Scenes from Provincial Stages: Essays in Honour of Kathleen Barker*, ed Richard Foulkes (1994), pp 65-87, *passim*.

53. *Reading Mercury*, 19 January 1829.

54. Ken Shaw, 'The Rise and Fall of the Theatre Royal', *Newbury Weekly News*, 23 August 1979.

55. *Reading Mercury*, 5 November 1827.

56. [Sybil Rosenfeld and Richard Southern], 'On Listing Theatres', *Theatre Notebook*, 1 (1945-7), 3: information supplied to the writers by Derek L Sherborn.

57. *Reading Mercury*, 19 January, 16 February, 9 and 23 March 1829.

58. University of Surrey, Guildford Institute: 'Scrapbook of Playbills', 1. 2, 3, 5, 9 August 1823.

59. University of Surrey, Guildford Institute: 'Scrapbook of Playbills', 1. 21 July 1823.

60. Russell, *Guildford*, p.188.

61. University of Surrey, Guildford Institute: 'Scrapbook of Playbills', 1. 3, 6 and 8 July 1826.

62. Russell, *Guildford*: p.188. [?] Clarke, *The Georgian Era*, 4. 577. University of Surrey, Guildford Institute: 'Scrapbook of Playbills', 1. 8, 9 and 10 February 1827.

63. University of Surrey, Guildford Institute: 'Scrapbook of Playbills', 1. 19 February 1827.

64. University of Surrey, Guildford Institute: 'Scrapbook of Playbills', 1. 5 and 10 March 1827.

65. University of Surrey, Guildford Institute: 'Scrapbook of Playbills', 1. 3 and 4 July 1832.

66. Grice, *Rogues and Vagabonds*, pp 114-5.
67. [John Mason], *Guildford* (privately printed, 1897). p.18. Guildford Museum: Playbill collection, 7 November 1836. University of Surrey, Guildford Institute, 'Scapbook of Playbills', 2. 16 November 1837.
68. Playbills in the Guildford Museum and the Guildford Institute.
69. University of Surrey, Guildford Institute: 'Scrapbook of Playbills', 1. 19 March, 29 March, 2 April 1827.
70. University of Surrey, Guildford Institute: 'Scrapbook of Playbills', 1. 7, 16 June 1825 and 14 June 1826.
71. Guildford Museum: Playbill collection, 22 June 1840.
72. Guildford Museum: Playbill collection, 7 July 1843.
73. Guildford Museum: Playbill collection, 4 October 1847.
74. Theatre Museum: Peter Davey's manuscript notebooks, vol 28, playbill inserted in the notebook. *Russell's Guildford Directory* (Guildford, 1842), p.33.
75. *Jackson's Oxford Journal*, 30 July 1831.
76. *Jackson's Oxford Journal*, 21, 28 July, 4 August 1827.
77. *Jackson's Oxford Journal*, 11 August 1827.
78. *Jackson's Oxford Journal*, 4 August - 6 October 1827, *passim*.
79 *Jackson's Oxford Journal*, 18 July - 29 August 1829, *passim*.
80. *Jackson's Oxford Journal*, 5 and 19 September 1829.
81. *Jackson's Oxford Journal,* 15 August 1829. Leman Thomas Rede, *The Road to the Stage* (1827), p.11.
82. *Jackson's Oxford Journal*, 16 July and 27 August 1831.
83. *Jackson's Oxford Journal*, 20 August 1831.
84. *Jackson's Oxford Journal*, 30 July, 6 and 27 August, 1831.
85. Hibbert, *The Encyclopaedia of Oxford* , p.168.
86. Royal Commission on Historical Monuments, England, *Inventory of the Historical Monuments in the City of Oxford* (1939), p.168.
87. *Jackson's Oxford Journal*, 26 June and 6 July 1833.
88. *Jackson's Oxford Journal*, 3 August 1833.
89. *Jackson's Oxford Journal*, 2 July 1836.
90. Bodleian Library: John Johnson Collection, 'Oxford Theatrical Amusments', 1892 -, unattributed newspaper cutting, M Adds 129 b. 9.
91. Alan Mackinnon, *The Oxford Amateurs* (1910), p.41. *City of Oxford Directory* (1846), p.3.
92. *Jackson's Oxford Journal*, 25 June, 2 and 9 July 1836.
93. *Hampshire Telegraph*, 13 and 21 October, 10 November 1823. British Library: Playbill collection, vol 426, Gosport.
94. *Hampshire Telegraph*, 24 December1825. Iain Mackintosh and Geoffrey Ashton, *The Georgian Playhouse* (1975), section 7.
95. *Hampshire Telegraph*, 16 and 30 October, 13 November 1826. British Library: Playbill collection, 20 October 1826, 5 February 1827.
96. Gosport Museum: Playbill, the date is difficult to decipher but is probably either 1832 or 1833. British Library: Playbill collection, 269, Gosport, 20 November 1833.
97. New York Public Library: William Douglas manuscript notebook.
98. Coleman, *Fifty Years*, pp 494-7.
99. *Hampshire Chronicle*, 15 August 1825.
100. *Hampshire Chronicle*, 5 September 1825. *Hampshire Telegraph*, 29 August and 5 September 1825.
101. *Theatrical Times*, 2 (1847), 287 and 296; 3 (1848), 404.
102. Jones-Evans, 'The Royal Theatre, Ryde', *Hampshire County Magazine*, 15, (1975), no 4, pp 54-55.

CHAPTER 13
EDWARD BARNETT: VENTURES

The company returns to Croydon

Thornton had relinquished the lease of the Croydon Theatre to Elliston in 1810 and then lost interest in the playhouse. Not so Barnett. During Elliston's managership, in 1812, he appeared as Percy and his wife as Angela in a production of *The Castle Spectre*.[1]

Nineteen years later he was to be found managing the theatre as well as appearing on the stage, this time lit by gaslight rather than oil lamps. He was following a disarrayed and poorly attended season under the direction of a Mrs Hall who had invited Edmund Kean to appear but the indifferent stage support he had received 'mortified' the actor with the result that he gave muted performances.[2] In the course of Barnett's season *Hamlet* was staged with the manager as Polonius bringing light relief to Cathcart's title role. The Croydon newspaper critic dealt more harshly with Cathcart than Mitford had; as a fencer he was not proficient and as a verse speaker he was boisterous and self-indulgent.[3] By the end of that first season the consensus was that the company had 'exerted themselves... effectually' and this in spite of noise and riot in the gallery.[4]

Barnett visited the theatre regularly until 1839. Many of the productions were as he had staged them at his other theatres complete with identical performers and roles, decorated with scenery by Miller which appeared to be taken from place to place. The artist's task of painting did not preclude him acting as well. Barnett's partiality for the plays of Sheridan Knowles - one of his few nods to contemporary writing - introduced the Croydon audience to *The Hunchback*, *William Tell* and *The Wife*. Knowles himself had taken part at Drury Lane in the first of these pieces, playing the title role of Master Walter. At Croydon Cathcart and later a newcomer, Bennett, took the lead.[5] Douglas Jerrold was another favourite with performances of *Black Ey'd Susan, Richard Parker, The Rent Day* and *The Housekeeper.* Several modern gothic pieces held an appeal; one such was *The Vampire* or *The Bride of the Isles* by the prolific James Robinson Planché. Barnett promised:

> The piece commences with the Enchanted Vision, raised by the powerful influence of Guardian Spirits, to protect the Innocent. Their Incantation produces the Marvellous Appearance of the Vampire.... Great effect is produced in the Basaltic Caverns of Staffa, and at the Tomb of Cromah. The piece concludes with the Annihilation of the Vampire.[6]

The Croydon Theatre, Crown Hill, from The Surrey Magazine *(September 1904).* (Croydon Archive Service)

Each season must have flown by, for a local historian was complaining in 1834 that the theatre was 'seldom open'.[7] There were some uncertainties: Barnett heard that the building, of which he was an annual tenant, was mortgaged to the classical architect Sir John Soane who by 1835 was believed to be preparing to sell it. What was Soane doing with a theatre? A possible explanation is that he held it in readiness for the use of his playwright son but later quarrelled with the young man. All however went well for Barnett until 1839 when performances ceased and the theatre was transferred to Burnett's neighbouring premises for use as a potato warehouse.[8]

Chichester

In addition to Croydon, where he was at least known and had played in earlier days, Barnett decided on two new ventures that same year, the theatres at Chichester in Sussex and Bath in Somerset.

Prior to 1764 Dymer had brought a company to Chichester, playing in the long room of an inn; but from that time Chichester possessed a dedicated theatre, situated at the lower end of South Street. The original was a malthouse, converted by Samuel Johnson, which held in the region of £40. Thomas Collins, leader of the Salisbury Comedians, succeeded in management. It was he who had leased the Portsmouth theatre with which Thornton had vied in his productions at Gosport. Collins was responsible for rebuilding on the same site the new Chichester playhouse of 1792 with money raised from a tontine. The new building, put up by Thomas Andrews of St Pancras and one of the subscribers to the tontine, held £50 to £60. Its external measurements were 102 feet by 32 feet. This was a venture in which the Duke of Richmond, with his seat near the city at Goodwood, showed a keen interest, advising on the design and giving scenery which had been used in his own private London theatre at Richmond House, Whitehall. These scenes were of some quality painted by artists of the calibre of the father and son team of Drury Lane, the Greenwoods. Sadly Richmond House was burnt down at the end of 1791.[9]

Barnett began his visits to the city in 1828 and repeated them until 1832, travelling here after he had finished his Croydon season.[10] The repertoire was that common to his circuit. In 1829 *Virginius*, with Cathcart in the title role, was played. On another evening *Pizarro* was presented with Cathcart playing the Inca chieftain. Several touches of humour lightened the casting of this play: Morris, the artist, took the Blind Man and Manager Barnett played the High Priest. Morris produced a fine set of scenes for *The Forty Thieves*, showing not only the interior and exterior of Ali Baba's dwelling but also woodland, lakeside and cavern scenes. Possibly Morris, whose work as actor, scene painter and theatre decorator at Newbury and Reading was noted in the previous chapter, became a local resident for after Barnett ceased to visit Chichester he continued scene painting and acting for the Davenports, managers in 1835.[11]

There was little to distinguish the everyday arrangements from those at the other theatres on the circuit. Box seats sold at 3/-, upper boxes at 2/6d, with the pit and gallery remaining at 2/- and 1/-. At 8.45 pm half price could be obtained, 2/-, 1/6d, 1/- and 6d. Doors were opened at 6.30 pm and the entertainment started at 7.00 pm. By this date a theatre manager's professional status was above reproach and Barnett and his wife were able to lodge amongst the august society of the cathedral close with a Mr Budden.

The Chichester Theatre from The Theatric Tourist *by James Winston (1805).* (East Sussex Record Office, Chichester)

Bath

Chichester was not Barnett's only venture into new territory; he also leased the Theatre Royal at Bath intending, he assured the house in a curtain speech, to 'associate himself permanently with the Bath Theatre' but after a single season he left the concern, defeated.[12] This was a difficult time: the previous manager, Benjamin Bellamy, had attempted a period of diversification, mounting from 1828 Italian and English opera, tragedy, comedy, spectacle and pantomime but to little profit with the result that he resigned in 1833. That same year the theatre was advertised to be let by tender and Barnett submitted his bid.[13] He found a building, constructed in the main by John Palmer, commanding a prominent position in Beaufort Square. Peculiarly stylish was the north or 'Grand' front by George Dance the Younger.[14] Within, pillars of cast iron supported each of the circles and there were twenty-six boxes entered through one of the houses owned by the theatre. A suite of retiring rooms added comfort and made for elegance. The ceilings were covered with paintings by Andrea Casali, bought at the sale of effects at Fonthill Abbey.[15] The season opened on 26 December 1833. Admission prices were boxes 4/- , pit 2/6d and gallery 1/-, reducing when half price was allowed to 2/6d and 1/6d with no half price in the gallery.[16] The Barnetts lodged in the house in Seymour Street of Edward B Prattinton who, although a letting agent, was an enthusiastic collector of theatrical ephemera which he eventually bequeathed to the Society of Antiquaries.[17]

The new manager drew together a company consisting of some of the players of the previous dispensation, Mr and Mrs Woulds, Aldridge, Montague senior, Mulleney, Mrs Ashton and Mrs Darley, as well as newcomers to the city most of whom we have already met, Miss Atkinson, Miss Gordon, Miss Malcolm, Miss Weston, Edmunds, Hannington, W Keene, Lee, Stuart and Wyatt. As might be expected, many of the plays staged were tested and tried drawers of audiences, including *Macbeth*, *The Country Girl*, *The School for Scandal* (Mrs Barnett played Lady Teazle), *Jane Shore*, *Speed the Plough* (Barnett played Sir Abel Handy) and *The Heir at Law* with the Barnetts playing Lord Duberly and Cicely Homespun. The guest appearance of James Wallack did not extend the repertoire. *Hamlet* was staged and Wallack presented a petulant prince; although his forte was the melodramatic hero, in this Shakespeare play he was judged to be no better than a provincial actor. The company was uneven. Higgie played Claudius in a 'low, sepulchral voice', difficult to hear and lacking in regality, Hannington brought a sharp quick pace to the role of Hamlet's father's ghost although a member of the audience claimed he was not tall enough, Miss Gordon's Queen Gertrude was 'without animation' and, greater deficiencies, Miss Malcolm's Ophelia lacked imagination and pathos. The actor playing Laertes did so under duress and was so wretched that sarcastic 'Bravos!' rang through the house. Wallack shone in Rolla (*Pizarro*) but the women of the company were feeble. Another visitor was Sheridan Knowles who successfully introduced a number of newish plays, including his own, such as *The Wife*, *Virginius* with Knowles in the title role, *The Beggar of Bethnal Green* with Knowles as Lord Wilford and *The Hunchback* with Knowles again in the title role. Unfortunately in the last play Miss Malcolm (Julia) was unequal to the task. She was not alone for Knowles was criticised when he appeared in his works at Drury Lane: his voice was pitched too high and although possessed of a good eye his face presented a 'rather fat intelligence'.[18] Several interesting dramas were presented. One was the documentary *Jonathan*

Bradford or Murder at the Road-side Inn; Connor and Morris provided the scenes which showed the George Inn on the Oxford Road. There was too a dramatisation of the novel *American Cooper* with the listed locations and incidents of the Rocky Scene, the Cabin of the *Ariel*, the Guard House, American Drilling, the Combat between Long Tom Coffin and Sgt Drill and Barnstable led to his execution. In spite of these successes, though, the company had difficulty in finding time to learn the new plays and the prompter's voice was frequently in evidence. Nor were the stagehands sufficiently rehearsed: the two halves of the demi-scenes on occasion did not match when they finally slid togther amidst much quivering.[19]

At the end of the season Barnett relinquished the lease unable to make the theatre pay and Woulds, together with Macready, took on the management for a couple of years but then they became insolvent.[20]

1. British Library: Playbill collection, 276, Croydon, 2 October 1812.
2. *Croydon Chronicle*, 4 December 1830 and 12 February 1831.
3. *Croydon Chronicle*, 3 December 1831.
4. *Croydon Chronicle*, 26 November and 10 December 1831.
5. Richard Brinsley Knowles, *The Life of James Sheridan Knowles* (1872), p.89.
6. Croydon Archive Services: J Corbet Anderson, 'Croydon Theatre, Old and New', paste-up of playbills.
7. G S Steinman, *A History of Croydon* (1834), p.15.
8. Page, 'Recollections of Old Croydon', typescript, p.3. *Gentleman's Magazine*, (1860), 218. George Soane (1790-1860) was both novelist and playwright. His cliffhanger, *The Falls of Clyde*, was highly popular in its day.
9. Winston, *Tourist*, p.56. *Universal British Directory*, p.603. William Pitt Lennox, *Celebrities I Have Known* (1876), 1. 270. Francis Steer, *The Chichester Theatre*, Chichester Papers 9 (Chichester, 1959), pp 6-7. Alexander Hay, *The History of Chichester* (Chichester, 1804), p.396. Winston, *Tourist*, p.57. Rosenfeld, *Temples of Thespis*, pp 48-52.
10. Brighton Central Library: Playbill collection, 18 November and 12 December 1829. *Croydon Chronicle*, 3 December 1831.
11. British Library: Playbills, 275, Chichester, 8 December 1829 and 1835, *passim*.
12. Belville S Penley, *The Bath Stage* (London and Bath, 1892), p.132.
13. William Lowndes, *The Theatre Royal at Bath* (1982), pp 46-7.
14. V C Chamberlain, 'Resetting a Stage' in *Country Life*, 4 November 1982.
15. *Bath Directory, 1841* (Bath, 1841), np. *Original Bath Guide* (Bath, 1815), pp 86-7. *Original Bath Guide* (Bath [1853]), pp 47-8. Ian Stewart, 'A Dream Fulfilled' in *Country Life*, 23 December 1982.
    Casali was a native of Civita Vecchia. His ceilings were decorated with a scheme of deities, described by James Lees-Milne as 'insipid'. Fonthill was sold entire to John Farquhar, a millionaire gunpowder merchant, in October 1822 and a year later, just before Farquhar's death, disposed of piecemeal by Phillips the auctioneer. The paintings may now be seen at Dyrham Park near Bath. See: James Lees-Milne, *William Beckford* (Tisbury, 1976), pp 13 and 75-6.
16. Bath Central Library: Playbill collection, Bath, 7 January 1834.
17. *Bath Directory, 1841*, np. The Society of Antiquaries still holds the Prattinton Collection.
18. *Morning Chronicle*, 6 April 1832.
19. *Bath Chronicle*, 2 - 23 January 1834. *Bath Journal*, 6 and 13 January 1834. Bath Central Library: Playbill collection, various bills, 2 January - 23 May 1834.
20. Lowndes, *The Theatre Royal*, p.46.

CHAPTER 14
WHAT BECAME OF THE THEATRES?

When Thornton or Barnett left a theatre, any temptation to explore the progress of that building further has been resisted. However, it is unsatisfactory to leave the various playhouses without a brief note of their later development or, more often, their slow disintegration. The theatres fall into two main groups: there are those which Thornton, suspecting that he would have slight success in building a regular audience, abandoned and those which he built up over the years and which passed, after vicissitudes, to Barnett's management.

Firstly, the theatres that Thornton relinquished are listed in alphabetical order below.

Alresford

Much uncertainty veils the theatre in Alresford. After Thornton, Minton took over the management in 1808. He had appeared alongside Hatton at the Haymarket Theatre, taking minor roles such as the Waiter in *Three and the Deuce* and a Servant in *Sylvester Daggerwood*.[1] By 1808 he assumed the management of the Alresford theatre, adding to this that of Andover in 1809 and Fareham in 1810. He fades from the Alresford scene at this point.

Andover

Although Thornton had taken the trouble to arrange for purpose-built premises which he might lease in Andover, he visited the town for only a few years and by 1809 Minton brought his company in May and June.[2] Dorothy Jordan came to Andover to perform in 1813 and a playbill for 1816 suggests that the theatre regularly staged performances until that date and possibly later.³ A sign of the acceptability of the fare to the townspeople at the latter date is indicated in the Bailiff's patronage of a new comedy *Smiles and Tears.*⁴

A Market House was opened in 1826; above the arcaded selling area was a large room which served for the council, for assemblies and as the theatre.⁵ Hannam became manager. Rawlins' small storehouse theatre fell into decay and was demolished in 1842.⁶

Arundel

Trotter and the Worthing company seem to have enjoyed greater success than Thornton in the new theatre next to Tompkins' mother's house. Bills for this are few; one exists for Harley's benefit under the patronage of the Bedford Regiment for *The Wonder* in which Trotter played Don Felix.⁷ By 1823 another member of the Worthing company, William Burton (later to become manager of the National Theatre in New York), had undertaken the management and one of the visiting personnel was Clara Fisher who came to Arundel in 1827.⁸ That same year James Cathcart was in the company together with his wife.⁹ Two years later the Chaplin family, Chaplin, his wife, his son, his eldest daughter and two further girls, Miss H and Miss E Chaplin, were the lessees presenting the 'Musical and Dramatic Prodigy', Master Burke, in the role of Young Norval (*Douglas*).¹⁰ By this time the theatre was functioning but spasmodically and the last opening took place in 1833 with a performance of *The Beggar's Opera.*¹¹ It is noteworthy that at this babes in arms were charged double price.¹² Charles New, Arundel's miller, pulled the place down the following year and built a house on the site of the stage which the Duke bought and leased to tenants.¹³ When the need arose - for example, for the appearances of Ira Aldridge, the 'Black Roscius', under the patronage of the Duke in 1847 - the Town Hall was fitted up.¹⁴ By this time Holmes was the manager, a singularly inept fellow who dragged several theatre companies, including that at Newbury, into serious debt.¹⁵

Dorking

The Industrial Revolution caught up with the King's Arms Inn; a large section of the establishment became a foundry in the early nineteenth century. Sometimes the King's Head Inn in the north-west angle of the

High Street was also used as a theatrical venue. Collins, a Dorking artist, described a visit to this fit-up in 1807: '...there being four candles to light us all, two of which by nine o'clock (no doubt frightened by the company) hid themselves in their sockets'.[16]

East Cowes

After several tentative visits to his theatrical base, Thornton seems to have abandoned Cowes. Yachting helped to establish the community of West Cowes at the expense of the area to the east during the first part of the nineteenth century and the theatre building may have been left out on a limb.[17] Possibly a replacement but temporary playhouse came under the management of Shatford of Lymington - or his successors, Shalders and Penson - as a company from the mainland made a one night stand at Cowes in 1797.[18]

Fareham

The existence of a Thornton theatre in Fareham, a shadowy proposition, is strengthened by the news that Minton, who often followed in Thornton's footsteps in early nineteenth-century Hampshire, was playing there in 1810. Originality was eschewed either by Minton or his audience and such old favourites as *The Castle Spectre* and *A Tale of Mystery* were staged.[19]

Farnham

After Thornton's initial seasons at Farnham at the beginning of his career as manager, he seems not to have returned to the town. By 1793 management is ascribed to Duckworth. Mysteriously, a young man named Luttrell claimed he was the son of the theatre manager and in spite of being an 'inanimate barker' acted in the town.[20] By the time of the Barnett regime, plays were staged in Farnham by J Morgan. It is difficult to tell whether he was merely staying in the Goat's Head Inn or if this was the location of the fit up. In the 1840s the Assembly Room at the Goat's Head was used for one man shows such as the visit of the 'Professor of Elocution', Mr J P Anderson, with his recitations from Homer, Cowper and

Scott.[21] From the arrangements at the theatre one is impressed by the conservatism at Farnham: bills show that there is the usual pattern of main and after-piece with an interspersion of songs and recitations, the seats are the traditional prices of 3/- , 2/- and 1/- , the doors open at 6.00 pm for a 7 pm start and the bills state that no one is allowed behind the scenes. In the 1850s a room in the Bush Hotel was used for fit ups. An ad hoc company composed of players from a number of London theatres presented such fare as the current hit *Time Tries All* and James Robinson Planché's *Faint Heart Never Won a Lady.*[22] By 1890 the venue had changed to the Corn Exchange in the Borough, inconvenient premises lacking emergency exits and toilets.[23]

Henley

We left the Henley Theatre at the point at which Thornton sold it in 1795 to Penley and Jonas. The composition of the company is reflected in the bill of 1798 advertising *Every One Has his Fault:* Penley played Sir Robert Rumble and Jonas Solus; W[illiam?] Penley was also in the troupe and non-family members included Newman, Healey, Griffith, Thompson and Shirelock. The main piece started at 6.30 pm and the nights of performance were Monday, Tuesday, Thursday and Saturday.[24] By 1805 the two managers had decided to build a replacement in New Street. Designed and constructed by William Parker, surveyor and timber merchant of the town, it was large enough to contain a double tier of boxes. Paintings in the playhouse were by Mottram of Drury Lane.[25] William Dicks disgraced the bargemen of Newbury in 1812 by coming over to this theatre where, during the performance, he threw a quart mug of beer from the gallery into the pit. He was taken into custody and only a printed apology saved the man from prosecution.[26]

A bill dated 1811 for Fenton's company exists. They gave *The Poor Gentleman* at a building nominated 'Theatre, Henley' but whether this is the New Street building is doubtful as only a pit and gallery are mentioned in the disposition of the house.[27] The Fentons were a breakaway group from the Cheltenham-based company managed by John Boles Watson II and the son, then only about eleven years old, developed into a lively and competent actor.[28]

Parker's building still stands in New Street and is used as a regular playhouse, the Kenton Theatre. It claims to be the fourth oldest theatre in England.

Horsham

There were three buildings at Horsham which served as theatres: the Town Hall, the King's Head Hotel and the rambling warehouse in Denne Road in which Thornton possibly set up his stage. He abandoned the town in 1791. Unclear about which of the three premises, Davey states that George Stanton (a member of the extended theatrical family) became manager in 1801. That same year Stanton was injured in a duel with Ensign William Bunn; both men had developed a common romantic attachment. Then Thomas Haymes, who also played in Dorking and was thus following in Thornton's walk, came to Horsham in 1804. The ball-room of the King's Head continued to be used for fit-ups; a season in 1819 is recorded.[29] A playbill of 1823 for *She Stoops to Conquer* refers to the 'New Theatre' but again the location is unspecified.[30]

Hungerford

Of Hungerford there is little to report. The Town Hall which Thornton visited at the beginning of the nineteenth century was leased for a season by Minton during the twelve months April 1807 to April 1808, for which he was charged £10/5/-.[31] A new Town Hall and Corn Exchange to one side of the former building was started in 1870 and the earlier demolished in 1872. Thriftily some of the materials were used to build cottages in Church Street.[32] The complex has served as a venue for professional travelling theatre, amateur productions and for films.

Southend

Wewitzer and Trotter each managed a theatre in Southend after Thornton's short managership at an uncertain location. The playhouse which Trotter built and opened in 1804 became the principal Southend theatre, although the building was very small.[33] Attendances at the town's theatres tended to be thin with the result that Trotter administered his for just six years before leasing it to Samuel Jerrold, manager of the Sheerness Theatre who was looking for a summer venue.[34] After Jerrold's managership a succession of lessees took over, including Chester in 1837 and Warren in 1841. Trotter died in 1851 and the theatre was sold first to Forrest and in 1859 to Susannah Clarke, who closed and demolished the building.[35]

Weybridge

When Thornton left Weybridge *c.*1810 the theatre failed and Lady Tuite converted the building into dwellings, presumably adding to the existing tenements the one in which Mrs Smith, the wife of the former manager continued to live. The property was sold to Robert Hyde, a baker, in 1822. At the beginning of the twentieth century the place was pulled down in order to widen Baker Street.[36]

The former Weybridge Theatre, the white building on the right of the street, painted by Ada Currey in 1882. (Elmbridge Museum, Weybridge)

Windsor

Only a year after he bought the Windsor Theatre, Mudie felt the lash of the *Monthly Mirror* complaining about the badness of the company, although Mrs Mudie and Chatterley, the male lead, were exempt from stricture.[37] That same year the Independents (later known as Congregationalists) of Bier Lane (subsequently River Street) bought the freehold of the theatre with a view to turn it eventually into a chapel. Minton extended the area of his circuit considerably when he leased the theatre in 1809. Possibly he overreached himself because three years later Penley and Jonas, who managed the nearby Henley Theatre, became lessees.[38] In spite of some poorly attended seasons, by 1815 the proprietor had completed a new theatre in Thames Street. The building was

196

semi-circular with iron columns supporting two tiers of boxes. On stage proscenium doors were still in use with a manager's box above each. 'Durability and neatness' were factors in its construction. The interior decorations were by Thomas Lupino, a scenic artist of Covent Garden and the scenery was painted by Thomas Greenwood of Drury Lane.[39] From the latter, according to Thomas Gilliland, one could expect settings which were 'bold, impressive [and] effective'.[40] The previous theatre was rapidly transformed into a chapel for the Congregationalists and used by them until 1832 when the worshippers acquired a new building. Occasional fractures in the body of the faithful resulted in factions returning to the old transformed theatre from time to time.[41]

After Amhurst: Chelmsford

After the unsuccessful season of 1821 Amhurst and his wife went on to open the West London Theatre (known later as the 'Dust Hole') in Tottenham Street, London, providing his patrons with a replica of the productions staged at the Surrey. By 1822 he was forced to sell by auction the theatre's costumes during which enterprise the stage collapsed. It was a symbol of Amhurst's unstable powers of management.[42]

One might assume that Barnett, who had been given a position of responsibility at Chelmsford, would have taken up the management. He spurned this. The reason can only be conjectured: his relationship with the Kelham family was reported to have been unhappy; the geographical location of Chelmsford, removed from the rest of the circuit, may have posed travel problems; and the theatre building may have been in a run-down condition in spite of an interior coat of paint.

A succession of managers followed. William Hall, who styled himself 'Pupil of the Late Mr Thornton' leased the playhouse in 1830. A few of the old company joined him; there were Hillington and Lacey and Mrs Fawcett, the sister of Mrs Orger, who as the Misses Ivers, readers of the *Chronicle* were reminded, had both been members of Thornton's company; they performed *Black Ey'd Susan* under the patronage of the Stewards of the Races. To make the building acceptable the interior was yet again re-painted.[43] Harvey took over in 1832 with a company drawn disparately from theatres at Manchester, Southampton, Birmingham, Newcastle and Bristol. In spite of this there were insufficiencies: amateurs had to be lured onto the stage and the orchestra wanted numbers. Weak himself as an actor, Harvey performing in Otway's *Venice Preserv'd* was advised by the newspaper to stick with comedy.[44] He only lasted the one season and in 1833 the management passed to Chapman and Manders, the first serving as stage manager and the latter as acting manager. Manders began by playing the laughing bailiff Tom Stag in *Captain Stevens* but he soon succumbed to an illness and even on his benefit night was unable to appear. In this season Edmund Kean visited Chelmsford.[45]

These single season stands point to the parlous condition of theatre companies in the 1830s. The general opinion of them was summed up by a writer in the newspaper of nearby Colchester:

> In the provinces theatrical amusements are at a discount. Men
> are not now such fools as to expend their time and money in
> seeing men and women make fools of themselves. If the march
> of intellect has done nothing else, it has well nigh marched
> players out of the English counties... Few respectable people are
> ever found within the walls of country theatres.[46]

Yet at this time Barnett was making a success of his carefully selected circuit of theatres and an indication of the pleasure the Chelmsford theatre could give its patrons, even in its last year of performing, is conveyed by the experience of John Round MP of Danbury Park who in 1836 went after dinner with several of his friends to a bespeak of *Perfection* and *A Roland for an Oliver*. The performances, he wrote, were 'very tolerable' and the theatre was well attended 'considering how much theatricals are discouraged at Chelmsford'.[47]

Progress, however, put an end to the theatre in the town. The building, together with a number of neighbouring houses, was purchased for demolition and in its place New Bridge Street led to a cast-iron bridge which crossed the River Can.[48]

After Barnett

For the sake of easy cross-reference this clutch of playhouses is dealt with in the same order as in the previous two chapters.

Reading Theatre

At the time of Barnett's retirement the Reading Theatre was in a parlous state of decay, cold and discomfort. At eighty-three Barnett himself was too old to see to the many repairs required and he moved to Ryde with his wife.

One of Barnett's own actors, T Fry, replaced him. At once the new manager moved the company to the New Hall in London Street; here an adaptation was made and the building became the Theatre Royal opening with *Uncle Tom's Cabin* in May 1853. Although at the curtain speech on the last night of the season Fry promised many improvements to the premises, it was not to be: there was a return to the old theatre in Friar Street the following summer. Unfortunately the skill of the company had reached a low ebb: lines were not known, production was faulty and in consequence the house indifferent. Finally, fifteen years after Barnett's relinquishment of his theatre, it closed and performances of plays were moved - but only for a short time as the building burnt down in 1870 - to the Assembly Rooms further along Friar Street. With the cessation of the Georgian playhouse the last links with Barnett and Thornton were broken.[49]

Newbury

After Barnett's last visit in 1833 the theatre at Speenhamland remained empty for ten years until the arrival of E T Holmes, a London actor who had taken on the management of the Brighton Theatre, leaving that for Newbury and later decamping from here in favour of Winchester. Unfortunately he chose a bad month for his visit as, with many a flourish, the new Literary and Scientific Institution was opening in the town.[50] However, the company managed to persuade the Mayor, G S Higgons, to offer his patronage to a performance of *The Lady of Lyons* with the afterpiece *Raising the Wind* in which Holmes appropriately played the part of Jeremy Diddler, a short-sighted sharper.[51] The summer of the following year Holmes spent in Penzance elaborating on his financial plight in a begging letter to the Marquis of Downshire: his wife was pregnant, his children delicate and for his part, he was attempting to raise money by giving readings from Shakespeare in Plymouth.[52] At the end of August he returned to Newbury where in desperation he put his wife on the stage but the season was not a success and, owing money to many of the townspeople, Holmes appealed to the curate of Speen to help him make a quick get-away from a difficult situation.[53] Ten years later the manager was in similar trouble in Winchester.

The buildings of Gilder's Square were sold in 1883 for £1800; these included the cottages, five dwelling houses with shops, a builder's shop and yard, a further yard and offices and the theatre. Bereft of its players this served later as cowshed, auction rooms and furniture warehouse.[54]

Gilder's Square and the Newbury Theatre in decline.
(Theatre Collection, University of Bristol)

Above these activities was the pretty plasterwork of the ornamented ceiling which was often photographed by various preservationists.[55] From the front facade the portico was removed and the cottages at the sides of the square became uninhabitable. On a frosty morning in 1976 bulldozers reduced the theatre to a memory.

Guildford

In spite of his advanced years, Barnett managed the Guildford theatre - with his wife's help - until 1852. It was reported that the last play his company performed was *High Life Below Stairs*.[56] By 1860 the building had become a warehouse (Platt's Furniture Repository) overtaken by the building of a hall in North Street in which visiting companies took the stage. Thornton's and Barnett's playhouse was demolished in 1889.[57]

Oxford

Life at the Victoria Theatre altered little after Barnett's retirement. A renovation of the building was made in 1866 by the sole lessee Henry Groom, the Oxford printer and the 'Directress' was Margaret Eburne who wrote and spoke the opening address.[58] This is a rare instance in which the theatre presented plays in the Christmas vacation; during term the veto on the drama was still in force. However, undergraduates might attend variety shows with impunity and a range of artistes which included Vance, Jolly Nash and a troupe of Japanese acrobats regularly performed. On the whole the undergraduates were presented with 'vulgarities and indecencies' to which the young audience responded with 'questionable jokes and rampant rowdyism', so much so that on many occasions the police had to be called.[59] Indeed Groom hired members of the City Police to stand at each entrance every evening to preserve 'order and regularity'. Companies which visited the city either played in the Town Hall (as did Toole's), or the temporary theatre leased by Hooper, a former member of Barnett's company, who performed at a variety of theatres which included a return to the St Mary Hall rackets court, the Assembly Room at the Star Hotel in Cornmarket Street and further use of the Town Hall.[60] A few travelling managers were accommodated at the Victoria - the building enjoyed a number of titles ranging through the Old Vic, the Vic, the Royal Victoria Theatre and the Theatre Royale - amongst whom was Frank Benson, a former member of the OUDS who came in October 1883, the year in which he established his own company. Many undergraduates illicitly attended Benson's repertoire of Shakespeare, Farquhar and Sheridan. In his memoirs he described the reception:

> ...the pit had to take umbrellas to shield themselves from being
> pelted and spat on by the gods in the gallery.... The front row of
> the stalls spent most of the time in destroying the instruments
> of the orchestra or putting them hopelessly out cf tune. The
> dress circle would rush on to the stage, via the boxes, dance
> with those *prima donnas* who were pretty, engage in pugilistic
> encounters with the officials and actors, or attempt to give
> impromptu performances of their own, until driven back to
> their places by volleys of stones, sticks, bricks, eggs, oranges, tea
> and potatoes from pit and gallery. The only calm moment was
> when all undergraduate sections of the house united in a sauve
> qui peut from a raid by the proctors and their bulldogs. Then
> windows, doors, drain-pipes, roofs and stage ventilators were
> quickly broken in a rapid and undignified flight.[61]

The days of the Vic were numbered. Vice-Chancellor Benjamin Jowett, a devotee of the serious drama, determined that the 'wretched, dismal, tumble-down structure', which he judged to be a fire risk, would give way to a replacement. Slightly to the east of its predecessor the New Theatre rose, opening its doors on 13 February 1886 for a student performance of *Twelfth Night*.[62] In 1933 on the same site T P Bennett and Sons built the second New Theatre, decorated with the sculptured panels (Harlequin and Opera) of Eric Aumonier.[63] This theatre, now the Apollo, still functions.

Gosport

The complex consisting of manager's house, coffee house and the theatre which Thornton originally built in Gosport's Middle Street was used as a chapel for nonconformist worship, shops, domestic residences and a warehouse. The buildings still stand at 125-6 High Street (1998 numbering). One of the original doors to the theatre vestibule can be seen.

The doors of the Gosport Theatre
(Gosport Records Society)

Ryde

By the 1860s the Ryde Theatre had begun to shows serious signs of wear and had become a 'paltry, insignificant erection'.[64] In this it resembled many other provincial playhouses which by the second half of the century had ceased to serve their original purpose and instead had become warehouses.

Croydon

Following its use as a potato warehouse, the Croydon Theatre, rescued for a decade by Barnett, became the premises of the Croydon Literary and Scientific Institution, one of the mushrooming evening schools which generally tended to replace the theatres.[65] By the 1850s the building was leased by a Dr Richard Paull and occupied as a boys' college.[66] Theatrical days returned in 1868 (the year in which the Croydon Fair was permanently closed down due mainly to unruliness, although a cattle mart was annually held on the site for many years) when the original theatre was in part demolished and the building finally known as the Hippodrome stood on the site for almost a century, ending its life as a cinema.[67]

Chichester

A variety of managers took the theatre for brief periods after Barnett terminated his lease. Davenport succeeded him, giving way to Pool in 1840 and Holmes followed in 1846 for three seasons. The inevitable sale of the theatre occurred in 1850 when it was bought and converted into a brewhouse by Richard Gatehouse whose family owned property to the south of the adjacent Theatre Lane and any theatrical entertainments were transferred to the gracious Assembly Rooms in North Street. This served the purpose well, although it was considerably smaller than the South Street playhouse.[68] From a brewhouse the building was reclaimed, becoming the reading room of the Mechanics Institute with a gas fire and lighting. After a spell as a gym, a reversion to a library occurred. 1936 saw it serving as a retail store. The premises suffered the addition of a large plateglass window when it became a furniture sale room.[69] At the time of writing it still stands, listed, and used as an arcade and theatre box office.

Bath

No lessee lasted for long at Bath for the post was 'anything but one of profit'.[70] Mrs Macready attempted in 1845 the management in which her husband had failed but the echo of the previous year's sermon by the rector of St Michael's Church rang through the building:

> The character of the theatre... is marked with almost every variety of evil: and, therefore, in proportion as it is adapted to the

intellectual character of man, and as it is calculated to interest
his passions and to make a deep impression on his heart, it is a
dangerous enemy to his virtue and happiness.[71]

Charles Kean had been engaged to appear for a season in 1862; he was
one of the first to report a disastrous Good Friday blaze in the auditorium.[72] C J Phipps, a young Bathonian in his twenties and subsequently a
designer of theatres at Nottingham, Glasgow and Wolverhampton won the
competition to create a new house within the ruins of the old. Under the
management of James Henry Chute Ellen Terry arrived the following year
to play Titania (*A Midsummer Night's Dream*) in the opening production
of the rebuilt theatre.[73] Four years later depleted finances forced the
managers to disband the theatre's company but remain open as a touring
date base, a policy continued until the present day. Lately a pleasing link
has been established with the Royal National Theatre which brought to
the theatre, amongst others, its production of *She Stoops to Conquer.*[74]

1. Theatre Museum: Theatre Files, Haymarket Theatre, playbills for 22 August and 5 September 1805.
2. *Salisbury Journal*, 8 May - 26 June 1809.
3. Aspinall, *Mrs Jordan and her Family*, p.255.
4. Melville T H Child, *The Community of Andover before 1825* (1972), p.12. 'Bailiff' was the local term for mayor.
5. *London and Provincial Commercial Directory* (1823), p.307.
6. New York Public Library: William Douglas manuscript notebook.
7. British Library: Playbill collection, 270, Arundel, 7 December 1811.
8. Odell, *More about the Old Theatre, Worthing*, p.25. New York Public Library: William Douglas manuscript notebook.
9. Arundel Museum: Playbill collection, 15 March 1827.
10. Brighton Central Library: Playbill collection, Arundel, 7 April 1829. Arundel Museum: Playbill collection, 26 May 1829.
11. Local information supplied by Ms Valerie Lishman.
12. Theatre Museum: Peter Davey manuscript notebooks, 22, Arundel.
13. Local information supplied by Brigadier Robinson who lived in the house Charles New built.
14. Odell, *More about the Old Theatre, Worthing*, p.25.
15. British Library: Burney Collection of Playbills, 283, Newbury, 9, 11 and 12 September 1844.
16. Jackson, *Dorking*, p.63.
17. *VCH. Hampshire and the Isle of Wight*, 5. 197.
18. *Salisbury and Winchester Journal*, 28 August 1797.
19. *Hampshire Telegraph*, 18 June 1810.
20. *Thespian Magazine*, 1 (1793), 54.
21. Musuem of Farnham: Playbill collection, 5 March 1832 and 4 May 1847.
22. Musuem of Farnham: Playbill collection, 29 March 1858.
23. Ewbank Smith, *Victorian Farnham* (Chichester, 1971), pp 146 and 212.
24. Kenton Theatre, Henley: playbill, 16 January 1798.
25. *Reading Mercury*, 12 November 1805. *Pigot's Directory*, p.443. *Directory of Oxfordshire* (1830), p.646. Information supplied by Dr Malcolm Graham, Local Studies Librarian, Oxford Central Library.

What Became of the Theatres?

26. Kenton Theatre, Henley: broadsheet, 17 February 1812.

27. Bodleian Library, Oxford: John Johnson Collection, playbill collection, Henley, 7 March 1811.

28. Anthony Denning, *Theatre in the Cotswolds*, edited and extended by Paul Ranger (1993), 105-113.

29. Theatre Museum: Peter Davey manuscript notebooks, 24, Horsham.

30. Horsham Museum: silk playbill, 6 January 1823.

31. Berkshire Record Office, Reading: Hungerford Constables' Accounts Books, 3, H/FR 1-8.

32. Hugh Pihlens, *Hungerford. A Pictorial History* (Chichester, 1992), figs 4 and 6.

33. New York Public Library: William Douglas manuscript notebook.

34. *Theatrical Inquisitor*, 1 (1812), 107. John Kennedy Melling, *Southend Playhouses from 1793* (1969), p.44. J W Burrows, 'Southend: the Old Theatre', *Transactions of the Southend-on-Sea Antiquarian and Historical Society*, 1 (1921), 146-7. Samuel Jerrold's son, Douglas William, wrote the famous nautical drama *Black Ey'd Susan*.

35. Melling, *Southend Playhouses*, 44-66, *passim*.

36. Weybridge Museum: Typescript on the history of the town.

37. *Monthly Mirror*, 24 (1807), 222.

38. New York Public Library: William Douglas manuscript notebook.

39. *Windsor and Eton Express*, 5 September 1813 and 8-21 August 1815.

40. Gilliland, *Dramatic Mirror*, 1.143.

41. Local information supplied by Mrs Jean Kirkwood.

42. *The Drama*, 1 (1821), 307 and 2 (1822), 208.
The West London Theatre became better known as the Prince of Wales's, by then a highly fashionable venue, managed from 1865 by Squire and Marie Bancroft.

43. Chelmsford Central Library: Playbill collection, 21 July 1830.

44. *Chelmsford Chronicle*, 13, 27 July, 3 August 1832.

45. Chelmsford Central Library: Playbill collection, 12 and 30 July 1833.

46. *Colchester Gazette*, 1 August 1835.

47. Essex Record Office, Chelmsford: Diary of John Round, 2 August 1836, D DRh F25/18.

48. Torry, *The Book of Chelmsford*, p.54.

49. Phillips, *Reading Theatres*, 24-6.

50. *Berkshire Mercury*, 26 August 1843. Newbury District Library: Collection of prospectuses for the Newbury Literary and Scientific Institute. Berkshire Record Office, Reading: Correspondence of E T Holmes.

51. Newbury District Museum: Playbill collection, playbill on silk with lace edge, Newbury, 7 September 1843.
The role of Diddler became a favourite with Sir Henry Irving later in the century.

52. Berkshire Record Office, Reading: Letters of E T Holmes to the Marquis of Downshire.

53. British Library: Playbill collection, 283, Newbury, 9, 11 and 12 September 1844. Frank H Stillman, *Newbury during the Victorian Era* (Newbury, 1893), p.10.

54. Notice of the sale of the theatre, 18 September 1883; the notice was housed in the Newbury Archive Room in the Mansion House but since the time of sighting the collection has been disbanded and the present whereabouts of the sale notice is unknown. Southern, *The Georgian Playhouse*, p.52. Newbury District Library: Victor Gordon, 'Old Plays in Old Days in Newbury', article from unknown newspaper mounted in Walter Money, *The Ancient Town and Borough of Newbury in Berkshire* (1887). *Newbury Weekly News*, 20 September 1883. Local information given by David Lewendon.

55. eg The Royal Commission on Historical Monuments. The state of the theatre was mentioned by the editors of *Theatre Notebook* in 1945. See: 1 (1945-7), 3.

56. University of Surrey, Guildford Institute: 'Scrapbook of Playbills', 2, note from B J Chaplin, former Institute Librarian, who was present at the production.

57. Chamberlin, *Guildford*, 169-170. Theatre Museum: Peter Davey manuscript notebooks, 28, Guildford.

58. Bodleian Library, Oxford: John Johnson Collection, Playbill collection, Oxford, 19 December 1866, GA Oxon b. 93.

59. The Revd and Hon J G Adderley, *The Fight for the Drama at Oxford* (Oxford, 1888), ix-x. The Revd and Hon J G Adderley, 'The Fight for the Drama at Oxford', *Church Reformer*, 6 (1887), 210. Mackinnon, *The Oxford Amateurs*, p.41. Bodleian Library: John Johnson Collection, Playbill collection, Oxford, 22 and 23 November [1860?], GA Oxon b. 86.
Vance (Alfred Peck Stevens, 1813-85) sang comic songs, most popular of which was 'The Chickaleery Bloke', in music halls.

60. Bodleian Library: John Johnson Collection, Playbill collection, Oxford, 8 August 1859. Mackinnon, *The Oxford Amateurs*, p.41.
The Star Hotel, later to become the Clarendon Hotel, stood near to the site of the present Clarendon Arcade.

61. Frank Benson, *My Memoirs* (1930), p.205.

62. Benjamin Jowett, *The Life and Letters of Benjamin Jowett, MA, Master of Balliol College, Oxford*, ed Evelyn Abbott and Lewis Campbell (1897), 2. 230-1. Laurence Irving, *Henry Irving. The Actor and his World* (1951, rep 1989), p.474.

63. 'The New Theatre, Oxford', *The Architect and Building News*, 137 (1934), 279.

64. Adams, *The Isle of Wight*, p.89.

65. Croydon Archives Service: A W Apterl, 'Early Days in a Loft in Crown Hill', *Croydon Advertiser*, 29 December 1939.

66. Information supplied by the Croydon Archivist.

67. Croydon Archives Service: Illustrations, 143.4, Crown Hill. A K Johnceline, 'The Theatre in Croydon', in *Proceedings of the Croydon Natural History and Scientific Society*, 16 (1976), 210. Bannerman, *Forgotten Croydon*, p.30.

68. *Excursions in the County of Sussex* (1822), p.26.

69. Steer, *Chichester Theatre*, p.8. Patricia Gill and Alison McCann, *Walks around Historic Chichester* (Chichester, 1980), p.31.

70. *Original Bath Guide* (Bath [1853]).

71. Cited in *Theatre Royal, Bath. Past, Present and Future* (Bath, nd), np.

72. Jeremy Brien, 'The Old and New at Bath Royal' in the *Stage*, 19 September 1974.

73. Iain Macintosh and Michael Sell, ed, *Curtains* (Eastbourne, 1982), p.88. Bath Central Library: Playbill collection, Bath, 4 March 1863.

74. *Theatre Royal, Bath*.

CHAPTER 15
THE PASSAGE OF TIME

The story of the management of the Thornton-Barnett circuit of theatres stems from 1785, when Thornton began to visit Newbury with his own company, until Barnett retired from the theatrical scene in 1853 with a small clutch of the original theatres remaining. This is an amazing continuance, giving a picture of the changing conditions of theatre management from the reign of George III until Victoria had become an accepted part of the institutional fabric of England. It would be a painstaking and dull exercise to attempt a point by point comparison of the Georgian and the Victorian manager. Instead, the gradual changes that came over the theatre buildings, the repertoire of the company, the players and the audience are considered.

Theatres

Either by transforming existing premises or by building on new foundations Thornton established his circuit of theatres; he would seem to have taken a pride in these buildings, employing either the company artist to decorate such features as plasterwork, the fronts of the boxes, the proscenium arch and the skyscapes of the auditorium ceiling or getting hold of a firm of decorative artists such as the Caves of Winchester, known for their work on the interior of churches; he was even prepared to buy paintings from other theatres to recut and use in the moulded frames of the roof. In between visits of the company, one wonders what damage the interiors suffered, used as warehouses, auction rooms and concert halls. As we have seen, Thornton caused the interiors to be redecorated on a regular basis and took the opportunity at the same time to renew some of the painted drop curtains and stock scenery. Barnett was more haphazard, giving the interior of the building a coat of paint after a lengthy closure but rarely taking the opportunity to add to the collection of scenes. Perhaps ownership of the buildings had come too easily to him. He had not been forced to scrimp in order to build or lease his playhouses; instead they passed to him lock, stock and barrel in a ready-made working order. When a couple of new locations were required to keep the circuit alive, Barnett leased operative theatres in Bath and Chichester; an individual stamp on a playhouse did not restrain him from using the buildings of other circuits. Here obviously is a change of outlook from the days of his father-in-law's management. Yet he possessed the initiative to build the Victoria Theatre in Oxford's Red Lion Yard, Barnett's sole venture into theatre construction, although it has to be admitted this was an exercise in jerry-building.[1] In contrast, when homeless in Gosport, he resorted to a simple adaptation of the Market House.

Although Barnett attempted to expand the circuit by a couple of theatres, his failure to do so is a reminder that companies were finishing with the circuit system. By 1853, the date of Barnett's retirement, companies travelled not to their own theatres but to those under the management of an administrator. Any vestigial remains of a circuit could be entirely hidden by the metropolitan theatres. Only twelve years after Barnett's farewell we find ourselves in a different world in which Squire and Marie Bancroft made the Prince of Wales's Theatre in Tottenham Street the base for their company, employing their energies entirely in developing it into a comfortable venue for lavishly presented dramas. Barnett could not have foreseen this, but social circumstances impinged in a small way on his later management.

Repertoire

Common traits were displayed by Thornton and Barnett in their choice of repertoire. The use the older manager made of the plays of Shakespeare has been considered and the same few plays tended to be revived also during Barnett's management. During the 1830s when the gothic villain was fast losing his foothold on the stage, Barnett continued with a long line of Othellos, Richard IIIs and Macbeths, all men of political position representing a strong vein of superhuman wickedness. One imagines, for example, that Cathcart's presentations of these roles would have found their niche in the theatres of the circuit fifty years earlier. The comedies, most in a rewritten state, also continued on the Barnett stage innocent of additions or reinterpretations under the pressure of social or literary change.

It was only to be expected that Thornton would mount the plays of Sheridan, some of which were written during his management. Use of these was made by Barnett at least a generation later, even to the extent of presenting *The Rivals* or *The School for Scandal* as the opening play of a new season, the custom of many Georgian managers. He found, too, that he could stage *Pizarro* after the threat of a contemporary French invasion of England had ceased, so reducing the play to a historical exercise.

Of course, the conservatism lay not only in Barnett's choice of play and the choices members of the company made as they prepared for their benefit nights. Many decisions lay with the audience, whether this was composed of those who formally 'desired' a play or the regular run of the mill applauders and hissers. On the whole Barnett was more successful than Thornton in forecasting which plays would be acceptable to the spectators of each of the half dozen locations in which he held a theatre. It is difficult to judge whether such county towns as Guildford, Chelmsford and Reading, together with the then small market town of Newbury, would have been more restricted by old-fashioned tastes than other places. Certainly one would imagine that Oxford, in spite of the academic opposition, would have generated a curiosity that would have demanded a wider range of new dramas than those in fact staged.

Innovations tended to be prompted by theatrical visitors. Celebrities, though fewer than in Thornton's day, often brought their own reper-toire with them and so introduced a welcome extension for the audience to savour. Thus it was only to be expected that an actor with whom a role had originated should perform that part and also take on other roles which possible casting difficulties in London would not allow. But not all visitors were innovatory: Edmund Kean, for example, continued to play the same villainous parts, period pieces all, by means of which he had established himself a generation earlier. In addition to some performers, writers could bring fresh air to the stage. For example Barnett knew Mary Russell Mitford and as each tragedy she wrote took hold in London, so a provincial staging would be given just a month or two later. Mitford was willing to travel to see her plays performed and often graced the Barnett theatres.

So luckily were a small number of other playwrights, among whom was James Sheridan Knowles. During the 1820s and 30s Barnett staged Knowles's plays on his circuit with the added attraction of the appearance of the author in the cast. In such plays as *The Hunchback* Knowles was able to use a strange mix of folklore and protest against social injustice to fire the souls of his auditors. The adoption of the works of James

Robinson Planché for his theatres was another of Barnett's few concessions to contemporary writing; possibly the coincidence of his assumption of management with the beginning of Planché's popularity makes the connection. Unlike Knowles, Planché did not visit the Barnett circuit. On an altogether lighter note, the manager continued to maintain his links with the Haymarket by sending occasionally for the script of a new operetta he could use as an afterpiece.

Gas lighting, introduced into many provincial theatres during the 1820s, was an innovation of which Barnett possibly took a while to appreciate the possibilities. Members of audiences who visited buildings in which this was used spoke of the brightness of the illumination.[2] Here was a contrast with the patchy dim lighting supplied by oil lamps. However, with the use of tinted silk baffles and the coloured shades of argand lamps lighting by oil tended to be more atmospheric than the new method and for a while was preferred. Only when managers discovered that the intensity could be varied did the gas seem preferable. Even so, the note sounded by the burning gas could be at the same pitch as the heroine's voice, impeding the audibility of her words.[3] Technological problems are not new.

We know that Thornton received an education at the Middle Temple. To what extent Barnett was educated remains a mystery and whether such an education would determine his selection of plays again is a question which has to remain in abeyance. Tentatively, it seems that Barnett had more of an interest than Thornton in discovering plays which would suit the personnel in his company; a more rigid form of type casting according to the stock principles was adopted by the older man. Barnett certainly seems to have lacked the theatrical flair and love of spectacle that Hatton so greatly enjoyed and with which Thornton co-operated to the full. It is rare (but not unknown) that Barnett advertises a list of exciting scenes and vistas and a mention of coordinating costumes is exceptional.

Towards the end of his management some of the London theatres were beginning to stage nightly a single drama for a period, a convention which would not have drawn the country audience to the same extent, although it should be pointed out that during Thornton's management in the early days of the run of such dramas as *The Castle Spectre* and *Pizarro* they could take total hold of the stage for a week. In the face of change Barnett appears to be striving to put on a wide and contrasting repertoire for those who had the money or leisure to attend the playhouse several times a week.

The players

The days of a company consisting of an extended family - such a one as Thornton's - were passing. Barnett's theatrical family was limited to his wife, his son Richard who was conductor of the orchestra, another lad and his daughter-in-law. Yet both managers created conditions in which other performing families could happily exist for years. Wages seemed to play little part in this. Thornton had paid each of his actors around £1 per week, a rate which remained constant under Barnett until 1827 when Leman Thomas Rede tabulated the salaries of the various companies. Compare this wage with the £1. 10s which Harvey paid his performers in the Channel Islands where inexpensive food was an added perquisite. Several managers were noted for the generous recompense they gave their employees but, naturally, they attracted players of some stature: it was possible to earn up to £3. 10s per week at Bath and up to £4 at Liverpool and Manchester.[4] The constancy of the Barnett salaries ought to represent a fall in the standard of living for the performer and his family, for after the Napoleonic Wars the usual financial slough occurred. Yet the addresses of specific actors given on playbills suggest that the same kind of lodgings were sought out, mostly the spare rooms of provision merchants above their premises.

People who had acted under Thornton appear to have regarded the company under Barnett as a base to which they could return and likewise Barnett's playbills were always warmly welcoming to the former members. An area of player untapped by him was the amateur aristocratic actor. His father-in-law had felt at home in their presence and so, obviously, had Hatton; but not Barnett. No longer was help given at private theatricals and Barnett kept his company within the confines of the professional theatre. Across the Channel the rise of the populace against the nobility during the Revolution seemed to encourage in England a bonding of aristocrat and player in the creation of productions, as at Wargrave. When peace was restored in France, then such joint ventures passed out of fashion here. In Barnett's case this may reflect more than social change. He possibly lacked Thornton's veneer of social ease or found that he had little sympathy with the military and aristocratic outlook. He did, however, entertain the idea of using troops as supernumeraries. One occasion was for the pantomime *The Forty Thieves* to be staged at Newbury but on approaching Col Sir John Elley his request to employ some of the Oxford Blues was instantly turned down on the grounds that the usage would lack dignity.[5]

A balance between pay and admission prices was a necessity and here it is noteworthy that both Thornton and Barnett maintained the 1/-

gallery, 2/- pit and 3/- box seats with either a rise in the price of the dearer seats or an intervening charge when an extra row of boxes was added to a theatre. Possibly the economic recession of the 1820s made a rise in charges unfeasible as admissions would exceed the finances of many of the audience. A limited income would be a further factor militating against spectacular productions. Any surplus Barnett appears to have channelled into providing visiting stage personalities at his playhouses. Here, too, there were bounds and Thornton's extravagant use of *illuminati* was not imitated. On the whole fewer people were invited to perform and, for the most part, they lacked the star quality of a Jordan or a Betty. Barnett made ends meet in difficult years by cutting back on scenes, dresses, auditorium redecorations and a wide range of 'names'. It may seem to us a bleak policy but it worked and the circuit was kept in operation.

Audiences

In 1800 the Croydon theatre was built. Its chief characteristics were neatness, convenience and the reasonably competent company managed by Henry Thornton.[6] The unmade lane outside the building soon gave way to a street and numbers of houses grew up around the theatre. This small enclave of respectability, Crown Hill leading into Church Street and so to the parish church, was to change later in the century as numbers of public houses opened within the immediate vicinity together with a vegetable and a fish market along the streets fronting the playhouse. The territory which Barnett leased during the 1830s was different in tone from that which Thornton had enjoyed for the first decade of the century; it had by then run down, a constant hazard for managers. In such circumstances Thornton would have left the neighbourhood as he did at Newbury and Windsor; but not Barnett. Decency and decoration within his theatres ensured that Thornton drew on an audience that was not just respectable but could also number titled people among its patrons. By the time Barnett inherited the theatres thirty years later many of them were in need of repair rather than just a repaint. But for Barnett at Croydon this was not necessarily a gloomy picture. The very cause of the delapidation to the area, the innkeepers, ministered to the theatre through their patronage of an occasional evening.

Almost any manager working at the same time as Thornton would have relied on military and naval personnel to fill a considerable part of his house. Post-Waterloo, these reserves of forces were not to be found in such numbers and although occasionally a barracks, such as that at Croydon, sponsored an evening, more often the performance was under the wing of the town's cricket club, cultural society, reading room or local council. Such audiences were from a smaller catchment and lacked the distinction of titled people at the top of the hierarchy. Later generations suffered. The detailed memoirs of generals giving readers vignettes of theatrical life were not, in turn, written up by a bevy of town clerks.

It would be a mistake to imagine that the evening educational establishments of the 1830s springing up in the wake of electoral reform were the sole force driving the playhouses into extinction. However, a new seriousness possessed the merchant and middle classes and if theatres were to maintain their audiences the plays had to reflect this movement. We have already seen the conservative revivals of comedy and melodrama and the new writing, sometimes whimsical, progressing in parallel on the Barnett stages. Only after Barnett's retirement did realism get under way in the theatre and that tended to be in the larger cities rather than in the remaining country playhouses. Perhaps Barnett should have been thankful that time had spared him the great and rapid changes in daily entertainment which the coming of the cinema, and later of the television, exerted in the twentieth century.

1. The term 'jerry-building' is said to have arisen from the cheaply constructed domestic streets of the Oxford suburb of Jericho, built prior to the Victoria behind the University Press and principally for its employees. These working-class people would regularly have formed a section of the theatre's audience. See Hibbert and Hibbert, *The Encyclopaedia of Oxford*, p.197.
2. The Revd Sidney Smith, for example, was astounded by the brilliance of the gas lighting at Lambton Hall. See Hesketh Pearson, *The Smith of Smiths* (1977), 166.
3. Verbal information supplied by Dr Richard Southern.
4. Rede, *The Road to the Stage*, 9-11.
5. Lennox, *Celebrities*, 1. 296.
6. D W Garrow, *The History and Antiquities of Croydon* (1818), p.108.

Under Two Managers

APPENDIX 1:
SOURCES

1. Printed Books and Articles

Acts of the Privy Council.

Adams, W Davenport, *A Dictionary of the Drama* (1904).

Adams, W H Davenport, *The History, Topography and Antiquities of the Isle of Wight* (Ryde, 1856).

Adderley, J G, *The Fight for the Drama at Oxford* (Oxford, 1888).

Adderley, J G, 'The Fight for the Drama at Oxford', *Church Reformer*, 6 (1887), 209-213.

Adolphus, John, *Memoirs of John Bannister* (1839).

Ancient and Modern History of Portsmouth, Portsea, Gosport and their Environs, The (nd).

Angelo, Henry, *The Reminiscences of Henry Angelo,* ed H Laver Smyth(1825).

Apterl, A W, 'Early Days in a Loft in Crown Hill', *Croydon Advertiser* (29 December 1939).

Archer, Thomas, *A Poetical Description of New South-End* (1793).

Aspinall, A, *Mrs Jordan and her Family* (1951).

Ayling, Stanley, *George the Third* (1972).

Baker, John, *The Diary of John Baker,* ed P C Yorks (1931).

Bannerman, Ronald, *Forgotten Croydon* (Croydon, 1933).

Barker, D M and J L, *A Window on Weybridge* (Addlestone, nd).

Bath Directory, 1841 (Bath, 1841).

Bennett, Arthur and Parsons, Edward, *A History of the Free School of Andover* (Andover, 1920).

Bennett, James, *A History of Tewkesbury* (Tewkesbury, 1830).

Benson, Frank, *My Memoirs* (1930).

Bernard, John, *Retrospections of America, 1797-1811* (New York, 1887).

Bernard, John, *Retrospections of the Stage* (Boston, Mass, 1830).

Betjmann, A G, *The Grand Theatre, Lancaster: Two Centuries of Entertainment* (Lancaster, 1982).

Biography of the British Stage, The (1824).

Blackman, M E and Pulford, J S, *A Short History of Weybridge* (Walton and Weybridge, 1991).

Boaden, A M, and Melville, Lewis, *The Beautiful Lady Craven. Memoirs of Elizabeth Baroness Craven* (1913).

Boas, Frederick, 'The University of Oxford and the Professional Players', *The Times Literary Supplement*, 14 March 1929.

Braybrooke, Richard, *The History of Audley End* (1836).

Brien, Jeremy, 'The Old and New at Bath Royal', *Stage* (19 September 1974).

Brim, John Southern, *A History of Henley on Thames* (1861).

Britton, J and Brayley, E W, *The Beauties of England and Wales* (1801).

Brown, A F J, *Essex People, 1750-1900* (Chelmsford 1972).

Brown, James D, and Stratton, S S, *British Musical Biography* (1897).

Bruce, Morys George L, *The Story of Tennis* (1959).

Burney, Frances, *The Diary and Letters of Madame D'Arblay*, ed C F Barrett (1846).

Burrows, J W, 'Southend: the Old Theatre', *Transactions of the Southend-on-Sea Antiquarian and Historical Society*, 1 (1921), 146-7.

Byron, George Gordon, *Byron's Letters and Journals*, ed Leslie A Marchand (1973).

Chamberlain, V C, 'Resetting a Stage', *Country Life* (4 November 1982).

Chamberlin, E R, *Guildford. A Biography* (1970).

Chancellor, E Beresford, *Old Q and Barrymore* (1925).

Charke, Charlotte, *A Narrative of the Life of Mrs Charlotte Charke* (1775).

Child, Melville T H, *The Community of Andover before 1825* (1972).

Childs, W M, *The Town of Reading during the Early Part of the Nineteenth Century* (Reading, 1910).

Clarke [?], *The Georgian Era* (1832-4).

Coleman, John, *Fifty Years of an Actor's Life* (1904).

Coles, W A, 'Mary Russell Mitford, the inauguration of a Literary Career', *Bulletin of the John Rylands Library*, 40 (1957), 33-46.

Companion in a Tour round Southampton, A (Southampton, 1801).

Corke, Shirley, *Guildford. A Pictorial History* (Chichester, 1990).

Coryn, M, *The Chevalier D'Eon, 1728-1810* (1832).

Cox, C V, *Recollections of Oxford* (1870).

Cox, Cynthia, *The Enigma of the Age. The Strange Story of the Chevalier d'Eon* (1966).

Cross, Richard, *The Early Diary of Richard Cross, Prompter to the Theatres*, ed H W Pedicord (Manchester, 1955).

Cunningham, A, ed 'The Southampton Guide, 1787', *The Hampshire Antiquary and Naturalist*, 2 (1892), 7.

Appendix 1: Sources

Denning, Anthony, *Theatre in the Cotswolds*, ed Paul Ranger (1993).

Dennis, Philip, *Gibraltar and its People* (Newton Abbot, 1990).

Dibdin, Charles, *Observations on a Tour throughout almost the Whole of England and a considerable Part of Scotland* [1801-2].

Directory of Oxfordshire (1830).

Djabir, Susan C, *The Horsham Companion* (Horsham, nd).

Donaldson, Walter Alexander, *Fifty Years of an Actor's Life* (1858).

Donaldson, Walter Alexander, *Fifty Years of Greenroom Gossip* (1881).

Donaldson, Walter Alexander, *Recollections of an Actor* (1865).

Dyer, Robert, *Nine Years of an Actor's Life* (1833).

Egan, Pierce, *The Life of an Actor* (1892).

Encyclopaedia Britannica (1797).

Encyclopaedia Britannica (1911).

Eustace, G W, *Arundel Borough and Castle* (1922).

Everard, Edward Cape, *Memoirs of an Unfortunate Son of Thespis* (1818).

Everitt, Alan, *English Urban History* (1973).

Excursions in the County of Sussex (1822).

Fernyhough's Reading Directory 1841 (Reading, 1841).

Forbes, Derek, 'The Earliest Grossmiths and their Pictorial Playbills' in *Scenes from Provincial Stages: Essays in Honour of Kathleen Barker*, ed Richard Foulkes (1994).

Fothergill, Brian, *Mrs Jordan* (1965).

Fowler, Marian, *Blenheim: Biography of a Palace* (1991).

Franks, Alfred, 'Historic Essex Mansion to Disappear', *Essex Countryside*, 13 (1965), 354.

Frost, Thomas, *The Old Showmen and the London Fairs* (1834).

Garlick, Kenneth, *Catalogue of Paintings of the Walpole Society* (1964).

Garrick, David, *Three Plays by David Garrick*, ed Elizabeth P Stein (1926).

Garrow, D W, *The History and Antiquities of Croydon* (1818).

Gates, W G, *Records of the Corporation* (Portsmouth, 1928).

[Gauntlett, Henry], *Letters to the Stranger in Reading* (Reading, 1810).

Gauntlett, Henry, *Sermons by the Late Revd Henry Gauntlett, Vicar of Olney, Bucks, with a Memoir of the Author* (1835).

Genest, John, *Some Account of the English Stage* (Bath, 1832).

Gibson, Strickland, *Statuta Antiqua Universitatis Oxoniensis* (Oxford, 1931).

Gilboy, E W, *Wages in Eighteenth-Century England* (Cambridge, Mass, 1934).

Gill, Patricia and McCann, Alison, *Walks around Historic Chichester* (Chichester, 1980).

Gilliland, Thomas, *The Dramatic Mirror* (1808).

Godwin, Henry, *The Worthies and Celebrities connected with Newbury,*

Berkshire and its Neighbours (1859).

Golland, Jim, 'A Dramatic Discovery', *Local History Magazine*, 42 (January-February, 1994), 14-15.

Graves, Richard, *The Spiritual Quixote* (1773).

Greenwood, G B and Martine, A B, *Walton-on-Thames and Weybridge. A Dictionary of Local History* (Weybridge, nd).

Grice, Elizabeth, *Rogues and Vagabonds* (Lavenham, 1977).

Grice, F, 'Roger Kemble's Company at Worcester', *Theatre Notebook*, 9 (1954-5), 73-5.

Grove's Dictionary of Music and Musicians, ed Eric Blom (1954).

Hall, Lillian Arvilla, *Catalogue of Dramatic Portraits in the Theatre Collection of Harvard College Library* (Cambridge, Mass, 1931).

Hall, S C, *A Book of Memories of Great Men and Women of the Age* (1871).

Handbook to Guildford and its Environs, A (Guildford, 1862).

Hannam-Clark, Theodore, *Drama in Gloucestershire* (1928).

Harding, Godfrey, *The Opening of the Yvonne Arnaud Theatre, Guildford; Supplement to the Surrey Advertiser* (Guildford, 1965).

Hare, Arnold, ed, *Theatre Royal, Bath. A Calendar of Performances at the Orchard Street Theatre, 1750-1805* (Bath, 1977).

Hare, Arnold, *The Georgian Theatre in Wessex* (1958).

Hartnoll, Phyllis, *The Concise Oxford Companion to the Theatre* (1972).

Hartnoll, Phyllis and Found, Peter, *The Concise Oxford Companion to the Theatre* (1992).

Hay, Alexander, *The History of Chichester* (Chichester, 1804).

Herrmann, Luke, *Paul and Thomas Sandby* (1986).

Hibbert, Christopher and Edward, *The Encyclopaedia of Oxford* (1988).

Highfill, jnr, Phillip H; Burnim, Kalman A; Langhans, Edward A, *A Biographical Dictionary of Actors, Actresses, Musicians, Dancers, Managers and Other Stage Personnel in London, 1660-1800* (Carbondale and Edwardsville, 1973-93).

Hill, Constance, *Mary Russell Mitford and her Surroundings* (1920).

Hoad, Margaret J, *Portsmouth, as others have seen it* (Portsmouth, 1972).

Hodgkinson, J L and Podgson, Rex, *The Early Manchester Theatre* (1960).

Hogan, Charles Beecher, *Shakespeare in the Theatre, 1701-1800* (Oxford, 1957).

Holbrook, Ann Catherine, *The Dramatist* (1809).

Holcroft, Thomas, *The Theatrical Recorder* (1805).

Hunt, Leigh, *Critical Essays on the Performers of the London Stage* (1807).

Irving, Laurence, *Henry Irving. The Actor and his World* (1951, rep 1989).

Jackson, Alan J, *Dorking. A Surrey Market Town through Twenty*

Appendix 1: Sources

Centuries (Dorking, 1991).

Johnceline, A K, 'The Theatre in Croydon', *Proceedings of the Croydon Natural History and Scientific Society*, 16 (1976), 210-211.

Jones-Evans, Eric, 'The Theatre Royal, Ryde', *Hampshire County Magazine* (February 1975), 55-6 and 61.

Jowett, Benjamin, *The Life and Letters of Benjamin Jowett, MA, Master of Balliol College, Oxford*, ed Evelyn Abbott and Lewis Campbell (1897).

Kelly, J A, *German Visitors to English Theatres* (Princeton, 1936).

Kelly, Michael, *Solo Recital*, ed Herbert van Thal (1972).

Knight, Charles, *Passages of a Working Life, during Half a Century* (1873).

Knight, Charles, *A Volume of Varieties* (1804).

Knowles, James Sheridan, *Dramatic Works* (1856).

Knowles, Richard Brinsley, *The Life of James Sheridan Knowles* (1872).

Lawrence, W J, *Old Theatre Days and Ways* (1935).

Lee, H, *Report to the General Board of Health on a Preliminary Enquiry into the Sewage, Drainage and Supply of Water* (1850).

Lee, Henry, *Memoirs of a Manager* (Taunton, 1830).

Leech, Clifford and Craik, T W, gen eds, *The Revels History of Drama in English* (1975-83).

Lees-Milne, James, *William Beckford* (Tisbury, 1976).

Lennox, William Pitt, *Celebrities I Have Known* (1876).

Lennox, William Pitt, *Fifty Years of Biographical Reminiscences* (1863).

Lennox, William Pitt, *My Recollections from 1806-1873* (1874).

Lennox, William Pitt, *Percy Hamilton* (1851).

Lennox, William Pitt, *Plays, Players and Playhouses* (1881).

London and Provincial Commercial Directory (1823).

Long, J C, *George III* (1960).

Lowndes, William, *The Theatre Royal at Bath* (1982).

Mackinnon, Alan, *The Oxford Amateurs* (1910).

Mackintosh, Iain, *The Royal Opera House Retrospective 1732-1982* (1982).

Mackintosh, Iain and Ashton, Geoffrey, *The Georgian Playhouse* (1975).

Mackintosh, Iain and Sell, Michael, eds, *Curtains* (Eastbourne, 1982).

Macmillan, Dougald, ed, *Catalogue of the Larpent Plays in the Huntington Library* (San Marino, 1939).

Macready, William Charles, *The Diaries of William Charles Macready*, ed William Toynbee (1912).

Man, John, *The Stranger in Reading* (Reading 1810).

[Mason, John], *Guildford* (privately printed, 1897).

Mavor, William, *A General View of the Agriculture of Berkshire drawn from the consideration of the Board of Agriculture and Internal*

Improvement (1809).

Melling, John Kennedy, *Southend Playhouses from 1793* (1969).

Melling, John Kennedy, 'The Theatre at Chelmsford', *Essex Chronicle* (19 December 1958).

Mitford, Mary Russell, *Belford Regis* (1835).

Mitford, Mary Russell, *The Dramatic Works* (1854).

Mitford, Mary Russell, *The Friendship of Mary Russell Mitford as recorded in Letters from her Literary Correspondents,* ed A C L'Estrange (1882).

Molloy, J Fitzgerald, *The Life and Adventures of Edmund Kean* (1888).

Money, Walter, *A Popular History of Newbury in the County of Berks from Early to Modern Times* (1905).

Moore, Mark, *Memoirs and Adventures of Mark Moore* (1795).

Mozeen, Thomas, *Young Scarron* (1752).

Mrs Jordan. The Duchess of Drury Lane (1955), exhibition catalogue.

Newbury Buildings Past and Present (Newbury, 1973).

'The New Theatre, Oxford', *The Architect and Building News*, 137 (1934), 279.

Nicoll, Allardyce, *A History of English Drama, 1660-1900* (Cambridge, 1955).

Odell, Maria Theresa, *More about the Old Theatre Worthing* (Worthing, 1945).

Odell, Maria Theresa, *The Old Theatre, Worthing* (Aylesbury, 1938).

O'Keeffe, John, *Recollections of the Life of John O'Keeffe* (1826).

Ordnance Survey Map of Ryde (1863).

Original Bath Guide (Bath [1853]).

Owen, Ino, *Britannia Depicted* (1730).

Oxberry, William, *Dramatic Biography and Histrionic Anecdotes* (1825-7).

Papendiek, Charlotte Louise Henrietta, *Court and Private Life in the Time of Queen Charlotte* (1887).

Parker, George, *A View of Society and Manners in High and Low Life* (1781).

Pasquin, Anthony [Williams, John], *The Life of the Earl of Barrymore* (1793).

Peake, Richard Brinsley, *Memoirs of the Colman Family* (1841).

Pearson, Hesketh, *The Smith of Smiths* (1977).

[Peck, Robert Jasper], *Narrative of the Late Deplorable Fire at Chelmsford, Essex* (1808).

Penley, Belville S, *The Bath Stage* (London and Bath, 1892).

Pennant, Thomas, *A Journey from London to the Isle of Wight* (1801).

Pewsey, Stephen, *The Book of Southend-on-Sea* (1993).

Philo-Dramaticus, 'A Letter to Charles Kemble Esq., and R W Elliston, Esq., on the Present State of the Stage', *Blackwood's Edinburgh Magazine*, 17 (1825), 727-731.

Appendix 1: Sources

Pigot's Directory (1823).

Pihlens, Hugh, *Hungerford. A Pictorial History* (Chichester, 1992).

Pihlens, Hugh, *The Story of Hungerford* (Newbury, 1983).

Porter, Henry, *History of the Theatres of Brighton* (Brighton, 1886).

Post Office Reading Directory, The (Reading, 1842).

Powys, Lybbe, *Passages from the Diaries of Mrs Philip Lybbe Powys, 1750-1808*, ed J Climenson (1899).

Ranger, Paul, *The Georgian Playhouses of Hampshire 1730-1830* (Winchester, 1996).

Ranger, Paul, 'The Theatres of Oxford: Forty Years of Family Management', *Oxoniensia*, 54 (1989), 393-8.

Raymond, George, *The Life and Enterprises of Robert William Elliston* (1857).

Rede, Thomas Leman, *The Road to the Stage* (1827).

Redgrave, Samuel, *A Dictionary of Artists of the English School* (1874).

[Reed, Isaac], *Biographia Dramatica*, 1782.

Reid, Herbert J, *The History of Wargrave* (1865).

Report of the Select Committee on Dramatic Literature, The (1832).

Rhodes, R Compton, 'The King's Players at Oxford, 1661-1712', *The Times Literary Supplement*, 21 February 1929.

Roberts, Cecil, *And So to Bath* (1940).

Roberts, W J, *The Tragedy of a Blue Stocking* (1913).

Robertson, A, *The Great Road from London to Bath* (1792).

Rogers, H T, 'Gosport's Lost Theatres', *Gosport Records*, 3 (1972), 13-17.

Rosenfeld, Sybil, 'Some Notes on the Players in Oxford', *Review of English Studies*, 19 (1943), 366-375.

Rosenfeld, Sybil, *Temples of Thespis* (1978).

Rosenfeld, Sybil, *The Theatre of the London Fairs in the 18th Century* (Cambridge, 1960).

Rosenfeld, Sybil, 'The Theatrical Notebooks of T H Wilson Manley', *Theatre Notebook*, 7 (1952-3), 2-12 and 43-5.

Rosenfeld, Sybil and Murray, Edward Croft, 'A Checklist of Scene Painters working in Great Britain and Ireland in the Eighteenth Century', *Theatre Notebook*, 19 - 20 (1964-5), *passim*.

[Rosenfeld, Sybil and Southern, Richard], 'On Listing Theatres', *Theatre Notebook*, 1 (1945-7), 3.

Royal Commission on Historical Monuments, England, *Inventory of the Historical Monuments in the City of Oxford* (1939).

Rusher's Reading Guide and Berkshire Directory 1817 (Reading, 1817).

Russell's Guildford Directory (Guildford, 1842).

Russell, J and S, *A History of Guildford* (Guildford, 1801).

221

Russell, J and S, *A History of Guildford*, ed F Laurence (Guildford, 1845).
Russell, William Clark, *Representative Actors* (1872).
Ryley, S W , *The Itinerant* (1805).
Salter, H E, *Cartulary of Osney Abbey* (1929-36).
Saxon, A H, *The Life and Art of Andrew Ducrow* (Hamden, Conn, 1978).
Scanlan, E G, 'Tennis Courts in England and Scotland', *Theatre Notebook*, 10 (1955), 10-15.
Shaw, Ken, 'The Rise and Fall of the Theatre Royal', *Newbury Weekly News* (23 August 1979).
Sheridan, Thomas, 'Five Hundred Years of Reading Theatre', *Reading and Berkshire Review*, 11 (1952), 14.
Smith, Ewbank, *Victorian Farnham* (Chichester, 1971).
Smith, W C, *Rambles round Guildford* (Guildford, 1828).
Snare, John, *Map of Reading* (1842).
Southern, Richard, *The Georgian Playhouse* (1948).
Statute Books, The.
Steer, Francis, *The Chichester Theatre*, Chichester Papers 9 (Chichester, 1959).
Steer, Francis, 'Sources of Information on 18th and Early 19th Century Theatres in Sussex', *Theatre Notebook*, 12 (1957-8), 58-64.
Steinman, G S, *A History of Croydon* (1834).
Stephen, Leslie and Lee, Sidney, eds, *Dictionary of National Biography* (1909).
Stewart, Ian, 'A Dream Fulfilled', *Country Life* (23 December 1982).
Stillman, Frank H, *Newbury during the Victorian Era* (Newbury, 1893).
Stochholme, Joanne M, *Garrick's Folly* (1964).
Stone, G W and Hogan, C Beecher, *The London Stage*, part 5 (1968).
Styles, John, *An Essay on the Character of the Stage* (Newport, IOW, 1806).
Summers, W H, *The Story of Hungerford in Berkshire* [1926].
Thespian Dictionary, The (1805).
Taylor, John, *Records of My Life* (1832).
Telfer, J Buchan, *The Strange Career of the Chevalier D'Eon de Beaumont* (1885).
Theatre Royal, Bath. Past, Present and Future (Bath, nd).
Thornton G A, *A Short History of Clare* (Brentwood, 1963).
Timbs, John, *A Picturesque Promenade around Dorking* (1823).
Tomalin, Claire, *Mrs Jordan's Profession* (1995).
Tompkins, John, *The Tompkins Diary*, ed G W Eustace (Cambridge, 1930).
Torry, Gilbert, *The Book of Chelmsford* (Buckingham, 1985).
'Tour in 1776, A', *Essex Chronicle* (15 April 1938).

Townsend, James, *News of a Country Town* (1914).

Turner, Barbara Carpenter, 'A Notable Family of Artists', *Proceedings of the Hampshire Field Club*, 22 (1961), 30-33.

Universal British Directory (1793).

Vaughan, Anthony, *Born to Please. Hannah Pritchard, Actress 1711-1768. A Critical Biography* (1979).

Victoria History of the Counties of England, The. Hampshire and the Isle of Wight, vol 3 (1908) and vol 5 (1912), ed William Page.

Victoria History of the Counties of England, The. Oxfordshire, vol 12, (1906), ed C R Elrington.

Waldron, F G, *The Literary Museum* (1792).

Warwick, Lou, *Theatre Unroyal* (1974).

Watson, Vera, *Mary Russell Mitford* (nd).

Wedgwood, Josiah, *Letters of Josiah Wedgwood*, ed Katherine Euphrensis Farrer (1903).

Wendeborn, A, *Der Zustand des Staats* (Berlin, 1784).

Wewitzer, Ralph, *A Brief Dramatic Chronicle of Actors, etc. on the London Stage* (1817).

Whincop, Thomas, *Scanderberg or Love and Liberty to which are added a List of all the Dramatic Authors... to the Year 1747* (1747).

White, L F W, *The Story of Gosport* (Southsea, nd).

White, William, *A Description of the Town of Reading including its origin and History* (Reading, 1841).

Wilkinson, Tate, *Memoirs of His Own Life* (York, 1790).

Wilkinson, Tate, *The Wandering Patentee* (York, 1795).

Williams, J, *The Life of the Late Earl of Barrymore* (1793).

Wilson, C Baron, *Our Actresses* (1844).

Windsor Guide, The (Windsor, 1811).

Winston, James, *The Theatric Tourist* (1805).

Witherby, Charles, *Map of Guildford* (1839).

Wright, Thomas, *The History and Topography of Essex* (1836).

Wright, Thomas, *The History and Topography of the County of Essex comprising its Ancient and Modern History* (1842).

a Wood, Anthony, *Life and Times*, ed A Clark (1891-1900).

2. Journals and Newspapers

Architect and Building News, The.

Athenaeum, The.

Bath Chronicle.

Bath Journal.
Berkshire Chronicle.
Berrow's Worcester Journal.
Bristol Gazette.
Bulletin of the John Rylands Library.
Chelmsford Chronicle.
Church Reformer.
Colchester Gazette.
Country Life.
Croydon Advertiser.
Croydon Chronicle.
Drama, The.
Essex Chronicle.
Essex Countryside.
European Magazine, The.
Gazetteer, The.
Gentleman's Magazine, The.
Gosport Records.
Hampshire Antiquary and Naturalist, The.
Hampshire Chronicle.
Hampshire County Magazine.
Hampshire Telegraph.
Jackson's Oxford Journal.
Monthly Mirror.
Morning Chronicle, The.
Morning Herald, The.
Newbury Weekly News.
Oxoniensia.
Portsmouth Gazette.
Portsmouth Telegraph.
Proceedings of the Croydon Natural History and Scientific Society.
Proceedings of the Hampshire Field Club, The.
Prompter, The.
Public Advertiser.
Reading and Berkshire Review.
Reading Mercury.
Salisbury Journal.
Salisbury and Winchester Journal.
Stage, The.
Surrey Magazine.

Sussex Weekly Advertiser.
Theatre, The.
Theatre Notebook.
Theatrical Inquisitor.
Theatrical Journal.
Theatrical Times.
Thespian Magazine.
Times, The.
Times Literary Supplement, The.
Transactions of the Southend-on-Sea Antiquarian and Historical Society.
West Sussex Advertiser.
Windsor and Eton Express.
World's Fair, The.

3. Institutions, Collections etc.

Andover, Archives of the Charter Trustees.
Andover, District Library.
Arundel, Arundel Castle:
>   archives of the Duke of Norfolk:
>>   title deeds of the site of the theatre.
Arundel, Museum:
>   collection of playbills.
Bath, Central Library:
>   collection of playbills.
Birmingham, Central Library:
>   Winston Collection relating to the publication of *The Theatric Tourist*;
>   collection of playbills.
Boston, Mass, Harvard University Theatre Collection:
>   Manuscript notebook of James Winston, TS 1335.211.
Brighton, Central Library:
>   collection of playbills.
Bristol, University of Bristol Theatre Collection:
>   Paul Ranger, 'Henry Thornton, 1750-1818', typescript dissertation submitted for the award of M.Litt, 1975.
Bury St Edmunds, Suffolk Record Office:
>   Baptismal Register of the Parish of Clare, Suffolk, FL 501/3;
>   Church Wardens' Books, no 1.
Chelmsford, Cathedral:

Burial Register, 16.67.

Chelmsford, Central Library:

collection of playbills;

broadsheets relating to the Chelmsford Theatre.

Chelmsford, Chelmsford and Essex Museum.

Chelmsford, *Essex Chronicle* Newspaper Collection:

files of the *Chelmsford Chronicle*.

Chelmsford, Essex Record Office:

W A Mepham, 'History of the Drama in Essex from the Fifteenth Century to the Present Time', typescript doctoral thesis, University of London, 1938;

Sale Catalogue of the Estate of William Clacher (1837), B4070;

collection of playbills;

petitions of Henry Thornton to perform, Q/SB6;

'Transcriptions of Monumental Inscriptions in the Churches of... Chelmsford', manuscript, T/P72/1;

Diary of John Round, D DRh F25/18.

Cheltenham, Museum and Art Gallery:

collection of playbills.

Chertsey, Public Library:

Wetton Scrapbook.

Chichester, West Sussex Record Office.

Croydon, Archives Service:

J Corbet Anderson, file of manuscript notes and cuttings;

J Corbet Anderson, 'Croydon Theatre, Old and New', paste-up of playbills;

Ronald Bannerman, ed, 'A Scrapbook of Old Croydon';

William Page, 'My Recollections of Croydon Sixty Years Ago', typescript;

playbill collection;

collection of deeds belonging to the firm of Marshall, Liddle and Downey;

material relating to Crown Hill, Croydon, 143.4.

Croydon, Central Library.

Dorking, Museum.

Dorking, Public Library.

Eton, Eton College Archives:

Thomas James, Paper on the holidays at Eton College, 1766.

Farnham, Museum of Farnham:

collection of playbills.

Gloucester, County Record Office.
Gloucester, Central Library, Gloucestershire Collection:
>Prohibitions of Theatrical Performances, Q/TS (addn).

Gosport, Central Library.
Gosport, Museum:
>collection of playbills.

Guildford, Central Library, Local Studies Collection:
>Letter from the Chief Librarian of Guildford to Richard
>Southern.

Guildford, Muniment Room:
>'Catalogue of the Papers of the Grantley Estate', biographical
>note on Fletcher Norton;
>Lease for theatre plot (1792), RB 274;
>Petition of Henry Thornton and licence to erect a theatre,
>BR/QS/2/7 (1) and (2);
>collection of playbills.

Guildford, Museum:
>collection of playbills.

Guildford, University of Surrey, Guildford Institute:
>collection of playbills;
>scrapbooks of playbills.

Henley on Thames, Kenton Theatre.
>collection of playbills and notices.

Hereford, City Library:
>the Kemble Scrapbooks.

Horsham, Museum:
>Letters and applications to perform in the town, HM333;
>collection of playbills.

Johannesburg, Central Library:
>William Douglas manuscript notebook;

King's Lynn, Central Library.
Kingston upon Thames, Surrey Record Office.
Lichfield, Public Library.
Lincoln, Central Library:
>Thomas Robertson, letters;
>collection of playbills.

Liverpool, Record Office.
London, The British Library, Bloomsbury.
London, The British Library, Euston:
>the Burney Collection of Playbills;

the Burney Collection of Private Theatre Playbills, 1750-1808;
collection of playbills, 426.

London, The British Library Newspaper Library:
provincial newspapers.

London, Christie, Mason and Woods Archive Collection:
A Catalogue of all the Valuable Materials of the Theatre and Several Erections at Wargrave (1792), interleaved with manuscript sale notes and accounts.

London, Garrick Club:
Samuel De Wilde, Charlotte Goodall in the role of Wildair.

London, Hammersmith and Fulham Archives and Local History Centre.

London, Museum of the Moving Image:
working model of the Phantasmagoria.

London, The Public Record Office, Chancery Lane:
the Lord Chamberlain's Papers, LCS/163.

London, Royal Commission on Historical Monuments.

London, St James's Palace, Lord Chamberlain's Office.

London, The Society of Antiquaries:
the Prattinton Collection.

London, The Theatre Museum:
Peter Davey manuscript notebooks;
London theatre files;
provincial theatre files.

London, Victoria and Albert Museum.

Louisiana, USA, Louisiana State University:
Richard Phillip Sodder, 'The Theatre Management of Alexandre Placide in Charleston, 1794-1812', PhD dissertation, 1983.

Newbury, District Library:
collection of prospectuses for the Newbury Literary and Scientific Institute.

Newbury, District Museum:
collection of playbills.

Newbury, Mansion House:
sale notice of the Newbury Theatre, Speenhamland, 1883.

New York, Library and Museum of the Performing Arts:
William Douglas manuscript notebook.

Oxford, Ashmolean Museum, Library.

Oxford, Bodleian Library:
Department of Western manuscripts:
Diaries of the Revd Henry White, Diaries 42111-12;

   Minns Topographical Scrapbooks, Mss Top Oxon d 498.
John Johnson Collection:
  collection of playbills;
  newspaper cuttings.
Oxford, Merton College, Library.
Oxford, Radcliffe Hospital NHS Trust, Archives.
Oxford, St John's College, Library.
Oxford, Westgate Library, Oxfordshire Local Studies Collection.
Plymouth, Central Library.
Plymouth, West Devon Records Office:
  collection of playbills.
Portsmouth, Central Library:
  collection of playbills.
Reading, Berkshire Records Office:
  Borough of Newbury, Council Minute Books;
  Hungerford Constables' Accounts Books, 3, H/FR 1-8;
  the correspondence of E T Holmes;
  collection of playbills.
Reading, Central Library:
  collection of playbills.
Reading, Museum of Reading.
Reading, the University of Reading:
  K G Burton, 'The Early Newspaper Press in Berkshire (1723-
  1855)', thesis submitted in 1954 for the award of MA and sub-
  sequently privately printed.
Southampton, City Archives:
  material relating to the Southampton theatres, SC/4/3/1153
Southend, Library.
Washington, DC, The Folger Shakespeare Library:
  James Winston's manuscript notebooks, T. a. 65;
  collection of playbills.
Weybridge, Museum:
  theatre folder, typescript, anonymous;
  typescript on the history of the buildings of Weybridge.
Weybridge, Parish Church:
  Register of Burials.
Winchester, Central Library, Hampshire County Collection.
Winchester, Hampshire Record Office:
  James Rodney, 'A History of Alresford' (nd), typescript.
Winchester, Offices of Jacob and Johnson:

files of the *Hampshire Chronicle.*
Windsor, Offices of the *Windsor and Eton Express:*
    files of the *Windsor and Eton Express.*
Windsor, Public Library.
Windsor, Theatre Royal:
        collection of playbills
        collection of admission tokens.
Windsor, Windsor Castle, the Royal Library.
Worcester, City Library.
York, the Minster Library:
        collection of playbills.

4. Verbal Information

R E Brinton.
Lesley Burton.
Paul Cannon.
Diana Coldicott.
John Counsell.
Gosport Society.
Dr Malcolm Graham.
Dr Arnold Hare.
Dr Walter Hassall.
Olwen Hedley.
Havant Local History Group.
Anthony Higgott.
S M Jarvis.
Eric Jones-Evans.
Jean Kirkwood.
David Lewendon.
Valerie Lishman.
John Kennedy Melling.
Daphne Phillips.
Brigadier Robinson.
Sybil Rosenfeld.
Jon M Searle.
Dr Richard Southern.
J E N Walker.
John Webb.

APPENDIX 2
MONEY AND SPELLING

1. Money

The money terms of the eighteenth and nineteenth century have been given when quoting prices in the text. The following table is designed to clarify the relationship of this with present decimal coinage.

Predecimal	Decimal
£1. 1/- (one guinea)	£1.05
£1 (one pound)	£1.00
10/- (ten shillings)	50p
5/- (five shillings)	25p
4/- (four shillings)	20p
3/- (three shillings)	15p
2/- (two shillings)	10p
1/- (one shilling)	5p
6d (sixpence)	2.5p

The comparative buying power of money presents problems. We have noticed the constancy of the charge of 1/- for a seat in the gallery, the preserve of the working men, apprentices or sailors of an area. One may compare this charge at the Oxford theatre with the wage of an agricultural labourer in the county. In 1808, ten years after the theatre in Merton Street, Oxford, opened, an Oxfordshire farm labourer could earn 1/7d per working day in the wintertime but come harvest, when the working hours were longer, the wage would rise to 3/2d per working day. These figures included an allowance of beer and nine-tenths of the Oxfordshire cottages had decent gardens in which food could be grown, reducing the cost of living. It has to be remembered that poor weather conditions could lower the number of working days per week (based on figures given in E W Gilboy, *Wages in Eighteenth-Century England*, Cambridge, Mass, 1934). In the light of these figures a charge of 1/- for the gallery seems high.

2. Spelling

In citations spelling as given has been employed and normally no attention has been drawn to this. Occasionally, for the sake of clarity, the name of a person or place has been tacitly modernised.

Under Two Managers

INDEX

Index

Index

DATE DUE

GAYLORD 234			PRINTED IN U. S. A.

ANGLESEA I

Carwan P.

G.t Orms Head

Air P.t

Wigan

Liver-pool

Prescot

Warrington

Manchester

Mottram

Holyhead 258

Port.

Stockport

Disley

Knutsford

Chap

Altringham

Northwich

CHESHIRE

Tideswell

Bakew

New

Middle wich

Namptwich

pas

What

Congleton

Lee

Newcastle under Line

STAFFORD

Stone

Drayton

Newin

Crucaeth

Bettus

Fluaton

Part of Flint

Wem

Stafford 111

Bruich y Pwll

CARNA

MERIONETH

Bala

Llan gollen

Ellesmere

Oswestry 153

Went

Newport

Bardsey I.

Penrhwye Point

Harleigh

SHIRE

Dol gelly

Llanvi ding

SHROP

Shrewsbury

Lichfi

Wellington

Wolverhampton

Shiffnal

Much Wenlock

Dudley

Bridgnorth

Stou

Aberdovy

Talybonts

Aberyswith

CARDIGAN

BAY

Dinar mouthy

Welch Pool

Llanvair

MONTGOMERY

Machynleth

SH

Mont gomery 168

Newtown

Llanidloes

Church Stretton

Bishops Castle

Newton

SHIRE

Cleobury Mortimer

Ludlow

Bewdle

Tenbury

Bromsgrove

WORCESTER

Card gan 229

Llanarth

CARDIGANSH

Tregaron

RADNOR

Rhydengowy

Buall

SH

Knighton

Prestign

Leominster

Radnor 160

Bromyard

HEREFORD

Weobly

Hereford 135

Droitwich

us Worcester

Pershore

Upton

Cam

Chel ham

St Floren

Newport

Newcastle in Emlyn

BRECKNOCK

Llanymddyvri

SHIRE

Hay

Rowlston

SH

Ledbury

Tewksbury

GLOCEST

PEMBROKE

SH

Carmarthen SH

CARMARTHEN

Narberth 218

Llandilo

Llangadock

Brecon

Ross

Mon mouth 129

Glocetter

Nort

SH

Cirenste

Haverford West 265

Kidwelly

Capel Tan Van

Crickhowel

Abergavenny

Newn ham

Mitchel Dean

104

Stroud

SHL

Cric

Laugharn

Merthyrtydvil

MONMOUTH

Cair leon

Newport

SH

Chepstow

Dursley

Sodbury

Tetbury

Malmsbu

Wotto

Pembro

GLAMORGAN

SH

Caerphilly

Landaff

River Severn

Marsh field

Chippenham

Caln

Worms H.

Penrice

Swa

Bridgend

Cowbridge

Cardiff

Breaksea P.

the Holms

Bristol 119

Bath 106

WILTS

Lu

ndy Island

BRISTOL CHANNEL

Wrington

Devizes

Oxwich P.

Ilfracomb

Porlock

Minehead

Axbridge

Wells

Frome

Warminster

Heytsb

Mer

Hindon

Sali

Hartland P.t

Hartland

Combe Martin

Barnstaple

Stowey

Bridgewater

Glastonbury

Britton

Shaftsbury

Stratton

Biddeford

South Molton

Taunton

SOMERSET SH

Somerton

Ilchester

Sherborne

Ivincmiton

Sturminster

Blandford

DORSE

Torrington

Sheepwash

Crumleigh

Tiverton

Wel ington

Ilminster

Yeovil

Milton Abby

Winb

Genny

Hatherleigh

Crediton

Collymp ton

Beaminster

Armin ster

Bere Regis

Boscastle

Holsworthy

Bow

DEVON

Exeter 172

Honiton

SHIRE

Dorchester 120

Bossiney

Oakhampton

Moreton

Chudleigh

Coliton

Lyme

Brid

amels

Launceston 214

Lidiord

WALL

SHIRE

Abbots bury

Corfe Cas

stle

Wardbridge

Callington

Tavistock

Ashburton

Newton Bushel

Tiegnmouth

Portland I.

Weymouth

Lestwithiel

Beeraston

Tor Bay

Race or Portland

dolphin

Liskeard

St Germans

Totness

Brixham

W looe

Plymouth

Dartmouth